LAWLESS BORDERS

The Rule of Law Deficit in European Immigration Control

Elspeth Guild, Valsamis Mitsilegas
and Niovi Vavoula

BRISTOL
UNIVERSITY
PRESS

First published in Great Britain in 2025 by

Bristol University Press
University of Bristol
1–9 Old Park Hill
Bristol
BS2 8BB
UK
t: +44 (0)117 374 6645
e: bup-info@bristol.ac.uk

Details of international sales and distribution partners are available at bristoluniversitypress.co.uk

British Library Cataloguing in Publication Data
A catalogue record for this book is available from the British Library

ISBN 978-1-5292-3778-8 hardcover
ISBN 978-1-5292-3779-5 ePub
ISBN 978-1-5292-3780-1 ePdf

Cover design: Liam Roberts Design
Front cover image: iStock/Pict Rider
Bristol University Press uses environmentally responsible print partners.
Printed and bound in Great Britain by CPI Group (UK) Ltd, Croydon, CR0 4YY

Bristol University Press' authorised representative in the European Union is:
Easy Access System Europe, Mustamäe tee 50, 10621 Tallinn, Estonia,
Email: gpsr.requests@easproject.com

FSC
www.fsc.org
MIX
Paper | Supporting responsible forestry
FSC® C013604

Contents

Introduction: Setting the Scene 1

PART I The Rule of Law Deficit in State Border Control Practices: From the External to the Externalized Border

1 **The Proliferation and Mutation of Extraterritorial Immigration Control** 11

1 Introduction 11

2 The evolution of extraterritorial immigration control: from pushbacks to pullbacks, from the high seas to third countries 12

3 Extraterritorializing the external border: pushbacks at the physical border 20

4 Outsourcing refugee status determination to third states: the UK–Rwanda model 25

5 Italy–Albania 32

6 Conclusion 35

2 **The Rule of Law Deficit on the Border: The European Union Pact on Migration and Asylum** 37

1 Introduction 37

2 The fiction of 'non-entry' 37

3 The uses and abuses of the instrumentalization of migration 43

4 The normalization of detention 50

5 Conclusion 54

3 **Border Control through the Hostile Environment** 56

1 Introduction 56

2 The criminal law of the hostile environment: the criminalization of facilitation of unauthorized entry and beyond 57

3 The hostile environment through the use of administrative law 63

4 Targeting the legal profession 65
5 Conclusion 68

PART II **Border Violence and Rule of Law: Examining the Role of Frontex in Lawless Border Control**

4 **Borders, Power and Accountability: The Case of Frontex** **71**
1 Introduction 71
2 Institutional powers 73
2.1 Shared responsibility 73
2.2 Schengen or the European Union? 77
3 Legal existence and responsibility 80
4 Consequence of responsibilities 84
5 Conclusion 91

5 **Frontex: Management and Internal Oversight** **93**
1 Introduction 93
2 An overview of the oversight mechanisms 94
3 Frontex's internal oversight mechanisms 98
3.1 The Commission as an internal fundamental rights monitoring mechanism 98
3.2 The executive director and the management board 100
3.3 A specific management board response to fundamental rights abuses: Working Group on Fundamental Rights and Legal Operational Aspects of Operations 102
3.4 The Consultative Forum 103
3.5 The Fundamental Rights Officer 104
3.6 The complaints mechanism 108
4 Conclusion 109

6 **EU External Oversight of Frontex and Border Violence** **111**
1 Introduction 111
2 Parliament: the LIBE Committee and the Frontex Scrutiny Working Group 113
3 European Anti-fraud Office 123
4 The Court of Justice of the European Union and halting operations under Article 46 of the 2019 Frontex Regulation 130
5 Conclusion 132

PART III The Erosion of the Rule of Law through the Development of Europe's Techno-Borders

7 **Technology-led Border Surveillance and the Rule of Law: Eurosur as a 'Foggy' Network of Information Exchange** 137
1 Introduction 137
2 The emergence of Frontex as a 'migration information hub' 139
2.1 The early days 139
2.2 Formalization and expansion of Frontex's information-related tasks 139
2.3 The expansion of informational tasks under the 2019 Frontex Regulation 142
3 Zooming in on Eurosur 146
3.1 Making sense of Eurosur: purpose and functions 146
3.2 Eurosur: an accountability diffuser fuelling Frontex's rule of law deficit 152
3.3 The murky landscape regarding the processing of personal data by Eurosur 153
4 Conclusion 158

8 **EU Large-scale IT Systems for Third-country Nationals Beyond the Rule of Law** 160
1 Introduction 160
2 The emergence of a complex architecture of interoperable large-scale IT systems for third-country nationals 161
2.1 The first generation of IT systems 162
2.2 The second generation of IT systems 164
2.3 Synthesis 166
2.4 Interoperability: the missing glue 167
3 IT systems as a highly complex ecosystem 169
3.1 The promotion of the technical nature of interoperable IT systems 170
3.2 Continuous and inconsistent reforms 173
3.3 Delegated and implementing acts 174
4 Large-scale IT systems as security systems 178
5 Interoperable large-scale IT systems and effective judicial protection: 'mission impossible'? 184
6 Conclusion 188

9 From Digitalization to Algorithmization in European Border Management: Automation, Artificial Intelligence and the Rule of Law 190

1 Introduction 190
2 The manifold experimentation with algorithms in European states: terminological ambiguities and lack of foreseeability 193
2.1 A bird's eye view into national initiatives at the borders 194
2.2 The case of triaging visa applications in the Netherlands and the UK 195
2.2.1 The Dutch 'Informatie Ondersteund Beslissen' algorithm 196
2.2.2 The UK litigation 199
3 The shift towards algorithmization and AI at EU level: the case of interoperable large-scale IT systems 201
3.1 Automated processing of applications for Schengen visas and travel authorizations and the central role of the CRRS 202
3.2 Significant discretionary power to Frontex and eu-LISA 206
3.3 Elusive judicial protection against discriminatory decision-making 207
3.4 Facial images: the hidden shift towards facial recognition 209
3.5 The Multiple Identity Detector: an artificial intelligence-powered interoperability component? 213
3.6 The curious case of Article 111 of the AI Act 215
4 Conclusion 217

Conclusion: Restoring the Rule of Law on the Border 219

Index 224

Introduction: Setting the Scene

The past decade has witnessed a proliferation of border controls in Europe, the primary aim of which is simultaneously permissive and preventive. They are permissive in the sense that the vast majority of third-country nationals, understood as persons who do not hold the citizenship of any European Union (EU) state, enter the EU rapidly with only a light control, increasingly electronic, at the physical border which results in less than 0.005 per cent of those who present themselves at an EU external border being refused admission.[1] This very light control at the border is complemented by a much more stringent control before departure for those who need a visa[2] and, from 2025 onwards for those who travel visa-free, a prior travel authorization through the European Travel Information and Authorisation System (ETIAS).[3] They are preventive for a small number of persons seeking to arrive at EU borders along irregular routes – according to Frontex, in 2022, 331,553 persons were apprehended[4] – by resorting to small, unseaworthy boats at sea, or crossing land borders at places without border crossing points. Their objective is to prevent refugees and migrants from accessing the EU border, its territory and the jurisdiction of the EU, and, increasingly, also some transit states. The evolution of border control

1 Frontex, 'Risk Analysis for 2023/2024' (Warsaw, August 2023), https://www.frontex.europa.eu/assets/Publications/General/ARA_2023.pdf, accessed 12 August 2024. Regular crossing of the EU external borders numbered more than 250 million entries in 2023, in 2022 126,654 persons were refused entry; see Elspeth Guild, 'Interrogating Europe's Borders: Reflections from an Academic Career' (Farewell Speech, Radboud University, 2019).

2 In 2023, the non-issuance rate for an EU short-stay visa was 16 per cent. See Commission, 'Short-stay Visas Issued by Schengen Countries' (15 May 2024), https://home-affairs.ec.europa.eu/policies/schengen-borders-and-visa/visa-policy/short-stay-visas-issued-schengen-countries_en, accessed 12 October 2024.

3 Regulation (EU) 2018/1240 of the European Parliament and of the Council of 12 September 2018 establishing a European Travel Information and Authorisation System (ETIAS) and amending Regulations (EU) No 1077/2011, (EU) No 515/2014, (EU) 2016/399, (EU) 2016/1624 and (EU) 2017/2226 [2018] OJ L 236/1.

4 Frontex (n 1).

reflects these two objectives, but the emphasis has been on enhancing the coercive nature of border controls, evidenced by the dramatic increase of powers and allocation of funds for the development of the EU border control agency, Frontex. Its change from a mainly civilian body into a coercive policing force poses profound rule of law challenges in a two-fold interconnected manner: in negating the application of the law, including human rights law, asylum law and international law of search and rescue to refugees and migrants, who are increasingly viewed as located outside the law; and in shielding states and EU agencies, including Frontex, from any legal responsibility towards third-country nationals – shielding border operations and state arbitrariness from accountability and scrutiny. The aim of this book is to put this fundamental rule of law deficit in the spotlight and provide a systematic and systemic critique of the evolution and proliferation of lawless borders.

The development of EU border controls on persons and the focus on the normalization of the use of coercive powers against persons in certain situations raises an additional issue. The EU approach weakens the legal framework of where borders are and what they do. Already it must be noted that the EU has no borders as such, as it is not a state; the Member States have borders defined under international law. What the EU does have is powers relating to border controls and surveillance which have been allocated to it by the Member States in accordance with the EU Treaties. Thus, the concerns which states have about ensuring the coherence and clarity of their borders as a core aspect of their state sovereignty are not applicable to the EU. EU law has developed on the basis of the allocation of competences to it and each competence may have a separate territorial application.[5] The territorial scope of the Customs Union and the messy scope of the Schengen area are only two examples. However, as history has taught many European states, protecting territorial integrity is central to the continuing existence of the state. At the time of finalizing the manuscript in October 2024, the Russian invasion in Ukraine demonstrates the centrality of borders as an intrinsic element of state sovereignty in European politics. The EU's approach to border controls on persons as a shared competence is sectoral, not intrinsic. Thus, the EU is willing to bend the rules on what and where borders are and where the rules applicable to border controls may be applied to satisfy the interests of certain EU Ministries of Interior which are very much focused on 'fighting' irregular migration, as there is no counterbalancing interest at the EU level regarding the inherent importance of coherent borders for the maintenance of state sovereignty.

---

[5] Elspeth Guild and Steve Peers, 'Out of the Ghetto? The Personal Scope of EU Law' in Steve Peers and Nicola Rogers (eds), *EU Immigration and Asylum Law* (Brill Nijhoff 2006).

Inadvertently, EU policy on border controls on persons is having the consequence of undermining Member States' claims to the integrity of state sovereignty.

This book is organized in three parts, each of which composes of three chapters. It constitutes a joint endeavour by the three authors in the sense that the intellectual and conceptual underpinnings of the book are a joint effort and the outcome of ongoing research strands undertaken by all three authors. The different chapters have thus been co-authored by the three authors and in the different parts one author has taken the lead; the first part by Valsamis Mitsilegas, the second part by Elspeth Guild and the third part by Niovi Vavoula.

In particular, the first part of the book (Chapters 1–3) focuses on the rule of law deficit of coercive border control by European states. In particular, Chapter 1 examines the evolution of extraterritorial immigration control, covering multiple sites – the high seas, the territory of third states, the physical border but also the territory of transit and destination states) and mutating into different models: from pushbacks to pullbacks, from state operations in the high seas to control by omission or by co-opting third states into coercive control, to outsourcing the examination of asylum claims to third countries. The rule of law deficit in extraterritorial immigration control is examined primarily from the perspective of the applicability of the European Convention on Human Rights, as a key human rights instrument which can shield the generation of lawless zones in terms of the protection of migrants in Europe. Then, Chapter 2 focuses more directly on EU law and examines the rule of law deficit in the development of the control of EU external borders exacerbated by the adoption of the Pact on Migration and Asylum in 2024. The chapter centres on three key instances where the rule of law is undermined under the Pact: the normalization and expansion of asylum border procedures, based on a fiction of non-entry; the introduction of the contested concept of the instrumentalization of migration as a vague EU legal concept which can lead to the normalization of exclusion of asylum seekers from the territory of the EU; and the generalization and normalization of the detention of migrants under the Pact, which poses fundamental rule of law challenges in terms of arbitrariness and lack of proportionality. As for Chapter 3, this examines the rule of law challenges arising from sustained efforts by states and the European Union to create a hostile environment targeting those who help migrants, in particular civil society and the legal profession. The analysis focuses on three key manifestations of the hostile environment:

1. the use of criminal law to prosecute civil society, in particular by prosecuting (on the grounds of the facilitation of unauthorized entry but also of other offences including collusion and organized crime)

non-governmental organizations (NGOs) who conduct search and rescue operations at sea;

2. on targeting these NGOs through the uses and abuses of administrative law, including the imposition of sanctions for alleged breaches of health and safety or environmental law, sanctions which aim to effectively stop search and rescue operations at sea; and measures to target the legal profession; and
3. the provision of legal advice and assistance to migrants, ranging from the criminalization of legal advice to the stigmatization and intimidation of the legal profession.

The second part of this book (Chapters 4–6) examines how the development of the EU border control agency, Frontex, has been coupled with significant border violence and complicity in fundamental rights violations along with European states and how EU law and institutions have responded to the rise of such violence in border operations at the EU's (Schengen) external borders. Border violence is exemplified by the loss of lives,[6] due to failure to rescue and other fundamental rights violations at the EU's external borders.[7] While there

[6] According to the International Organization for Migration's (IOM) Missing Migrants Project, there have been at least 5,684 deaths on migration routes to and within Europe between 2021 and 2023, with increasing numbers of deaths seen on routes across the Mediterranean, on land borders to Europe and within the continent. According to IOM, there were more than 1,400 persons missing at sea on the Central Mediterranean route alone in 2022. 'More than 5,000 Deaths Recorded on European Migration Routes since 2021' (IOM, 25 October 2022), https://www.iom.int/news/more-5000-deaths-recorded-european-migration-routes-2021-iom, accessed 12 October 2024. 'Deadliest Quarter for Migrants in the Central Mediterranean since 2017' (IOM, 12 April 2023), https://www.iom.int/news/deadliest-quarter-migrants-central-mediterranean-2017, accessed 12 October 2024.

[7] Aside from the Mediterranean, border violence also takes place at the Greek–Turkish land border crossing point on the Evros river or at specific places on the Hungarian–Serbian border and the border of the Baltic states and Poland with Belarus. Border violence also takes place in the Balkans and at the Spanish enclaves in Morocco. This is not to ignore the loss of life in the Atlantic where persons seeking to arrive at the Canary Islands fail to be rescued. In addition, within the border control free European area, certain crossing places between France and its neighbours, Italy and Spain, are also places where border violence against foreigners by allegedly French authorities is rife. See, among others, European Union Agency for Asylum (EUAA), 'Input by Civil Society Organisations to the Asylum Report 2023 Section: Greece' (2023); Boldizsár Nagy, 'Special Issue Constitutional Dimensions of the Refugee Crisis Hungarian Asylum Law and Policy in 2015–2016: Securitization Instead of Loyal Cooperation' (2016) 17(6) *German Law Journal*; Sarah Ganty, Aleksandra Jolkina and Dimitry Kochenov, 'EU Lawlessness Law at the EU-Belarusian Border: Torture and Dehumanisation Excused by "Instrumentalisation"' (2024) *Hague Journal on the Rule of Law*; Sarah Bachellerie, 'Chasing down Foreigners at the French-Italian Border (Hautes-alpes) as a Matter of Social and Racial Policing' (2020) 108 *Journal of Alpine Research*.

has been substantial academic attention to this process of externalizing border violence in the EU resulting in tragedies in the Mediterranean,[8] there has been less focus on the rise of political and international pressure for effective monitoring mechanisms to counter and diminish border violence[9] and the EU's response through the legal structures of border control and efforts to increase fundamental rights in the practices at those borders.[10] Overall, Part II provides an overview of the development of Frontex as an agency with coercive powers[11] and how the exercise of those powers has led to pressure for effective counterbalancing monitoring powers by actors within the EU. Furthermore, it highlights the challenges of effective internal and external (but within the EU) monitoring mechanisms and the inevitability of the engagement of independent actors in monitoring. Chapter 4 examines the institutionalization of Frontex, the tensions with national border police agencies and the EU legislator's growing concerns regarding fundamental rights protections. The main question addressed in that chapter is how has the EU legislature chose to address the allocation of institutional powers in the creation and subsequent reconfiguration of Frontex. It examines the establishment of the agency and the anomalies which are inherent in the way in which it was set up and developed. The relationship of Frontex with EU migration law is one of the central issues. In other words, Chapter 4 outlines the shadow dance for the first period of the agency's existence regarding the allocation of responsibility and the rather muddied waters of the legal arrangements. Chapter 5 examines the consequences for the distribution of responsibilities as a result of these choices. In this chapter, the issue of protection (or lack thereof) of fundamental rights is central. For enabling the visibility of fundamental rights violations in law, they must first be codified. The EU has done this through the EU Charter of Fundamental Rights (EU Charter), tying the meaning of the rights there into the European

[8] Alison Mountz and Jenna M. Loyd, 'Constructing the Mediterranean Region: Obscuring Violence in the Bordering of Europe's Migration "Crises"' (2014) 13(2) *ACME: An International Journal for Critical Geographies* 173; Polly Pallister-Wilkins, 'The Humanitarian Politics of European Border Policing: Frontex and Border Police in Evros' (2015) 9(1) *International Political Sociology* 53.

[9] Human Rights Council, 'Report of the Special Rapporteur on the Human Rights of Migrants: Banking on Mobility over a Generation: Follow-up to the Regional Study on the Management of the External Borders of the European Union and its Impact on Human Rights of Migrants' (A/HRC/29/36, 8 May 2015).

[10] Elspeth Guild (ed), *Monitoring Border Violence in the EU: Frontex in Focus* (Routledge 2023).

[11] Annex V of the Regulation (EU) 2019/1896 of the European Parliament and of the Council of 13 November 2019 on the European Border and Coast Guard and repealing Regulations (EU) No 1052/2013 and (EU) 2016/1624 [2019] OJ L 295, rules on the use of force, including training and the supply, control and use of service weapons and non-lethal equipment, applicable to statutory staff deployed as members of the teams.

Convention on Human Rights, as well as international human rights law. A second and perhaps less visible mechanism by which fundamental rights in the EU are crystallized – and possibly expanded notwithstanding Article 51(2) of the EU Charter – has been through the signature and ratification of international conventions by the EU. Of particular relevance here has been the EU ratification of the UN Conventions on the Law of the Sea[12] and the Rights of Persons with Disabilities[13] and the Council of Europe's Istanbul Convention on Violence against Women.[14] Once crystallized, responsibility for ensuring compliance must be allocated and provided for in law. This chapter interrogates this aspect of the issue of lawless borders as regards fundamental rights compliance. In a nutshell, this chapter examines the fragmented response, usually resulting from pressure from one part of the legislator, the European Parliament, for ever increasing monitoring and supervision.[15] Chapter 6 looks at how the EU institutions and agencies have overseen the work of Frontex, mapping their efforts to fill the accountability gap through the exercise of their specific powers. Indeed, while some EU institutions have been particularly active in promoting the enhancement of Frontex powers, personnel and budget, the European Parliament and other EU institutions and agencies have been increasingly seeking to ensure the integration of a culture of fundamental rights compliance within the agency and accountability for failure to uphold fundamental rights.

The third part of this book (Chapters 7–9) focuses on the rule of law challenges posed by the development and use of modern technologies in border management at European level. This section focuses on three separate, yet increasingly inter-related, technological advents: the processing of personal data by Frontex, with a particular emphasis on the European Border Surveillance System (Eurosur); the setting up, operation and reconfiguration of EU/Schengen-wide large-scale IT systems for the processing of personal data by different groups of third-country nationals; and the rise of algorithmization, including artificial intelligence (AI) at the external borders. In particular, Chapter 7 follows the gradual evolution of the agency as an EU migration information hub, underpinned by the proliferation of information-related tasks and the growing processing of personal data.

---

[12] UNGA, Convention on the Law of the Sea (adopted 10 December 1982, entered into force 16 November 1994) 1833 UNTS 3.

[13] UNGA, Convention on the Rights of Persons with Disabilities (adopted 13 December 2006, entered into force 3 May 2008) A/RES/61/106.

[14] Council of Europe, Convention on Preventing and Combating Violence against Women and Domestic Violence (adopted 11 May 2011, entered into force 1 August 2014) CETS No 210.

[15] Nicolette Busuttil, 'The EU Legislator, Frontex and Fundamental Rights' in Elspeth Guild (ed), *Monitoring Border Violence in the EU* (Routledge 2023).

At the heart of Frontex's data-related tasks is supporting the development and operation of Eurosur, which provides an integrated framework for the exchange of real-time information and for operational cooperation between Member States' border surveillance authorities and the agency. Eurosur entails the setting up and operation of an information processing factory, whereby maritime monitoring and different surveillance tools are deployed. It involves the collection and processing of a wide-ranging, heterogeneous and non-exhaustive ensemble of human and technological components: satellites, drones (unmanned aerial vehicles), radars and stationary and mobile sensors, vessels and boats reporting systems, private companies, national and European experts' groups, patrols, information from Frontex, other Member States or third countries. The rule of law challenges identified in this chapter are centred on two axes: first, how the operation of Eurosur exacerbates and complicates the rule of law deficit of Frontex; and, second, the opacity and lack of foreseeability regarding the processing of personal data within the Eurosur ecosystem. Chapter 8 shifts the attention to the emergence of a complex and significantly opaque architecture of EU/Schengen-wide large-scale IT systems (databases) for third-country nationals, which are scheduled to become interoperable by 2027. This 'millefeuille' of databases comprises of the Schengen Information System, Visa Information System, Eurodac, Entry/Exit System, ETIAS and the European Criminal Record Information System for Third-country Nationals. Chapter 8 explains how the setting up and multiple reconfiguration of the databases through consecutive and constant revisions of the legal instruments that govern their operation demonstrate the prevalence of the 'technical' over the 'legal' and the role of interoperability in further obscuring the real impact of interconnecting the different data pots on the protection of fundamental rights. It also analyses how consultation of immigration data for law enforcement purposes blurs the distinction between different policy areas in the area of freedom, security and justice, and, notably, asylum, migration, police cooperation, internal security and criminal justice, and embraces the assimilation of the different groups of third-country nationals, all of whom are considered to present a security risk. Finally, this chapter examines the significant challenges of ensuring judicial protection of third-country nationals whose personal data are unlawfully processed in different Member States, by looking into concrete examples from the operational Schengen Information System and Eurodac.

The last chapter of this book is devoted to an examination of the growing reliance on algorithms to automate immigration decision-making, including extraterritorially, including through the deployment and use of AI systems. In particular, Chapter 9 provides a concise synopsis of the experimentation of European states with algorithms and AI and demonstrates the significant rule of law deficit which results through the example of algorithm-powered risk assessments for visa applications (so-called triaging). The chapter highlights the significant opacity of the legal framework underpinning interoperable large-scale IT systems, which will deploy different types of algorithms and AI though the legislation remains particularly obscure on the matter. The lack of judicial protection in this context is also highlighted here to demonstrate that the law deliberately hinders protection of individuals affected by opaque decision-making.

Finally, this volume would not have been completed without the assistance by Vasiliki Apatzidou, PhD Candidate at Queen Mary University of London, who took excellent care of its final editing and formatting. The authors wish to hereby express their gratitude.

PART I

The Rule of Law Deficit in State Border Control Practices: From the External to the Externalized Border

1

The Proliferation and Mutation of Extraterritorial Immigration Control

1 Introduction

A key element in the development of contemporary immigration control has been the focus on preventing migrants from accessing the physical border and the territory of states. To achieve this preventive aim, the past three decades have witnessed a growing emphasis on extraterritorial immigration control, generating what Guild has called 'the border abroad'.[1] The shift towards extraterritorial immigration control has been marked by a temporal and a spatial change.[2] Immigration control takes place increasingly before an individual has reached the actual physical border. Border controls take place increasingly outside and beyond the territorial border, aiming to prevent migrants reaching the border in the first place. States exercise border controls extraterritorially, on the high seas and on the territory of third states.[3] The present chapter aims to provide an overview of the proliferation and mutation of extraterritorial immigration control in recent years and highlight the rule of law deficit in such extraterritorialization. The analysis will focus on the rule of law deficit by examining attempts by states to use extraterritorial immigration control to circumvent migrants' protection under the European Convention on Human Rights (ECHR), by putting in place mechanisms

---

1 Elspeth Guild, 'The Border Abroad – Visas and Border Controls' in Kees Groenedijk, Elspeth Guild and Paul Minderhoud (eds), *In Search of Europe's Borders* (Brill 2002).

2 Valsamis Mitsilegas, 'The Law of the Border and the Borders of Law: Rethinking Border Control from the Perspective of the Individual' in Leanne Weber (ed), *Rethinking Border Control for a Globalizing World* (Routledge 2015).

3 Bernard Ryan and Valsamis Mitsilegas (eds), *Extraterritorial Immigration Control: Legal Challenges* (Brill 2010); Maarten den Heijer, *Europe and Extraterritorial Asylum* (Hart Publishing 2012).

aimed at negating the application of the law to migrants. The first part (the first two sections) analyses the evolution of coercive extraterritorial immigration control, from the high seas to third states and back to the physical border of states. The second part analyses the more recent paradigm of combining coercive immigration control with outsourcing the examination of asylum application in the territory of third states. Two different models are analysed in this context: the UK–Rwanda model, where the examination of asylum applications would happen in the territory of a third state under the laws of a third state; and the Italy–Albania model, where it is envisaged that the examination of asylum applications will take place in the territory of a third state under the laws of the state of destination.

2 The evolution of extraterritorial immigration control: from pushbacks to pullbacks, from the high seas to third countries

A growing state practice in extraterritorial immigration control has been the conduct of pushbacks, which are defined as refusals of entry and expulsions without any individual assessment of protection needs.[4] The European Court of Human Rights (ECtHR) had the opportunity to address the human rights challenges of such practices on the high seas in the case of *Hirsi*.[5] The case involved the interception by the Italian authorities in 2009 of three vessels carrying 11 Somali nationals and 13 Eritrean nationals aiming to reach the Italian coast. The interception occurred when the vessels were 35 nautical miles south of Lampedusa, that is, within the Maltese Search and Rescue Region of responsibility. The occupants of the intercepted vessels were transferred onto Italian military ships and returned to Tripoli and handed over to the Libyan authorities.[6] The Strasbourg Court had no difficulty in asserting jurisdiction. It stated that Italy cannot circumvent its jurisdiction under the Convention by describing the events at issue as rescue operations on the high seas[7] and noted that, while in its earlier ruling in *Medvedyev*,[8]

---

[4] Parliamentary Assembly of the Council of Europe, 'Pushbacks Practice and Policy in Council of Europe Member States' Resolution 2299/2019, https://assembly.coe.int/nw/xml/XRef/Xref-XML2HTML-en.asp?fileid=28074, accessed 12 October 2024. See Tineke Strik, 'Mechanisms to Prevent Pushbacks' in Sergio Carrera and Marco Stefan (eds), *Fundamental Rights Challenges in Border Controls and Expulsion of Irregular Immigrants in the European Union: Complaint Mechanisms and Access to Justice* (Routledge 2020) 234, 254.

[5] *Hirsi Jamaa and Others v Italy* App no 27765/09 (ECtHR, 23 February 2012).

[6] Ibid paras 9–12.

[7] Ibid para 79.

[8] *Medvedyev v France* App no 3394/03 (ECtHR, 29 March 2010) para 67. The Court held that the ECHR applied extraterritorially in enforcement actions by France in a case of suspected drug trafficking on the high seas as this was a case of France having exercised

the events took place on board a vessel flying the flag of a third state, here the events took place entirely on board ships of the Italian armed forces, the crews of which were composed exclusively of Italian military personnel. In the Court's opinion, in the period between boarding the ships of the Italian armed forces and being handed over to the Libyan authorities, the applicants were under the continuous and exclusive *de jure* and *de facto* control of the Italian authorities. Speculation as to the nature and purpose of the intervention of the Italian ships on the high seas would not lead the Court to any other conclusion.[9]

Having established jurisdiction, the Court found that Italy was in breach of both Article 3 ECHR (prohibition of inhuman and degrading treatment) and Article 4 of Protocol No 4 (prohibition of collective expulsion of aliens). As regards Article 3, the Court rejected Italy's claim that Libya was a safe third country. It noted that the mere ratification of international treaties by a third country is not by itself a guarantee of compliance with human rights[10] and added that Italy cannot evade its own responsibility by relying on its obligations arising out of bilateral agreements with Libya.[11] The Court added that the Italian authorities knew or should have known that, as irregular migrants, they would be exposed in Libya to treatment in breach of the Convention and that they would not be given any kind of protection in that country and that it was for the national authorities, faced with a situation where human rights were being systematically violated, as described, to find out about the treatment to which the applicants would be exposed after their return.[12] The Court found that in the case substantial grounds had been shown for believing that there was a real risk that the applicants would be subjected to treatment in Libya contrary to Article 3 of the Convention.[13] The Court also found a violation of Article 3 on account of the fact that the applicants were exposed to the risk of arbitrary repatriation to Eritrea and Somalia. According to the Court, when the applicants were transferred to Libya, the Italian authorities knew or should have known that there were insufficient guarantees protecting the parties concerned from being arbitrarily returned to their countries of origin.[14]

'full and effective control' over the boat in question and its crew, 'at least de facto, from the time of its interception, in a continuous and uninterrupted manner until they were tried in France, the applicants were effectively within France's jurisdiction for the purposes of Article 1 of the Convention'.

9 *Hirsi Jamaa and Others v Italy* (n 5) paras 79–80.

10 Ibid para 128.

11 Ibid para 129.

12 Ibid paras 130–131.

13 Ibid para 136.

14 Ibid para 156.

Italy was not exempt from complying with its obligations under Article 3 of the Convention because the applicants failed to ask for asylum or to describe the risks faced as a result of the lack of an asylum system in Libya. The Court reiterated that the Italian authorities should have ascertained how the Libyan authorities fulfilled their international obligations in relation to the protection of refugees.[15]

As regards the application of Article 4 of Protocol No. 4 on the prohibition of collective expulsion of aliens, the Court stated:

> It is therefore clear that, while the notion of 'jurisdiction' is principally territorial and is presumed to be exercised on the national territory of States, the notion of expulsion is also principally territorial, in the sense that expulsions are most often conducted from national territory. Where, however, as in the instant case, the Court has found that a Contracting State has, exceptionally, exercised its jurisdiction outside its national territory, it does not see any obstacle to accepting that the exercise of extraterritorial jurisdiction by that State took the form of collective expulsion. To conclude otherwise, and to afford that last notion a strictly territorial scope, would result in a discrepancy between the scope of the application of the Convention as such and that of Article 4 of Protocol no 4, which would go against the principle that the Convention should be interpreted as a whole. Furthermore, as regards the exercise by a State of its jurisdiction on the high seas, the Court has already stated that the special nature of the maritime environment cannot justify an area outside the law where individuals are covered by no legal system capable of affording them enjoyment of the rights and guarantees protected by the Convention which the States have undertaken to secure to everyone within their jurisdiction.[16]

In the light of this, the Court found that the removal of aliens carried out in the context of interceptions on the high seas by the authorities of a state in the exercise of their sovereign authority, *the effect of which is to prevent migrants from reaching the borders of the state or even to push them back to another state*, constitutes an exercise of jurisdiction within the meaning of Article 1 of the Convention which engages the responsibility of the state in question under Article 4 of Protocol No. 4.[17] The Court found that the transfer of applicants to Libya was carried out without any form of examination of

---

15 Ibid para 157.

16 Ibid para 178, by reference to *Medvedyev*, para 81.

17 Ibid para 180 (emphasis added).

each applicant's individual situation and that there was therefore a violation of Article 4.[18]

Hirsi is of great significance in affirming the extraterritorial application of human rights law and emphasizing that states cannot evade their human rights responsibilities towards migrants by exercising extraterritorial immigration control including by cooperating with third states. In an extremely important finding, the Court extended the protection of migrants under the ECHR in cases of collective expulsion. As den Heijer has noted, the Court's reasoning allows for an interpretation that any interception activity that factually prevents migrants from effectuating an entry may be construed as expulsion.[19] In *Hirsi*, the Court applied the Convention in cases where state deliberate action has resulted in the deflection of migrants, that is, to acts the effect of which is to prevent migrants from reaching the borders of the state or even to push them back to another state.[20] State jurisdiction applies here even if the migrant has not reached the physical, territorial border of the state. States can no longer hide behind deflection techniques under a logic of prevention.[21] As it has been noted, the Court's approach, in effect, exports the border to places and instances where the state exercises enforcement action.[22] This has been characterized as a functional approach to border control focusing not on a general test of personal or geographical control, but rather on the specific power or authority assumed by the state acting extraterritorially in a given capacity.[23] This emphasis is coupled with a focus on the impact on the affected individuals, in what has been characterized the 'individualisation of jurisdiction'.[24] By placing the individual at the heart of

---

18 Ibid paras 185–186.

19 Maarten den Heijer, 'Reflections on *Refoulement* and Collective Expulsion in the *Hirsi* Case' (2013) 25 *International Journal of Refugee Law* 283. But see the subsequent ruling by the Strasbourg Court in the case of *N.D. and N.T. v Spain* App nos 8675/15 and 8697/15 (ECtHR, 13 February 2020).

20 *Hirsi Jamaa v Italy* (n 5) para 156, assessing Italy's transfer of migrants to Libya, where the authorities 'knew or should have known that there were insufficient guarantees protecting the parties concerned from the risk of being arbitrarily returned to their countries of origin'.

21 Itamar Mann, *Humanity at Sea: Maritime Migration and the Foundations of International Law* (Cambridge University Press 2016). Mann argues that in *Hirsi* the Court identifies how Italy manipulated jurisdiction (in p 169).

22 Valsamis Mitsilegas, 'Immigration Control in an Era of Globalisation: Deflecting Foreigners, Weakening Citizens, Strengthening the State' (2012) 19(1) *Indiana Journal of Global Legal Studies* 3–60.

23 Thomas Gammeltoft-Hansen, *Access to Asylum: International Refugee Law and the Globalisation of Migration Control* (Cambridge University Press 2011) 124.

24 Angelika Nussberger, 'The Concept of "Jurisdiction" in the Jurisprudence of the European Court of Human Rights' (2012) 65 *Current Legal Problems* 265.

the system of protection of the Convention, the ECtHR had to address the borders of the law related to extraterritorial immigration control operations.

Hirsi involved a situation of direct state coercive intervention on the high seas. After the ruling of the Strasbourg Court, states have attempted to circumvent its findings through a mutation of extraterritorial immigration control on the high seas and in collaboration with third states. The change in extraterritorial immigration control involved a shift from pushbacks through state intervention on the high seas, to situations where states refuse to intervene – putting an end to specific search and rescue initiatives,[25] delaying search and rescue at sea and disembarkation in their territory, diverting flows to other states,[26] targeting non-governmental organizations which attempt to address state inaction on the high seas by saving lives at sea through the generation of a hostile environment,[27] or delegating coercive intervention on the high seas to third states in the form of pullbacks. As Giuffré has noted, the practice of pullbacks aims to eliminate any physical contact, direct or indirect, between refugees and the authorities of potential destination states by transferring the coercive management of exiles to third countries, the ultimate goal being to sever any jurisdictional link with European countries, in an attempt to elude any concomitant responsibility.[28] Pullback practices present serious rule of law challenges, as the aim of the state is to negate, through the exclusion of its jurisdiction, the application of its laws vis-à-vis migrants, resulting in breaches of their rights. In order to address this rule of law deficit, scholars such as Moreno-Lax have advocated a functional approach to jurisdiction giving rise to the applicability of human rights obligations whenever and wherever state power is exercised in the performance of border

---

[25] Third Party Intervention by the Council of Europe Commissioner for Human Rights, under Article 36, paragraph 3, of the European Convention on Human Rights in *S.S. and Others v Italy* App no 21660/18 (ECtHR, 15 November 2019) CommDH (2019) 29 para 14: 'In the Commissioner's view, this shift is closely related to a number of interconnected actions taken by Council of Europe member states, individually and collectively, including within the framework of their membership of the European Union. This includes the gradual withdrawal, both in terms of vessels at sea and in geographical coverage, of maritime operations involving member states. This decline began with the discontinuation of Italy's Operation Mare Nostrum in October 2014.'

[26] UN Special Rapporteur on the Human Rights of Migrants, 'Report on Means to Address the Human Rights Impact of Pushbacks on Land and at Sea' (12 May 2021) A/HRC/47/30.

[27] Valsamis Mitsilegas 'Contested Sovereignty in Preventive Border Control: Civil Society, the "Hostile Environment" and the Rule of Law' in Mary Bosworth and Lucia Zedner (eds), *Privatising Border Control: Law at the Limits of the Sovereign State* (Oxford University Press 2022) 36–56.

[28] Mariagiulia Giuffré, *The Readmission of Asylum Seekers under International Law* (Hart 2020) 246.

control functions.[29] Under this model, effective control is understood not solely on the basis of the intensity or directness of any physical force that may be applied, but also on the basis of its material impact to determine the course of events unlocked by its exercise, even when the relevant activity of the state is carried out from a distance and applying minimal coercion.[30] In developing this model, Moreno-Lax has drawn inspiration from the law of the sea[31] and from other international human rights bodies.[32]

This extensive interpretation of jurisdiction remains to be tested with regard to the different scenarios of state attempts to negate the rule of law vis-à-vis migrants, ranging from omission, to delegation of coercive intervention to third states on the high seas, to more remote ways of cooperation including training and the provision of financial support and intelligence.[33] An emblematic instance of rule of law negation concerns cooperation between Italy and Libya, consisting in particular of support by the Italian authorities to, and cooperation with, the Libyan Coast Guard to strengthen its ability to intercept migrants at sea and changes in Italy's response to distress calls and its coordination of specific rescue operations. This cooperation is tested in the pending (at the time of writing) case before the ECtHR of *S.S. and Others v. Italy*.[34] The case concerns a search and rescue operation performed

[29] Violeta Moreno-Lax, 'Meta-Borders and the Role of Law: From Externalisation to "Responsibilisation" in Systems of Contactless Control' (2024) *Netherlands International Law Review*.

[30] Ibid.

[31] UNGA, Convention on the Law of the Sea (adopted 10 December 1982, entered into force 16 November 1994) 1833 UNTS 3.

[32] Such as the Convention against Torture and Other Cruel, Inhuman or Degrading Treatment or Punishment (adopted 10 December 1984, entered into force 26 June 1987) 1465 UNTS 85; the International Covenant on Civil and Political Rights (ICCPR) (adopted 16 December 1966, entered into force 23 March 1976) 999 UNTS 171; Human Rights Committee *A.S. and others v. Italy and Malta*, where the Committee found that Italy violated the communicants' right to life under Article 6(1) ICCPR, for not acting with the required due diligence in protecting life at sea and for depriving the victims of access to an effective remedy, due to the unjustified delays in carrying out a criminal investigation over the incident. For a commentary see Gabriela Citroni, 'No More Elusion of Responsibility for Rescue Operations at Sea: The Human Rights Committee's Views on the Case A.S., D.I., O.I. and G.D. v. Italy and Malta' (*Opinion Juris*, 9 March 2021), https://opiniojuris.org/2021/03/09/no-more-elusion-of-responsibility-for-rescue-operations-at-sea-the-human-rights-committees-views-on-the-case-a-s-d-i-o-i-and-g-d-v-italy-and-malta/, accessed 12 October 2024.

[33] See, for example, 'The EU Approach on Migration in the Mediterranean' (*Parliament*, June 2021), https://www.europarl.europa.eu/RegData/etudes/STUD/2021/694413/IPOL_STU(2021)694413_EN.pdf, accessed 12 October 2024.

[34] *S.S. and Others v Italy* App no 21660/18 (ECtHR, 15 November 2019); see Andreina De Leo, 'S.S. and others v Italy: Shaping Responsibility for Migrants Abuses in Libya'

on 6 November 2017 by the Libyan Coast Guard patrol vessel *Ras Jadir* and the non-governmental organization Sea-Watch's *Sea-Watch 3* in response to a distress call diffused by the Italian Maritime Rescue Coordination Centre (MRCC) coming from a sinking migrant dinghy, carrying around 150 passengers. According to the 17 survivors of the incident (the applicants), the Libyan Coast Guard arrival caused a strong water movement which led to the death of at least 20 people who had fallen from the boat. Furthermore, the Libyan Coast Guard obstructed the *Sea-Watch* rescue operations by throwing objects, as well as hitting and threatening the migrants with ropes and weapons, without providing life jackets to those who were in the water. *Sea-Watch* was eventually able to rescue and bring to safety in Italy 59 passengers. Forty-seven migrants were ultimately returned to Libya, where several of them faced serious human rights violations, including being detained in inhumane conditions, beaten, and sold to a captor who tortured them.[35] It is alleged that before reaching the scene, the Libyan Coast Guard communicated with the MRCC in Rome, which informed it of the location of the boat in distress. Furthermore, the patrol vessel of the Libyan Coast Guard performing the operation was one of the four patrol boats that had been donated by Italy to the Libyan Coast Guard on 15 May 2017. An Italian navy helicopter was also present during the incident.[36]

S.S. and Others reflects the challenges in upholding the rule of law in cases of cooperative coercive extraterritorial immigration control operations. Moreno-Lax has argued in favour of an expansive application of jurisdiction, in an attempt to address state evasion of responsibility in this case. She notes that the difference of *S.S.* from *Hirsi* is that the former involves control by proxy, consisting of Libyan interception on the high seas.[37] Moreno-Lax has argued that in *S.S.* the coordination of the rescue/interdiction operation was undertaken by MRCC Rome through a combination of prescriptive and executive action, with knowledge of the likely outcome and that Italy's conduct facilitated the whole process that led to the involvement of the Libyan Coast Guard and created the conditions for the several violations complained of to materialize, which is an indication of the existence of jurisdiction under Article 1 ECHR.[38] Moreno-Lax has argued that the Italian

(*PILIPG*, 6 January 2020), https://www.publicinternationallawandpolicygroup.org/lawyering-justice-blog/2020/4/23/ss-and-others-v-italy-sharing-responsibility-for-migrants-abuses-in-libya, accessed 12 October 2024.

35 Ibid.

36 Ibid.

37 Violeta Moreno-Lax, 'The Architecture of Functional Jurisdiction: Unpacking Contactless Control – On Public Powers, *S.S. and others v Italy* and the "Operational Model"' (2020) 21(3) *German Law Journal* 387.

38 Ibid 406.

authorities knew or ought to have known the human rights violations that calling the Libyan Coast Guard to intervene would entail.[39] She has adopted a holistic view of jurisdiction, arguing that the isolation of particular elements is not required to establish effective control triggering jurisdiction under the ECHR: she has argued that the evaluation of a concrete situation requires that attention be paid to the entire constellation of all the relevant channels through which state functions are exercised, be they factual, legal, or both at the same time.[40] Papastavridis, on the other hand, has argued that the law of the sea can afford a different or broader reading of the jurisdictional threshold of the Convention when its application at sea is at issue, adding that for jurisdiction to be established in *S.S.* the applicants should substantiate that the Italian authorities were in full knowledge of the distress situation, that they had designated an on-the-scene coordinator, and that they had instructed him or her to take specific action vis-à-vis the persons in distress. Papastavridis has added that even then, the Court should assess whether the loss of lives at sea amounted to a violation of the positive obligations of Italy under Article 2 ECHR and has noted that in that assessment, the search and rescue rules may prove very helpful for the Court in examining the due diligence of Italy in this regard.[41]

The challenges in upholding the rule of law in the evolution of cooperative extraterritorial immigration control are further exacerbated by the proliferation of cooperation mechanisms between European states (and the European Union [EU] itself) and third states through the provision of support to the latter, with the aim of strengthening the capacity of third states to perform preventive immigration control in their own territory and thus stopping migrants from embarking in the Mediterranean and ultimately preventing them from reaching the border of the destination state.[42] Current litigation in *S.S.* contains the promise of extending ECHR jurisdiction in cases of cooperative coercive immigration control conducted together with third states and extending into the territory of the Member States. When the EU is involved in such instances (including operations by Frontex or Eunavfor Med), the Charter of Fundamental Rights will apply extraterritorially to acts of EU bodies, missions and agencies.[43] However, the legal landscape becomes even more complex in situations where the link

[39] Ibid 408.

[40] Ibid 414.

[41] Efthymios Papastavridis, 'The European Convention of Human Rights and Migration at Sea: Reading the "Jurisdictional Threshold" of the Convention Under the Law of the Sea Paradigm' (2020) 21(3) *German Law Journal* 417.

[42] European Parliament (n 33).

[43] Article 51 of the EU Charter states that the latter applies to EU institutions, bodies, offices, and agencies, as well as Member States as soon as they are implementing EU law.

between support and extraterritorial immigration control is not as direct. Examples include capacity building in third states through the provision of financial support and/or training, as well as the provision of intelligence on migration flows to third states (through, for instance, Eurosur).[44] All these instances of cooperation have the potential to lead to human rights violations in the territory of third countries, in stopping migration flows and in undermining the right to asylum. Of relevance here is the argument put forward by Giuffré and Moreno-Lax, who have argued that in such cases states have international responsibility under international law under complicity (Article 16 of the International Law Commission's Articles on State Responsibility) and direction and control (Article 17).[45] Their model of 'contactless control'[46] is an important tool to address the rule of law deficit inherent in these forms of extraterritorial immigration control. In particular, extraterritorial surveillance originating in the EU, transmitted by state parties to a third state resulting in the deflection of migrant flows by the authorities of the third state would also fall under the jurisdiction of the ECtHR under the effective control criterion, as these operations have an extraterritorial effect and constitute a continuum between the surveillance actions leading directly to enforcement actions in the third state.[47]

3 Extraterritorializing the external border: pushbacks at the physical border

The evolution of extraterritorial immigration control from pushbacks to pullbacks and the increasing co-option of third states in immigration enforcement on behalf of destination states has been aiming at preventing migrants from reaching the physical border and the territory of these states. In instances where these efforts have failed, and migrants have managed to actually reach the border, a new trend has emerged recently: of negating the application of the law to these migrants, even though they have reached the physical border of a state.[48] This trend is manifested clearly by the growing state practice of pushbacks at the external border, linked many times with

---

[44] Eurosur, see https://home-affairs.ec.europa.eu/policies/schengen-borders-and-visa/border-crossing/eurosur_en, accessed 12 October 2024.

[45] Violeta Moreno-Lax and Mariagiulia Giuffré, 'The Raise of Consensual Containment: From "Contactless Control" to "Contactless Responsibility" for Forced Migration Flows' in Singh Juss (ed), *Research Handbook on International Refugee Law* (Edward Elgar, 2019).

[46] See also Giuffré (n 28) 245.

[47] Valsamis Mitsilegas, 'Cartografía de la Externalización del Control Migratorio: Ideas a Partir del Régimen de la UE sobre Tráfico Ilícito de Migrantes' (2020) 73–74 *Revista Española de Derecho Europeo* 23.

[48] FRA, 'Fundamental Rights Report 2024' (2024).

violence against migrants.[49] Pushback practices are being normalized[50] and are no longer observed exclusively in the context of extraterritorial immigration control,[51] but are increasingly documented at the EU external border and within the EU territory.[52] They entail essentially a denial of the rule of law towards third-country nationals, whose access to the territory is not accompanied by access to law. In this manner, pushbacks challenge a number of fundamental rights, including the right to asylum and the prohibition of collective expulsions, which as has been eloquently noted can be seen as a fence prohibiting the expulsion of persons without a minimum examination of each case because only such minimum examination can guarantee that there is no *refoulement*.[53] Yet in spite of the profound negative effect of pushbacks on the rule of law and fundamental rights, we have witnessed recently the trend by the ECtHR to justify such state practices. This justification is linked with the negation of the applicability of the law to third-country nationals who have reached the external border. In the case of *N.D. and N.T.*,[54] the ECtHR found that the expulsion of third-country nationals from the Spanish land border was not in breach of the Convention. The Court did so by privileging in its reasoning the assessment of whether the migrant's 'own conduct' contributed to how they reached the border. The Court referred to its earlier case-law according to which the applicant's own conduct is a relevant factor in assessing the protection to be afforded under Article 4 of Protocol No. 4.[55] In a key paragraph, the Strasbourg Court stated that:

> In the Court's view, the same principle must also apply to situations in which the conduct of persons who cross a land border in an unauthorised manner, deliberately take advantage of their large numbers and use force, is such as to create a clearly disruptive situation which is difficult to control and endangers public safety. In this context, however, in assessing a complaint under Article 4 of Protocol No. 4, the

---

49 On the latter see FRA, 'Guidance on Investigating Ill-treatment at Borders' (July 2024).

50 See Council of Europe (n 4).

51 See Mariagiulia Giuffre, *The Readmission of Asylum Seekers under International Law* (Hart 2020).

52 Council of Europe (n 4). It is noted that as these practices are widespread, and in some countries systematic, these 'pushbacks' can be considered as part of national policies rather than incidental actions.

53 Dana Schmaltz, 'Enlarging the Hole in the Fence of Migrants' Rights: *A.A. and others v. North Macedonia*' (*Verfassungsblog*, 6 April 2022), https://verfassungsblog.de/enlarging-the-hole-in-the-fence-of-migrants-rights/, accessed 12 October 2024.

54 *N.D. and N.T. v Spain* (n 19).

55 Ibid para 200.

> Court will importantly take account of whether, in the circumstances of the particular case, the respondent State provided genuine and effective access to means of legal entry, in particular border procedures. Where the respondent State provided such access but an applicant did not make use of it, the Court will consider, in the present context and without prejudice to the application of Articles 2 and 3, whether there were cogent reasons not to do so which were based on objective facts for which the respondent State was responsible.[56]

The Court's reasoning is highly problematic. It reverses the power asymmetry between the state and the migrant by claiming that states are threatened by collective migrant violence. This rhetoric goes beyond a mere securitization of migration and views, in an unsubstantiated and exaggerated manner, migrants as a direct threat to state stability. This securitization and militarization of migration fuels further attempts to limit access to the rule of law through the contamination of the legal discourse by nebulous concepts such as the 'instrumentalization' of migration.[57] Crucially, by over-emphasizing the significance of migrants' 'own conduct' the Court's discourse reveals again the strength of the preventive paradigm based on the concept of the 'good' and the 'deserving' migrant who will not abuse the system[58] – only in this case probity is to be proven not by having a claim to asylum, or by submitting an asylum application (whose possibility is essentially denied by pushbacks), but by accessing the border at points specifically designated by states, where access to the territory is becoming more and more difficult through the establishment of transit zones and border procedures.[59] The Strasbourg Court attempts to balance its suspicion towards migrants with a requirement to states to provide genuine and effective access to legal entry, a requirement which appears to disregard current reality.[60] In subsequent case-law, the Strasbourg Court found that pushbacks by Poland and Hungary were in breach of the prohibition of collective expulsion as they did not result from the migrants' 'own conduct'[61]

---

56 Ibid para 20, emphasis added.

57 See Chapter 2.

58 Sergio Carrera, 'The Strasbourg Court Judgement N.D. and N.T. v Spain: A Carte Blanche to Push Backs at EU External Borders?' (EUI Working Paper RSCAS, 2020/21), https://cadmus.eui.eu/handle/1814/66629, accessed 12 October 2024.

59 On border procedures, see Chapter 2.

60 Daniel Thym, 'A Restrictionist Revolution? A Counter-intuitive Reading of the ECtHR's N.D & N.T. Judgment on "Hot Expulsions"' (*EU Migration Law Blog*, 17 February 2020), http://eumigrationlawblog.eu/a-restrictionist-revolution-a-counter-intuitive-reading-of-the-ecthrs-n-d-n-t-judgment-on-hot-expulsions/, accessed 12 October 2024.

61 *M.K. and Others v Poland* App nos 40503/17, 42902/17 and 43643/17 (ECtHR, 23 July 2020) para 207.

and as individuals were denied a genuine and effective opportunity to seek protection,[62] while it also confirmed that irregular entry as such did not preclude the applicability of Article 4 of Protocol No. 4 of the Convention.[63]

In spite of these attempts to clarify and nuance its jurisprudence, the ECtHR's 'own conduct' test in *N.D. and N.T.* remains applicable. This has been confirmed in the recent ruling of *A.A. and Others v North Macedonia.*[64] In its ruling, the Strasbourg Court applied *N.D. and N.T.* and again found that there was no case of collective expulsion. The Court added here another element to the 'bad character' of the migrant, namely that the applicants had not been interested in applying for asylum in the respondent state, but had rather been interested only in transiting through it.[65] The Court ignored reports and concerns regarding pushbacks, and found that 'in spite of some shortcomings in the asylum procedure and reported pushbacks' it was not convinced that the respondent state failed to provide genuine and effective access to procedures for legal entry into North Macedonia.[66] Denial of access to the rule of law was the migrants' fault: it was in fact the applicants who placed themselves in jeopardy by participating in the illegal entry onto Macedonian territory, taking advantage of the group's large numbers; they did not make use of the existing legal procedures for gaining lawful entry to North Macedonian territory, thus the lack of individual removal decisions can be attributed to the fact that the applicants, if they indeed wished to assert rights under the Convention, did not make use of the official entry procedures existing for that purpose, and was thus a consequence of their own conduct.[67] The exclusionary spirit of *N.D. and N.T.* is thus alive and well.

[62] In *Shahzad v Hungary* App no 12625/17 (ECtHR, 8 October 2021) para 65, the Strasbourg Court held that the removal of the applicant to the external side of the border fence amounted to an expulsion within the meaning of Article 4 of Protocol No 4 ECHR (para 52). The ECtHR noted that the only way the applicant could have entered Hungary legally was through the two transit zones in Tompa and Röszke, which were located approximately 40km and 84km respectively from the location the applicant had been returned to (para 63). The ECtHR held it was nearly impossible to make use of the asylum procedure there and concluded that Hungary had failed to provide the applicant with an effective means of legal entry and that the lack of an individual expulsion decision could not be attributed to his own conduct.

[63] *M.H. and Others v Croatia* App nos 15670/18 and 43115/18 (ECtHR, 18 November 2021) paras 279–280.

[64] *A.A. and Others v North Macedonia* App nos 55798/16 and 4 others (ECtHR, 5 April 2022).

[65] Ibid para 121.

[66] Ibid para 122.

[67] Ibid para 123, by reference to *N.D. and N.T. v Spain* (para 231).

The approach of the Strasbourg Court sits uneasily with EU law.[68] The Strasbourg case-law justifies the non-applicability of the law to third-country nationals who have reached the EU external border and thus enables the further removal of third-country nationals from the territory of the Union including through collective expulsion and pushbacks. Pushbacks constitute a direct challenge to the rule of law and render access to asylum illusory. State practices on pushbacks thus challenge a number of key provisions of both primary and secondary EU law.[69] Of greater relevance to the limitation by EU law of the preventive agenda in pushbacks are Articles 18 and 19 of the Charter that enshrine the right to asylum and *non-refoulement* and prohibition of collective expulsions respectively Article 78 Treaty on the Functioning of the European Union (TFEU) (asylum policy ensuring compliance with the principle of *non-refoulement*), and a number of provisions of secondary EU law, including in the Schengen Borders Code whose application is without prejudice to the rights of refugees and persons requesting international protection, in particular as regards *non-refoulement*.[70]

The Court of Justice will be the key venue where the compatibility of state practice on pushbacks with EU law will be tested. In a related matter on the non-application of the law on the external border, the Court has already ruled against state efforts to exclude access to the law in the case of Hungary's transit zones. The Court found such practices contrary to Article 6(1) of the recast Asylum Procedures Directive,[71] noting the consistent and generalized administrative practice of the Hungarian authorities aimed at limiting access to the transit zones of Röszke and Tompa, so systematically and drastically, that third-country nationals or stateless persons who, arriving from Serbia, wished to access, in Hungary, the international protection procedure, in practice were confronted with the virtual impossibility of making an application for international protection in Hungary.[72] In a departure from the Strasbourg Court's approach in *N.D. and N.T.*, the Court of Justice of the European Union noted that, while it is for Member States to ensure

[68] Nora Markard, 'A Hole of Unclear Dimensions: Reading N.D. and N.T. v Spain' (*EU Migration Law Blog*, 1 April 2020), https://eumigrationlawblog.eu/a-hole-of-unclear-dimensions-reading-nd-and-nt-v-spain/, accessed 12 October 2024.

[69] Tineke Strik, 'Mechanisms to Prevent Pushbacks' in Sergio Carrera and Marco Stefan (eds), *Fundamental Rights Challenges in Border Controls and Expulsion of Irregular Immigrants in the European Union: Complaint Mechanisms and Access to Justice* (Routledge 2020) 234, 239.

[70] Regulation (EU) 2016/399 of the European Parliament and of the Council of 9 March 2016 on a Union Code on the rules governing the movement of persons across borders (Schengen Borders Code) [2016] OJ L77/1 (SCB), art 3, the obligation to refuse entry 'shall be without prejudice to the application of special provisions concerning the right of asylum and to international protection'.

[71] Case C-808/18, *Commission v Hungary* (17 December 2020) EU:C:2020:1029, para 119.

[72] Ibid para 118 (emphasis added).

that external borders are crossed legally under the Schengen Borders Code (with Regulation 2016/399), compliance with such an obligation cannot, however, justify the Member States' infringement of Article 6 of Directive 2013/32.[73] It is submitted that this reasoning is also applicable in cases of pushbacks from the external border and from the territory of EU Member States. The right to asylum and obligations under secondary EU asylum law take precedence over pushbacks and barriers to access to the asylum procedure and to the rule of law.[74]

4 Outsourcing refugee status determination to third states: the UK–Rwanda model

A further example of the negation of the application of the law to migrants who have reached the territory of the state can be found in the recently abandoned arrangements for the transfer of asylum seekers between the UK and Rwanda. At the time of writing, the recently elected Labour government has put in place secondary legislation which disapplies the legislation which creates the scheme. However, the analysis here remains relevant as proposals for outsourcing refugee status determination to third states remain on the table in various parts of Europe. The analysis of the UK–Rwanda scheme is also key to highlight the fundamental rule of law deficit in this model, which consists of the negation of the application of the law of the state of destination, coupled with the removal of asylum seekers to a third state and the determination of their asylum applications in the third state *under the law of the third state*.

Under this paradigm, individuals have reached the territory of the destination state, but that latter negates the application of its asylum law to them, detention and removal to a third state, regardless of any link between the individuals concerned and this state. It is for the third state then to examine the asylum claims under its own law and determine the legal position of the transferred asylum seekers accordingly, thus absolving the destination state which has transferred the asylum seekers of any legal responsibility. This paradigm is based on the negation of law towards third-country nationals who have reached the territory of the UK. Under the Illegal Migration Act 2023, the Secretary of State is under a duty to remove anyone who enters the UK irregularly.[75] As it has been validly observed, the Act in effect

[73] Ibid para 127. The Directive has now been repealed by Regulation (EU) 2024/1348 of the European Parliament and of the Council of 14 May 2024 establishing a common procedure for international protection in the Union [2024] OJ L 2024/1348.

[74] On access to asylum see Case C-72/22 PPU *M.A v Valstybės sienos apsaugos tarnyba* (30 June 2022) EU:C:2022:431.

[75] Illegal Migration Act 2023, s.1(2)(a).

extinguishes the right to seek asylum in the UK for those who do not follow a 'safe and legal route'.[76] The incompatibility of the Illegal Migration Act with the ECHR and refugee law has been highlighted.[77] The Act effectively excludes third-country nationals from the application of the law of the UK, although they are located within the territory of the UK, and prevents the lodging of asylum claims in the UK. This exclusion from the asylum system is backed up by the normalization of detention,[78] introducing a paradigm which has been reflected to some extent in EU law through the adoption of the Pact on Migration and Asylum.[79] Moreover, in a direct clash with the ECHR, section 55 of the Illegal Migration Act allows any Minister of the Crown to refuse to comply with an interim measure from the ECtHR. If the Minister decides to proceed with the removal, courts must disregard the interim measures.[80] In this manner, the Illegal Migration Act challenges the rule of law in a multitude of ways: in negating the application of domestic asylum law to individuals who have reached the territory and are within the jurisdiction of the UK; in negating thus the application of international and domestic human rights and refugee law safeguards to these individuals; and in negating the UK's duties as a signatory to the ECHR.

The UK–Rwanda scheme was based on the conclusion of a Memorandum of Understanding (MoU) between the UK and Rwanda setting out a scheme of removals of asylum seekers from the UK to Rwanda in order for their asylum claims to be determined there under the law of Rwanda. The legality and compatibility of this arrangement with human rights and refugee law have been litigated in UK courts culminating in a ruling of the Supreme Court.[81] The Supreme Court engaged with two related, but distinct, rule of law points. The first point concerned the compatibility of the UK–Rwanda scheme with refugee law and the ECHR. The second point concerned the extent to which the determination of Rwanda as a safe country by the executive could be scrutinized by the judiciary, raising a broader point of judicial accountability of government as a fundamental rule of law prerequisite.

---

[76] Stephanie Palmer, 'Editorial: Illegal Immigration Act' (2023) 5 *European Human Rights Law Review* 423.

[77] Ibid.

[78] The Act expands the powers of detention of the Secretary of State. Individuals may be detained if an 'immigration officer suspects' that the person meets the four conditions in s.2 of the IMA.16- IMA 2023 s.11(2). Emphasis added.

[79] See Chapter 2.

[80] Valsamis Mitsilegas and Elspeth Guild, 'The UK and the ECHR after Brexit: The Challenge of Immigration Control' (2024) 5 *European Convention of Human Rights Law Review* 116.

[81] *R on the application of AAA and Others* [2023] UKSC 42.

In terms of the first point, the Supreme Court held unanimously that the UK–Rwanda scheme was contrary to the principle of *non-refoulement*.[82] The Supreme Court emphasized that the principle of *non-refoulement* is enshrined in a multitude of international law instruments which are binding on the UK: the Refugee Convention,[83] the United Nations Convention against Torture and Other Cruel, Inhuman or Degrading Treatment or Punishment of 1984,[84] the United Nations International Covenant on Civil and Political Rights of 1966,[85] and the ECHR.[86] Significantly, the Supreme Court held that it may be that the principle of *non-refoulement* also forms part of customary international law, noting that the UK has subscribed to this view, along with the other states parties to the Refugee Convention, in the 2001 Declaration of States Parties to the 1951 Convention and/or its 1967 Protocol Relating to the Status of Refugees.[87] The Court concluded that the principle of *non-refoulement* is therefore given effect by the ECHR, but also by other international conventions to which the UK is party and that it is a core principle of international law, to which the UK government has repeatedly committed itself on the international stage, consistently with this country's reputation for developing and upholding the rule of law.[88] Under domestic law, asylum seekers are protected against *refoulement* by a variety of legal sources: not only by the Human Rights Act, but also by provisions in the 1993, the 2002 and the 2004 Immigration Acts, under which Parliament has given effect to the Refugee Convention as well as the ECHR.[89] The Supreme Court placed the examination of the Rwanda scheme thus firmly within an international rule of law framework, in which the ECHR takes central place.

The Supreme Court devoted a significant part of its ruling on examining whether Rwanda was a safe third country. Hickman has noted eloquently that the Court devoted 30 paragraphs to what it called a brief summary of the large amount of evidence demonstrating systemic weaknesses in Rwanda's asylum system.[90] The examination entailed detailed scrutiny of the system on the ground. The Supreme Court came to the conclusion that the Court of Appeal was entitled, on the evidence before it, to consider that there were substantial grounds for believing that asylum seekers would face a real risk of

[82] Ibid para 105.
[83] Ibid para 20.
[84] Ibid para 21.
[85] Ibid para 22.
[86] Ibid para 23.
[87] Ibid para 25.
[88] Ibid para 26.
[89] Ibid para 33.
[90] Tom Hickman, 'Rwanda Redux' (2023) 45(24) *London Review of Books*.

ill-treatment by reason of *refoulement* in the event that they were removed to Rwanda.[91] The Court examined in this context: the general human rights situation in Rwanda[92] and the adequacy of Rwanda's asylum system.[93] In terms of the latter, the Supreme Court held first that there are concerns which relate to the asylum process itself[94] and about the willingness of the judiciary to find against the Rwandan government.[95] The Supreme Court further noted the risk of a lack of independence in politically sensitive cases not only in the judiciary, but in terms of the provision of independent legal advice,[96] and also noted the absence of legal representation.[97] The Supreme Court further raised concerns related to the outcome of the asylum process,[98] about Rwanda's practice of *refoulement*,[99] and fundamentally, about the inadequacy of the Rwandan government's understanding of the requirements of refugee law, with its response to the United Nations High Commissioner for Refugees' (UNHCR) evidence demonstrating a misunderstanding of the meaning of the concept of *refoulement*.[100]

A key aspect of the Supreme Court's judgment was the question of whether to focus on reality on the ground or on the assurances given by the Rwandan government with regard to the treatment of asylum seekers in Rwanda in the future under the MoU. The Court noted that the defects in past and current practice are important factors in assessing future risk, particularly because the Migration and Economic Development Partnership with Rwanda does not establish a new asylum process, but is based on the continuation of the existing system operated by the Rwandan authorities. The Court held that there is reason to apprehend that there is a real risk that the practices described will not change, at least in the short term. The provision of resources by the UK government does not mean that the problems which we have described can be resolved in the short term. Monitoring arrangements may be capable of detecting failures in the asylum system, and over time may result in the introduction of improvements, but that will come too late to eliminate the risk of *refoulement* currently faced by asylum seekers removed to Rwanda. Furthermore, the suppression of criticism of the government by lawyers and others is liable to discourage the reporting of problems, and so undermine

91 *R on the application of AAA and Others* (n 81) para 73.
92 Ibid paras 75–76.
93 Ibid paras 77–94.
94 Ibid para 79.
95 Ibid para 82.
96 Ibid para 83.
97 Ibid para 84.
98 Ibid paras 85–86.
99 Ibid paras 87–90.
100 Ibid para 91.

the effectiveness of monitoring. It is also unclear whether the monitoring arrangements could provide a solution to problems emanating from the Rwandan government's interpretation of its obligations under the Refugee Convention, or from a lack of independence in the legal system in politically sensitive cases.[101] The Supreme Court proceeded with a strong criticism of the government's approach in a passage that is worth quoting at length:

> The Secretary of State advances a somewhat surprising argument to the effect that it does not matter if asylum claims are not processed correctly, because asylum seekers will not be subject to refoulement in any event. In relation to that argument, we note that if an asylum claim is wrongly rejected, and the asylum seeker does not have some other entitlement to remain in Rwanda, the government of Rwanda undertakes under paragraph 10.4 of the MOU … remove the person only 'to a country in which they have a right to reside'. That country will normally be the country of which the asylum seeker is a national or citizen: that is to say, the country which he has fled, and in which (ex hypothesi) he faces persecution.[102]

Finally, the Court addressed the argument that the Rwandan government entered into the arrangements with the UK in good faith. The Court accepted the reputational and financial incentives of the Rwandan government to adhere to the arrangements, but added:

> Nevertheless, intentions and aspirations do not necessarily correspond to reality: the question is whether they are achievable in practice. The central issue in the present case is therefore not the good faith of the government of Rwanda at the political level, but its practical ability to fulfil its assurances, at least in the short term, in the light of the present deficiencies of the Rwandan asylum system, the past and continuing practice of *refoulement* (including in the context of an analogous arrangement with Israel), and the scale of the changes in procedure, understanding and culture which are required.[103]

The second aspect of rule of law scrutiny by the Supreme Court, which formed a key question underpinning the Rwanda litigation in all instances from the Divisional to the Supreme Court, has been the extent to which the judiciary is under the duty to scrutinize executive decisions and assessments

[101] Ibid para 93.
[102] Ibid para 94.
[103] Ibid para 102.

which have human rights implications – in the present case the assessment by the UK government that Rwanda is a safe third country. This question is fundamentally a rule of law question, testing the extent to which the executive is bound by the rule of law. The Court of Appeal overturned the approach by the Divisional Court, by finding that the Divisional Court did not apply the correct scrutiny test by being essentially deferential to the executive's assessment – with the Divisional Court seemingly seeing its function as reviewing the Secretary of State's assessment and deciding whether it was a tenable view, rather than making its own assessment of the grounds for apprehending a risk of *refoulement* in the light of the evidence as a whole.[104] The Supreme Court did not address this issue directly, but still held that it was satisfied that the Court of Appeal was entitled in any event to interfere with the Divisional Court's conclusion and to consider the question for itself.[105]

The Supreme Court held that the Divisional Court's approach to rely primarily on the government's assessment of Rwanda as a safe third country on the basis of assurances was mistaken.[106] The Court has to make its own assessment of whether there are substantial grounds for believing that there is a real risk of *refoulement*. It is not required to accept the government's evaluation of assurances unless there is compelling evidence to the contrary.[107] The government is not necessarily the only or the most reliable source of evidence about matters which may affect the risk of *refoulement*.[108] The Court did not accept the government's suggestion, that assessing the value of assurances given by another country, in the present context, is analogous to assessing whether a particular course of action is in the interests of national security.[109] The Court further placed particular weight on the assessment made by UNHCR, both due to its institutional position and due to its expertise,[110] and noted the particular weight given to UNHCR evidence by the Strasbourg Court.[111] In a further point with a rule of law relevance, the Supreme Court recalled that the MoU was not binding in international law, that it did not create or confer any right on any individual, and that compliance with it was not justiciable in any court of law.[112]

[104] Ibid para 39.
[105] Ibid para 41.
[106] Ibid paras 51–52.
[107] Ibid para 52.
[108] Ibid para 55.
[109] Ibid para 56.
[110] Ibid paras 64–66.
[111] Ibid para 67.
[112] Ibid para 12.

The Supreme Court's ruling thus highlighted multiple failings in the UK government's upholding of the rule of law in terms of applicability of human rights standards, but importantly also in terms of the relationship between the executive and the judiciary. The Court's findings are extremely important for upholding the rule of law in the context of extraterritorial immigration control. The Court places executive action within the parameters of meaningful, independent, evidence-based judicial review focusing on the protection of human rights on the ground. In response to the ruling, the government concluded a treaty with Rwanda (aimed at providing a stronger legally binding framework compared to the previous MoU) concluded in December 2023 and legislation, in the form of the Safety of Rwanda (Asylum and Immigration) Act 2024, aiming at neutralizing – and effectively disregarding – judicial scrutiny of the executive designation of Rwanda as a safe country: Rwanda is safe since the executive has said so.[113] The stated purpose of the Act was 'to prevent and deter unlawful migration, and in particular migration by unsafe and illegal routes, by enabling the removal of persons to the Republic of Rwanda'.[114] In defiance of the Supreme Court's ruling and approach, the Act deprived the UK judiciary from examining claims regarding the safety of Rwanda and the risk of *refoulement*.[115] The Act stated that it was for a Minster of the Crown only to decide whether to comply or not with interim measures by the ECtHR[116] and expressly disallowed domestic courts from having regard to interim measures imposed by Strasbourg.[117] The blatant attack of the Safety of Rwanda Act on the rule of law has been highlighted both during its negotiations[118] as well as

[113] See Pia Lotta Storf, 'Bend It like Britain?' (*Verfassungsblog*, 14 May 2024), https://verfassungsblog.de/bend-it-like-britain/, accessed 12 October 2024.

[114] Safety of Rwanda (Asylum and Immigration) Act 2024, Section 1(1).

[115] Ibid Section 2(3) states that 'a court or tribunal must not consider a review of, or an appeal against, a decision of the Secretary of State or an immigration officer relating to the removal of a person to the Republic of Rwanda to the extent that the review or appeal is brought on the grounds that the Republic of Rwanda is not a safe country'.

[116] Ibid Section 5(2) states that it is for a Minister of the Crown (and only a Minister of the Crown) to decide whether the United Kingdom will comply with the interim measure.

[117] Ibid Section 5(3). Accordingly, a court or tribunal must not have regard to the interim measure when considering any application or appeal which relates to a decision to remove the person to the Republic of Rwanda under a provision of, or made under, the Immigration Acts.

[118] Elspeth Guild and Valsamis Mitsilegas, '"Get that Judge Out of My Sight": The Safety of Rwanda (Asylum and Immigration) Bill' (*EU Migration Law Blog*, 4 March 2024), https://eumigrationlawblog.eu/get-that-judge-out-of-my-sight-the-safety-of-rwanda-asylum-and-immigration-bill/, accessed 12 October 2024.

post-adoption.[119] The fact that the new Labour government has decided not to go ahead with the Rwanda scheme addresses the specific rule of law concerns, but the Rwanda saga and litigation highlights the rule of law challenges inherent in attempts to outsource asylum determination to third states without meaningful judicial scrutiny.

5 Italy–Albania

On 6 November 2023, Italy and Albania entered into an agreement the objective of which is the interception of boats on the high seas (mainly between Italy and Tunisia) and the transfer of their passengers to Albania to detention centres there for determination of their status and expulsion from Albania. Under the agreement, it is for Italian boats to intercept small boats in international waters and to take the passengers to Albania. It is also for Italian authorities to manage the detention centres in Albania (including paying for them and their staff) and to carry out asylum determination procedures for those seeking international protection, with a right of appeal which is envisaged to be carried out online before an existing tribunal based in Rome. Thus, the centres and the asylum and expulsion procedures are planned to be under the exclusive jurisdiction of the Italian authorities. Similarly, the carrying out of expulsion and the destinations is also the exclusive responsibility of Italy. Numbers of detainees is capped (3,000 at any one time). No persons with vulnerabilities will be sent to Albania, according the Italian authorities only single men will be sent there.[120] There is already some information on the physical nature of the detention centres which has been made available by news outlets, which coin the term 'Italy's Guantanamo' for the centre and system.[121]

Under human rights law and international refugee law, it is clear that Italy is responsible for ensuring full compliance to its obligations under the ECHR

---

[119] The British Institute of Human Rights, 'The Safety of Rwanda (Asylum and Immigration) Act', https://www.bihr.org.uk/get-informed/legislation-explainers/the-safety-of-rwanda-asylum-and-immigration-act-a-human-rights-explainer, accessed 12 October 2024.

[120] Amnesty International, 'The Italy-Albania Agreement on Migration: Pushing Boundaries, Threatening Rights' (19 January 2024), <, https://www.amnesty.org/en/documents/eur30/7587/2024/en/, accessed 12 October 2024; Alice Taylor, 'Albania-Italy Migrant Deal Moves ahead as Rome Publishes Tender for Processing Centre' (*EURACTIV*, 21 May 2024), https://www.euractiv.com/section/politics/news/albania-italy-migrant-deal-moves-ahead-as-rome-publishes-tender-for-processing-centre/, accessed 12 October 2024.

[121] Simone Baglivo, 'Italy's "Guantanamo": Inside the Centres for Migrants Rescued from Boats Set to Open in Albania' (*Skynews*, 3 August 2024), https://news.sky.com/story/italys-guantanamo-inside-the-centres-for-migrants-rescued-from-boats-set-to-open-in-albania-13189430, accessed 12 October 2024.

and international law from the moment that an interception operation is planned for its authorities, during the operation itself, during the transport of people to Albania, during their detention there, regarding enabling those people to seek asylum and to receive a fair procedure and to respect the *non-refoulement* duty when assessing, planning or carrying out any expulsion action. The key articles of the ECHR which are engaged are the right to life (Article 2 – the duty to rescue), the prohibition of torture, inhuman or degrading treatment or punishment (Article 3), the right to liberty (Article 5), the right to an effective remedy (including a fair asylum procedure, Article 13), the prohibition on collective expulsion (Article 4 Protocol 4, discussed earlier). Also, the right to leave a country (Article 2(2) Protocol 4) is engaged as regards the right to leave Albania for those detained there. However, both Albania and Italy have ratified the ECHR and while Italy may incur liability regarding the treatment of persons intercepted on the high seas and taken to Albania against their wishes, Albania may also incur liability for human rights violations which take place within its jurisdiction (primarily on its territory) where it either is or ought to be aware of those violations or the high risk of their occurrence by agents of another country. The ECtHR has developed a substantial case-law regarding this form of liability arising from the complicity of a number of European states in the US Extraordinary Rendition Program through permitting the US authorities to establish detention centres on their territory. This case-law is highly relevant to Albania's situation regarding what happens in the Italian detention centres on its territory.[122]

It is less clear whether EU law is engaged by the actions of the Italian and Albanian authorities regarding detention centres and asylum procedures. The problem is that asylum is a field which has been an EU competence since 1999 and the territorial scope is limited to that of the Member States. The existing EU asylum law, the Common European Asylum System (CEAS), which has gone through a major revision in 2024, prohibits sending asylum seekers to a country with which they have no link. This has led experts to consider that the agreement is not consistent with EU law.[123] In an attempt to deflect criticism and avoid EU competence, Italy has undertaken to apply equivalent standards to asylum applications as required by the Qualification Directive (the only part of the CEAS which is not limited to the EU territorial space).

---

122 Elspeth Guild, Didier Bigo and Mark Gibney, *Extraordinary Rendition: Addressing the Challenges of Accountability* (Routledge 2018).

123 Andreina de Leo, 'On the Incompatibility of the Italy-Albania Protocol with EU Asylum Law' (*SIDIBlog*, 15 November 2023), http://www.sidiblog.org/2023/11/15/on-the-incompatibility-of-the-italy-albania-protocol-with-eu-asylum-law/, accessed 12 October 2024.

The European Commission has yet to pronounce on the subject of the applicability of EU law to the Italian programme on the basis that it is studying the situation.[124] The Council of Europe Commission for Human Rights had few qualms about openly criticizing the agreement.[125] There is more than one source of potential EU legal engagement. The first is on grounds of the applicability of the CEAS, the general territorial limitations of the CEAS and the impact of that territorial limitation on the Charter, the scope of which is limited to that of EU law. However, there also exists an EU–Albania Stabilisation and Association Agreement which entered into force in 2009 and which covers asylum cooperation.[126] Article 80 states that the parties shall cooperate in the areas of visa, border control, asylum and migration, and shall set up a framework for cooperation in the field of asylum on the implementation of national legislation to meet the standards of the 1951 Geneva Convention and the 1967 New York Protocol, thereby to ensure that the principle of *non-refoulement* is respected as well as other rights of asylum seekers and refugees. A Stabilisation and Association Council was charged with other joint efforts that can be made to prevent and control illegal immigration, including trafficking and illegal migration networks. According to the EU doctrine on internal and external aspects of EU law, the ERTA doctrine, 'to the extent to which [Union] rules are promulgated for the attainment of the objectives of the Treaty, the Member States cannot, outside the framework of the [Union] institutions, assume obligations which *might affect those rules or alter their scope*'.[127] It is difficult to see how the Italian authorities can justify that the establishment of their Albania programme does not affect or alter the scope of their CEAS obligations.

The main similarity of the Italy–Albania programme and the UK–Rwanda one is that in both cases, the objective appears to be to physically move people (people suspected of having the intention of seeking irregular entry

[124] Jorge Liboreiro and Vinzenzo Genovese, 'Italy-Albania Migration Deal Must Comply with EU and International Law, Says Brussels' (*Euronews*, 7 November 2023), https://www.euronews.com/my-europe/2023/11/07/italy-albania-migration-deal-must-comply-with-eu-and-international-law-says-brussels, accessed 12 October 2024.

[125] Commissioner for Human Rights, 'Italy-Albania Agreement Adds to Worrying European Trend towards Externalising Asylum Procedures' (13 November 2023).

[126] Stabilisation and Association Agreement between the European Communities and their Member States, of the one part, and the Republic of Albania, of the other part [2009] OJ L 107.

[127] Case C-22/70, *Commission v Council* (31 March 1971) EU:C:1971:32 (emphasis added). See Graham Butler and Ramses A. Wessel, 'Happy Birthday ERTA! 50 Years of the Implied External Powers Doctrine in EU Law' (*European Law Blog*, 31 March 2021), https://europeanlawblog.eu/2021/03/31/happy-birthday-erta-50-years-of-the-implied-external-powers-doctrine-in-eu-law/, accessed 12 October 2024.

to the state and asylum seekers) from one jurisdiction to another (in the case of Italy from the high seas to Albania, in the case of the UK directly from the UK to Rwanda). The political objective is that these people, defined exclusively on the basis of their proximity to the physical territory of the state, are prevented from entering or stop being present on the territory. The main differences between the two schemes is that in the Italian case, the state accepts fully responsibility in human rights law for the programme. There is no attempt to avoid the jurisdiction of the ECHR or other human rights law. The only law which Italy seeks to avoid is the CEAS. In the case of the UK, avoiding legal responsibility is a primary aim. Excluding the jurisdiction of the ECtHR is a central component of the programme as set out in this chapter. Of course, the CEAS is no longer relevant for the UK since Brexit, though even before the UK was only bound by the 2004–2005 iteration of the system. Whether either system will achieve any significant change regarding the arrival of people seeking international protection is questionable. It is now unlikely that the UK–Rwanda scheme will ever be put into the effect. However, the Italy–Albania one is being implemented as this book is being written.

6 Conclusion

The aim of states to prevent the arrival of migrants to their external border and territory has led to the proliferation of coercive extraterritorial immigration control practices. The expansion of these practices comes as a response to the imposition of human rights safeguards by courts and aims to evade such safeguards, by essentially negating the application of the law – and the rule of law – to migrants and the absolution of states of any legal responsibility towards migrants. This chapter has analysed the evolution of four different models of extraterritorial immigration control: coercive control on the high seas and in cooperation with and/or in the territory of third states, notably in the form of pushbacks and pullbacks; the extension of pushbacks when migrants reach the external/physical border of states; the outsourcing of the asylum determination process to third states by removing migrants from the territory of the state of destination and examining applications under the law of the state where migrants have been removed – negating thus the application of the law of the destination state (the UK–Rwanda scheme); and the outsourcing of asylum determination in third states, by intercepting migrants before their arrival into the destination state, removing them to a third state and examining the application under the laws of the state of destination (the Italy–Albania scheme). These shifts in extraterritorial immigration control generate a proliferation of borders, ranging from the territory of third countries to the high seas to the physical border of states to their territory. The proliferation of these instances of border control premised upon the negation of the application of the law towards migrants raise profound rule of law challenges by multiplying what can be seen as lawless zones – or legal black holes[128] – in terms of the human rights protection of migrants. While courts are key actors in redressing this fundamental rule of law deficit, their approach thus far has not always been consistent, with a key question for the emerging litigation in domestic and European courts being the degree of discretion or leeway left to national governments claiming that they exercise sovereignty in the field of immigration control (a prominent feature in the problematic *N.D. and N.T.* ruling of the Strasbourg Court). It remains to be seen how the Strasbourg Court will respond to state efforts to undermine its seminar ruling in *Hirsi*, with the challenge being to establish the very applicability of the law in countering state efforts to generate what is in effect lawless borders.

[128] Itamar Mann, 'Maritime Legal Black Holes: Migration and Rightlessness in International Law' (2018) 29 *European Journal of International Law* 347.

2

The Rule of Law Deficit on the Border: The European Union Pact on Migration and Asylum

1 Introduction

The previous chapter examined the rule of law challenges inherent in the proliferation and mutation of practices of extraterritorial immigration control, where states attempt to prevent migrants from reaching their physical border and negate the application of their law once these migrants manage in fact to make it into the border or the territory of the state. This chapter will examine a further attempt by states to limit the legal standards applicable to migrants when reaching the border, this time as developed in the European Union (EU) Pact on Migration and Asylum adopted in 2024. The chapter will highlight the decisive shift in secondary EU law in the Pact in excluding migrants who have reached the EU external border from the full application of EU law, including the full application of EU asylum and fundamental rights law. The chapter focuses on three main elements of this new paradigm: on the imposition of a 'fiction of non-entry' through the new EU procedures and screening measures; on the emergence, and survival in EU law, of the questionable concept of 'instrumentalization' of migration; and on the normalization of detention in the EU external border. In all three instances the rule of law is eroded, as migrants reaching the external border are placed outside of the ordinary legal framework.

2 The fiction of 'non-entry'

Asylum border procedures under the Migration Pact entail a legal fiction of 'non-entry':[1] migrants have reached the EU external border, but reaching

[1] On the fiction of 'non-entry' see Minos Mouzourakis, 'More Laws, Less Law: The European Union's New Pact on Migration and Asylum and the Fragmentation of "Asylum Seeker" Status' (2022) 26(3–4) *European Law Journal* 171.

the border is accompanied by limited access to law. As Apatzidou has noted, the law is not suspended *in toto*, but selectively: some rules may apply but some parts of the legal order are suspended.[2] Border procedures thus reflect a preventive paradigm targeting the unwanted migrant who is portrayed increasingly as unworthy of full legal protection. The Pact has not appeared out of the blue in this context, but has followed an evolution of exclusionary law and practice by the Union and Member States in the field of border procedures.[3] Yet in its proposals in the Pact the Commission took the exclusionary approach in border procedures a step further. The amended Commission proposal for an asylum procedures Directive[4] was underpinned by a preventive agenda informed by the perception of asylum seekers as 'abusive' and expanding the concept of unwanted third-country national to those who are deemed as having a low chance of receiving international protection.

The aim of the proposal was to provide 'tools to respond to abuses of asylum procedures and preventing unauthorised movements'.[5] The Commission put forward a joint asylum and return procedure – aiming to stop third-country nationals at the border and to swiftly return them if their application is rejected – whose purpose was 'to quickly assess abusive asylum requests or asylum requests made at the external border by applicants coming from third countries with a low recognition rate in order to swiftly return those without a right to stay in the Union' – with the joint asylum and return border procedure perceived as an important migration management tool to prevent unauthorized entries and unauthorized movements, in particular as mixed flows include a significant share of asylum applicants who come from countries with a low recognition rate.[6] The Pact thus put forward what the Commission called 'a new pre-entry phase' consisting of pre-screening, a more developed accelerated procedure and a border procedure for asylum and return.[7] New rules on asylum procedures were justified on the grounds of preventing migrants from delaying procedures for the sole purpose of preventing their removal

2 Vasiliki Apatzidou, 'The Normalisation of Denial of Legal Safeguards in the Proposed Asylum and Migration Legislation' (*European Law Blog*, 2 March 2023), https://europeanlawblog.eu/2023/03/02/the-normalization-of-denial-of-legal-safeguards-in-the-proposed-asylum-and-migration-legislation/, accessed 12 October 2024.

3 For an overview see Valsamis Mitsilegas, 'The EU External Border as a Site of Preventive (In)justice' (2022) 28 *European Law Journal* 263.

4 Commission, 'Amended proposal for a Regulation establishing a common procedure for international protection in the Union and repealing Directive 2013/32/EU' COM(2020) 611 final.

5 Ibid 4.

6 Ibid.

7 Ibid 12.

from the Union and misusing the asylum system.[8] The Commission proposal extended significantly the grounds of applying border procedures, normalizing them on the external border,[9] and states expressly that applicants subject to the border procedure will not be authorized to enter the territory of the Member State.[10]

The Commission's preventive approach based on the fiction of 'non-entry' was further confirmed by its proposal for a pre-screening Regulation accompanying the amended Asylum Procedures Regulation.[11] Pre-entry screening would apply (as with the Asylum Procedures Regulation) to both third-country nationals who are present at the external border without fulfilling the entry conditions and to third-country nationals after disembarkation, following a search and rescue operation.[12] The perception of third-country nationals (regardless of their protection needs) as unwanted and as dangerous was thus again being normalized and extends to health and security risks, with pre-screening entailing entering third-country nationals to the wide web of EU migration surveillance infrastructures, including the EU migration databases such as the Schengen Information System (SIS) and the registration of biometric data.[13] The preventive framework of pre-entry screening was confirmed throughout the text of the draft Regulation. Screening should be conducted at or in proximity to the external border, before the persons concerned are authorized to enter the territory, with Member States called to apply measures pursuant to national law to prevent the persons concerned from entering the territory during the screening, a process which may include detention.[14] The pre-screening procedure was aimed at being speedy,[15] and during screening the third-country nationals involved would not be authorized to enter the territory of a Member State.[16]

---

8 Ibid 17.

9 Ibid, amended art 41(1).

10 According to Article 41(6), applicants will not have a right to remain after a rejection decision on a number of grounds. Ibid art 54(1).

11 Commission, 'Proposal for a Regulation introducing a screening of third country nationals at the external borders and amending Regulations (EC) No 767/2008, (EU) 2017/2226, (EU) 2018/1240 and (EU) 2019/817' COM(2020) 612 final.

12 Ibid 1 and art 3(1).

13 Ibid 2.

14 Ibid recital 12.

15 According to art 6(3), the screening must be carried out without delay and shall in any case be completed within five days from the apprehension in the external border area, the disembarkation in the territory of the Member State concerned or the presentation at the border crossing point. In exceptional circumstances, where a disproportionate number of third-country nationals needs to be subject to the screening at the same time, making it impossible in practice to conclude the screening within that time-limit, the period of five days may be extended by a maximum of an additional five days.

16 Ibid art 4.

The negative consequences of the preventive approach embraced in the Pact proposals for the rights of asylum seekers have been well-documented by scholars. Vested-Hansen has noted that the asylum border procedure will in practice merge or overlap with, or have blurred boundaries towards, the pre-entry screening procedure and the return border procedure, leading to a serious risk of deviating from crucial procedural safeguards for asylum seekers and further undermining the effectiveness of the substantive EU rules on qualification of refugees and other third-country nationals in need of protection.[17] The generalization of the fiction of 'non-entry' generates significant rule of law challenges. In a manner reminiscent of the Strasbourg Court's approach in *N.D. and N.T.*,[18] notwithstanding having managed to reach the EU external border, third-country nationals would be deemed not to have reached fully the territory of EU Member States. 'Non-entry' would not lead to complete negation of the law (as with pushbacks), but to prevention of access to the full asylum procedure and safeguards under EU law. Cassarino and Marin have called this a process of 'deterritorialization', whereby territory is separated from the legal order.[19] This process leads to a serious rule of law deficit, whereby national practices of confinement and detention at the border (or even within the territory of Member States) are deemed not to constitute entry to the territory.[20] In this manner, the EU asylum process is transformed from a process of asylum applications within the territory of the Member States governed by the full safeguards of EU law to a situation whereby the majority of asylum seekers are kept at the border and out of the territory only in law but not in terms of physical presence, with limited legal safeguards and with the aim of the process being essentially speedy removal.[21] This approach reflects clearly the preventive paradigm in EU border control viewing third-country nationals

[17] Jens Vested-Hansen, 'Border Procedure: Efficient Examination or Restricted Access to Protection' (*EU Migration and Asylum Law Blog*, 18 December 2020), https://eumigrationlawblog.eu/border-procedure-efficient-examination-or-restricted-access-to-protection/, accessed 12 October 2024.

[18] See Chapter 1.

[19] Jean-Pierre Cassarino and Luisa Marin, 'The Pact on Migration and Asylum: Turning the European Territory into a Non-territory?' (2022) 24(1) *European Journal of Migration and Law* 4.

[20] According to Mouzourakis (n 1), the fiction of non-entry will have a transformative effect on Greece, where the large population of asylum seekers subject to the fast-track border procedure on the islands is deemed to be present on national territory and is not indiscriminately deprived of their liberty until a decision is taken on their claim.

[21] According to Cassarino and Marin (n 19), with the new pre-entry screening and the reformed border procedures, the EU is asking the Member States most concerned by migration fluxes to consolidate the containment function of the external borders.

as a threat.[22] The presumption is that anyone who arrives irregularly must by definition be unwanted in the EU.[23]

The eventual adoption of the new EU asylum procedures and screening measures has confirmed these concerns. The key elements of the implementation of the fiction of non-entry in the adopted legislation are as follows. The Asylum Procedures Regulation[24] provides, with a number of exceptions, the right of an asylum seeker to remain in the territory of the state during the asylum procedure,[25] including where the applicant is a danger to public order or public security.[26] The Regulation further provides for the temporal merger between the admissibility and the substantive asylum interview,[27] and for the application of accelerated border procedures on a number of grounds, many of which involve framing the asylum seeker as dangerous and/or in bad faith.[28] The Regulation includes a number of Articles on asylum border procedures, which are essentially normalized in EU law. The border procedure may take place: following an application made at an external border crossing point or in a transit zone; following apprehension in connection with an unauthorized crossing of the external border; following disembarkation in the territory of a Member State after a search and rescue operation; and following relocation in accordance with Article 67(11) of Regulation (EU) 2024/1351.[29] The application of border procedures is mandatory in a series of circumstances, related to the framing of asylum seekers in bad faith and to asylum success rates.[30] Applicants subject to the border procedure will not be authorized to enter the territory of a Member State.[31] Member States must require applicants to reside at or in proximity to the external border or transit zones as a general rule or in other designated locations within its territory.[32] But the requirement to reside at a particular place will not be regarded as authorization to enter into and stay on the territory of a Member

22 Mitsilegas (n 3).

23 Elspeth Guild, 'Promoting the European Way of Life: Migration and Asylum in the EU' (2020) 26 *European Law Journal* 355, 367.

24 Regulation (EU) 2024/1348 of the European Parliament and of the Council of 14 May 2024 establishing a common procedure for international protection in the Union and repealing Directive 2013/32/EU [2024] OJ L2024/1348 (APR).

25 Ibid art 10(4)(a)–(c).

26 Ibid art 10(4)(c).

27 Ibid art 12(1).

28 Ibid art 42.

29 Ibid art 43(1).

30 Ibid art 45(1) by reference to art 42(1), point (c), (f) or (j).

31 Ibid art 43(2).

32 Ibid art 54(1); see also APR, art 54(2) and (3).

State.[33] Moreover, where an applicant subject to the border procedure needs to be transferred to the determining authority or to a competent court or tribunal of first instance for the purposes of such a procedure, or transferred for the purpose of receiving medical treatment, such travel will not in itself constitute an entry into the territory of a Member State.[34] Applicants subject to a decision which rejects an application as unfounded or manifestly unfounded if at the time of the decision they are subject to an accelerated or to a border procedure will not have the right to remain in the territory of the Member State.[35]

The Asylum Procedures Regulation thus imposes the fiction of non-entry through the normalization of border procedures in EU law. As it has been noted, in the new system, border procedures will become the rule for the vast majority of asylum seekers in Europe and that the summary rejection of asylum applications will become 'the new normal'.[36] Together with the use of accelerated procedures and the use of safe third country concepts, the Asylum Procedures Regulation reflects the noted fact that 'summary rejections of asylum applications remain a central objective of the Pact through the generalization of special procedures and the introduction of vague and disputable notions, leaving a considerable margin of discretion to Member States'.[37]

The fiction of non-entry is further reflected in other instruments in the Pact. The Regulation on a return border procedure[38] expressly states that third-country nationals and stateless persons whose application has been rejected in the context of the asylum border procedure will not be authorized to enter the territory of the Member State concerned.[39] However, the above persons who were detained during the asylum border procedure, who no longer have a right to remain and who are not allowed to remain may continue to be detained for the purpose of preventing their entry into the territory of the Member State concerned, of preparing their return or of carrying out the removal process.[40] So here the Pact introduces a double rule of law deficit: detention by the state without access to its territory.

---

33 Ibid art 54(4).

34 Ibid art 54(5).

35 Ibid art 68(3)(a).

36 Vincent Chetail and Mariana Ferolla Vallandro do Valle, 'The Asylum Procedures Regulation and the Erosion of Refugee's Rights' (*EU Migration and Asylum Law Blog*, 13 May 2024), https://eumigrationlawblog.eu/the-asylum-procedure-regulation-and-the-erosion-of-refugees-rights/#more-8953, accessed 12 October 2024.

37 Ibid.

38 Regulation (EU) 2024/1349 of the European Parliament and of the Council of 14 May 2024 establishing a return border procedure and amending Regulation (EU) 2021/1148 [2024] OJ L 2024/1349 (Regulation on a Return Border Procedure).

39 Ibid art 4(1).

40 Ibid art 5(3).

The fiction of non-entry, in conjunction with the framing of asylum seekers as dangerous and their risk assessment, is present in the new Screening Regulation,[41] whose stated objective is to strengthen the control of third-country nationals crossing the external borders, to identify all third-country nationals subject to the screening and to check against the relevant databases whether the persons subject to the screening might pose a threat to internal security.[42] Screening will happen in principle at the external border[43] and is generalized: it applies to all third-country nationals, regardless of whether they have made an application for international protection, who do not fulfil the entry conditions set out in Article 6 of the Schengen Borders Code and who: are apprehended in connection with an unauthorized crossing of the external border of a Member State;[44] are disembarked in the territory of a Member State following a search and rescue operation;[45] and who have made an application for international protection at external border crossing points or in transit zones.[46] The fiction of non-entry applies in the screening process as well: during the screening, the persons referred to above will not be authorized to enter the territory of a Member State.[47] Yet, in a further example of a double rule of law deficit, the Regulation obliges Member States to lay down in their national law provisions to ensure that these persons remain available to the authorities responsible for carrying out the screening for the duration of the screening, to prevent any risk of absconding, potential threats to internal security resulting from such absconding or potential threats to public health resulting from such absconding.[48]

3 The uses and abuses of the instrumentalization of migration

A further instance of attempts to prevent access of third-country nationals to the territory of EU Member States has been linked with the introduction of

[41] Regulation (EU) 2024/1356 of the European Parliament and of the Council of 14 May 2024 introducing the screening of third-country nationals at the external borders and amending Regulations (EC) No 767/2008, (EU) 2017/2226, (EU) 2018/1240 and (EU) 2019/817 [2024] OJ L 2024/1356 (Screening Regulation).

[42] Ibid art 1. See also Article 15 on the security checks involved.

[43] Ibid art 6; but see also Article 7 establishing the possibility of screening in the territory.

[44] Ibid art 5(1)(a).

[45] Ibid art 5(1)(b).

[46] Ibid art 5(2).

[47] Ibid art 6.

[48] Ibid art 6.

the term 'instrumentalization' of migration into the EU legal vocabulary.[49] Events in the EU external border with Belarus have led the European Council of October 2021 to frame migrant flows as a hybrid threat stemming from attempts by third countries to instrumentalize migrants for political purposes.[50] The European Council called upon the Commission to propose legislation in the field.[51] The Commission has since responded with a package of three measures: a proposal for a Decision on provisional emergency measures for the benefit of Latvia, Lithuania and Poland;[52] a general Regulation addressing situations of instrumentalization in the field of migration and asylum;[53] and a proposal to amend the Schengen Borders Code.[54] A definition of instrumentalization was included in the latter document. According to the Commission, 'instrumentalization of migrants' refers to a situation where a third country instigates irregular migratory flows into the EU by actively encouraging or facilitating the movement of third-country nationals to the external borders, onto or from within its territory and then onwards to those external borders, where such actions are indicative of an intention of a third country to destabilize the Union or a Member State, where the nature of such actions is liable to put at risk essential state functions, including its territorial integrity, the maintenance of law and order or the safeguard of its national security. This definition was inserted in the revision of the Schengen Borders Code[55] and the general Regulation on instrumentalization.[56]

Putting forward this new legal concept of instrumentalization in the field of EU immigration law reflected the confluence between a securitization and a militarization agenda – and framed migration flows as a weapon of war.[57] The Commission claimed that 'a highly worrying phenomenon observed is the increasing role of State actors in artificially creating and

---

49 Mitsilegas (n 3).

50 European Council, European Council meeting (21 and 22 October 2021) – Conclusions, EUCO 17/21, para 19 (Brussels, 22 October 2021), https://www.consilium.europa.eu/media/52622/20211022-euco-conclusions-en.pdf, accessed 12 October 2024.

51 Ibid para 20.

52 Commission, 'Proposal for a Council Decision on provisional emergency measures for the benefit of Latvia, Lithuania and Poland' COM(2021) 752 final.

53 Commission, 'Proposal for a Regulation addressing situations of instrumentalisation in the field of migration and asylum' COM(2021) 890 final (Instrumentalisation proposal).

54 Commission, 'Proposal for a Regulation of the European Parliament and of the Council amending Regulation (EU) 2016/399 on a Union Code on the rules governing the movement of persons across borders' COM(2021) 891 final (Schengen Borders Code proposal).

55 Ibid art 2(27).

56 Commission, 'Instrumentalisation proposal' (n 53) art 1 and recital 1.

57 Mitsilegas (n 3).

facilitating irregular migration, using migratory flows as a tool for political purposes, to destabilize the European Union and its Member States'[58] and stated that 'others' may attempt to conduct hybrid attacks on the Union that include the instrumentalization of migrants in the future.[59] The framing of the potential use of migrants as a means to destabilize the Union or its Member States renders migration as a threat to national security[60] and is used to justify further erosion of the rule of law. The Commission advocated in favour of 'flexibility' for Member States in addressing instrumentalization, going further than the proposals put forward in the Pact.[61] This flexibility is linked with the establishment of a permanent state of emergency on the external border,[62] leading to a permanent paradigm of preventive (in) justice systematically limiting access to the territory and law of the Union and its Member States – with the exception thus becoming the norm.[63] The preventive and securitized/militarized framing behind the use of instrumentalization is further reflected in the Preamble to the Regulation. According to the Preamble, in situations of instrumentalization 'it is essential to prevent the entry of those who do not fulfil entry conditions'.[64] Migration flows are linked to violence which EU Member States are called to address: where Member States are confronted at their external borders with violent actions, including in the context of attempts by third-country nationals to force entry *en masse* and using disproportionate violent means, they should be able to take the necessary measures in accordance with their national law to preserve security, law and order.[65]

The preventive and securitized framing of instrumentalization leads to the normalization of a state of emergency. The Regulation expressly

[58] Commission, 'Instrumentalisation proposal' (n 53) 1.

[59] Ibid.

[60] According to the Explanatory Memorandum, 'where the EU is under attack, it is important that the EU, at the level of the European Council acknowledges that the actions by a third country can be considered as instrumentalisation of migrants. Those actions are not necessarily targeting one or more Member States, but the EU as a whole and therefore require collective EU support'.

[61] Ibid 2.

[62] According to the Explanatory Memorandum, 'the objective of the proposal is to support the Member State facing a situation of instrumentalisation of migrants by setting up a specific emergency migration and asylum management procedure, and, where necessary, providing for support and solidarity measures to manage in an orderly, humane and dignified manner the arrival of persons having been instrumentalised by a third country, with full respect for fundamental rights', reproducing to a large extent the range of possibilities made available to Latvia, Lithuania and Poland under the proposal for a Council Decision on provisional emergency measures for the benefit of those Member States.

[63] Mitsilegas (n 3).

[64] Commission, 'Instrumentalisation proposal' (n 53) recital 6.

[65] Ibid recital 10.

posits an emergency migration and asylum procedure in a situation of instrumentalization of migrants.[66] This emergency procedure departs not only from applicable EU law standards, but also from the highly exclusionary reform of asylum procedures – through the emphasis on border procedures – witnessed in the Pact. The new emergency procedure applies widely in terms of territorial scope to third-country nationals 'apprehended or found in the proximity of the external border with the third country instrumentalising migrants in connection with an unauthorised crossing or who have presented themselves at border crossing points'.[67] By way of derogation from the proposed Asylum Procedures Regulation in the Pact, applications for asylum are registered no later than four weeks after applications are made, with Member States prioritizing the registration of applications; likely to be well founded.[68] Moreover, decisions on the admissibility and on the merits of asylum applications are taken at the border or transit zones regarding *all* registered applications.[69] The maximum duration of this emergency procedure is 16 weeks.[70] In this manner, border procedures – at the border and transit zones – are normalized. They apply to all asylum applicants – who are deemed to constitute a risk to national security – and for whom limited legal safeguards and detention will apply.[71] Reaching the border no longer means access to territory and results in serious derogations from and challenges to EU law. The preventive framing of instrumentalization was further discerned clearly in the Commission's proposal to amend the Schengen Borders Code, which emphasized the objective to prevent unauthorized border crossings[72] via the increased use of technology.[73] The proposal to amend the Schengen Borders Code further normalized the state practices justified by the Strasbourg Court

66 Ibid art 2.

67 Ibid art 2(1).

68 Ibid art 2(1)(a).

69 Ibid art 2(1)(b).

70 Ibid art 2(1)(c).

71 The Commission claims that the detention of applicants should be a measure of last resort, where other sufficient or less coercive measures cannot be applied in a specific case – and that the application of the emergency asylum management procedure will not imply a systematic detention of applicants.

72 According to Article 2 point 12 of the Schengen Borders Code proposal, the Code is modified to now include within border surveillance 'preventative measures to detect and prevent unauthorised border crossings'.

73 Article 13 on border surveillance is amended to include a specific paragraph on instrumentalization (Art 13(5)), justifying the intensification of border surveillance through the enhancement of technical means of surveillance which may include 'modern technologies including drones and motion sensors, as well as mobile units to prevent unauthorised border crossings into the Union'.

in *N.D. and N.T.*,[74] by stating that in a situation of instrumentalization of migrants Member States may limit the number of border crossing points or their opening hours where the circumstances so require.[75]

The proposed measures on the instrumentalization of migration serve to normalize a state of emergency in the control of the EU external border and undermine further the rule of law and challenge fundamental rights enshrined in primary and secondary EU law.[76] This normalization has occurred on the basis of a knee-jerk political reaction which has resulted in an attempt to translate contested political judgments into legal terms.[77] The result has been a legal definition of instrumentalization which is not compatible with the rule of law, it consists of terms which are vague and which do not meet the standards of legal certainty and foreseeability. Moreover, the Commission did not include much detail on the process of deciding whether instrumentalization is taking place,[78] and what the legal safeguards are to ensure that migrant representations are made during the decision-making process on whether instrumentalization is taking place and whether the decision to trigger the emergency procedure itself is subject to a legal remedy. The triggering of the emergency procedure on the grounds of instrumentalization normalized state practices on border procedures and the use of transit zones[79] linked with detention and the application of very limited legal safeguards to the migrants affected. The framing of instrumentalization does away even with existing problematic attempts to risk assess migrants, and it treats *all* migrants reaching the external border as high risk, posing national security threats. Fundamentally, treating individuals as instruments or weapons is a blatant denial of agency and rights, and

[74] See Chapter 1.

[75] Commission, 'Schengen Borders Code proposal' (n 54) modified art 5 adding a new paragraph 4.

[76] Mitsilegas (n 3).

[77] Ibid.

[78] Article 7 of the Schengen Borders Code proposal (n 54) provides for an authorization procedure by the Commission who will assess Member States' requests for derogations on the grounds of instrumentalization. As was noted by ECRE, 'neither the criteria for making the assessment nor the information that the Member State in question is required to provide are set out in this provision'. See European Council on Refugees and Exiles (ECRE), ECRE Comments on the Commission Proposal for a Regulation of the European Parliament and of the Council addressing situations of Instrumentalisation in the field of Migration and Asylum COM (2021) 890 final, https://ecre.org/wp-content/uploads/2022/01/ECRE-Comments-Instrumentalisation-January-2022.pdf, accessed 12 October 2024.

[79] Ibid. On the strengthening of existing Member State border practices, see also Andrew Fallone, 'Understanding the Future of European Union Counter-Smuggling Policy' (EUI STG Policy Papers Issue 2021/19, November 2021), https://cadmus.eui.eu/bitstream/handle/1814/73105/PA_2021_19_STG.pdf?sequence=1, accessed 12 October 2024.

becomes itself an instrument of dehumanization[80] constituting a direct attack on human dignity.

In view of the severe criticisms voiced here, the failure by the EU legislators to adopt the instrumentalization Regulation might be seen as a welcome step towards avoiding an extreme rule of law challenge in EU borders law. Yet elements of the original Commission approach on instrumentalization persist in the EU Pact, framed within the context of crisis and force majeure in EU asylum law. The Regulation adopted to address situations of crisis and force majeure[81] includes a number of references to instrumentalization. The Preamble defines a situation of instrumentalization arising:

> where a third country or a hostile non-state actor encourages or facilitates the movement of third-country nationals or stateless persons to the external borders of the Union or to a Member State, where such actions are indicative of an intention of a third country or a hostile non-state actor to destabilise the Union or a Member State, and where such actions are liable to put at risk essential functions of a Member State, including the maintenance of law and order or the safeguard of its national security.[82]

This remains a broad approach to instrumentalization, framing it as a national security issue and linking it to the need to address hybrid security threats.[83] These threats come from state, and vaguely defined, non-state actors; to address concerns regarding the overt breadth of the scope of instrumentalization, the Preamble specifies that situations in which non-state actors are involved in organized crime, in particular smuggling, should not be considered as instrumentalization of migrants when there is no aim to destabilize the Union or a Member State;[84] and that humanitarian assistance

80 On instrumentalization as dehumanization, see Mirko Forti, 'Weaponisation of Migrants? Migrants as A (Political) Weapon and the EU Regulatory Response: What to Expect Now' (*EJIL Talk*, 10 March 2022), https://www.ejiltalk.org/weaponisation-of-migrants-migrants-as-a-political-weapon-and-the-eu-regulatory-response-what-to-expect-now/?utm_source=mailpoet&utm_medium=email&utm_campaign=ejil-talk-newsletter-post-title_2, accessed 12 October 2024. See also 'EU: The "Weaponised Migration" Discourse Dehumanises Asylum-Seekers' (*Statewatch*, 10 November 2021), https://www.statewatch.org/news/2021/november/eu-the-weaponised-migration-discourse-dehumanises-asylum-seekers/, accessed 12 October 2024.

81 Regulation (EU) 2024/1359 of the European Parliament and of the Council of 14 May 2024 addressing situations of crisis and force majeure in the field of migration and asylum and amending Regulation (EU) 2021/1147 [2024] OJ L 2024/1359 (Crisis Regulation).

82 Ibid recital 14.

83 Ibid recital 17.

84 Ibid recital 15.

should not be considered as instrumentalization of migrants when there is no aim to destabilize the Union or a Member State.[85] Yet in both cases the limitation of the scope may be meaningless if it is left to Member States to unilaterally define what constitutes a situation where they – or the Union – are being destabilized. The framing of a situation as instrumentalization, and 'to prevent a third country or a hostile non-state actor from targeting specific nationalities or specific categories of third-country nationals or stateless persons', allows Member States to derogate from the standard EU asylum procedure and applying the border procedure on the merits of *all* applications for international protection.[86] On the basis of questionable and unclear grounds, and of a potentially catch-all definition of instrumentalization, the exception thus becomes the norm.

This approach is confirmed in the operative text of the Regulation. The preambular definition of instrumentalization is replicated in the text.[87] The Regulation further states that Member States may apply derogations from EU law in respect of third-country nationals or stateless persons who are subject to instrumentalization and who are either apprehended or found in the proximity of the external border, meaning the Member State's land borders, including river and lake borders, sea borders and its airports, river ports, sea ports and lake ports, provided that they are not internal borders, in connection with an unauthorized crossing by land, sea or air, or who are disembarked following search and rescue operations or who have presented themselves at border crossing points.[88] The Regulation normalizes the exception by introducing a number of derogations in situations of crisis and force majeure, including derogations related to the registration of applications for international protection,[89] to measures applicable to the asylum border procedure,[90] to the extension of time limits set out for take charge requests, take back notifications and transfers,[91] to derogations from the obligation to take back an applicant in a situation of extraordinary mass arrivals.[92] On border procedures, a significant derogation is the extension of the maximum duration of the border procedure for the examination of applications set out in that Article by an additional period of maximum six weeks – raising this thus up to 18 weeks.[93] Moreover, as per the Preamble,

[85] Ibid recital 16.
[86] Ibid recital 49.
[87] Ibid art 1(4)(b).
[88] Ibid art 1(4).
[89] Ibid art 10.
[90] Ibid art 11.
[91] Ibid art 12.
[92] Ibid art 13.
[93] Ibid art 11(1). For a critique, see Meltem Ineli-Ciger, 'Navigating the Labyrinth of Derogations: A Critical Look at the Crisis Regulation' (*EU Migration and Asylum Law*

a far-reaching derogation is that Member States may, in a border procedure, take decisions on the merits of *all* applications that are made by any third-country national or stateless person who is subject to instrumentalization.[94] It should be reminded that, from a rule of law perspective, the application of the Regulation must be compatible with EU constitutional law and the Charter, which enshrines the right to asylum and the concomitant importance of access to asylum.[95] The Court of Justice has held that EU law precludes legislation of a Member State under which, in the event of a declaration of martial law or of a state of emergency or in the event of a declaration of an emergency due to a mass influx of aliens, illegally staying third-country nationals are effectively deprived of the opportunity of access, in the territory of that Member State, to the procedure in which applications for international protection are examined.[96]

4 The normalization of detention

Detention has been one of the most problematic aspects of immigration control from a rule of law perspective. Detention is a measure with a strong punitive dimension and bears heavy consequences for the protection of fundamental rights as it involves deprivation of liberty. It is problematic for this far-reaching measure to be imposed for the purposes of the administrative management of migration, both in terms of proportionality and in terms of legality and the control of state arbitrariness in imposing immigration detention. In the EU, state practices of immigration detention have been accompanied by not always detailed requirements for immigration detention in secondary EU law. In a number of judgments, the Court of Justice has attempted to place immigration detention within certain rule of law parameters. Yet the adoption of a number of measures in the Pact challenges the rule of law by extending – and in effect normalizing – detention in EU law.

Blog, 10 June 2024), https://eumigrationlawblog.eu/navigating-the-labyrinth-of-derogations-a-critical-look-at-the-crisis-regulation/, accessed 12 October 2024.

94 Crisis Regulation, art 11(6).

95 See in this context the concerns expressed regarding the passage of an instrumentalization law in Finland in Amnesty International, 'Finland: Emergency Law on Migration Inconsistent with EU Law and Must be "Rigorously Scrutinised"' (12 July 2024), https://www.amnesty.org/en/latest/press-release/2024/07/finland-emergency-law-on-migration-inconsistent-with-eu-law-and-must-be-rigorously-scrutinized/#:~:text=The%20new%20emergency%20law%20defines,an%20attempt%20to%20destabilize%20it, accessed 12 October 2024.

96 Case C-72/22 PPU *M.A. v Valstybės sienos apsaugos tarnyba* [2022] EU:C:2022:505, para 75.

In terms of the legal position prior to the Pact, it can be that practices of immigration detention within the territory of EU Member States have been increasingly accompanied by detention at the border.[97] It has been documented that the implementation of border procedures by EU Member States has led widely to immigration detention.[98] It has been noted in particular that secondary EU law, by not clearly defining the relationship between border procedures and detention, leaves Member States too much scope for applying *de facto* detention practices.[99] This lack of clarity leads to considerable diversity as regards the legal treatment of detention between Member States. The result is that practices that are qualified as detention by one Member State may not be seen as such by another.[100] This diversity does not only demonstrate a lack of harmonization, but also generates significant rule of law challenges. Member States mislabel detention practices and do not treat confinement of migrants as immigration detention, resulting in the non-applicability of EU law, including fundamental rights, standards in the detention of third-country nationals.

The Court of Justice has attempted to address this rule of law deficit resulting from the reluctance of Member States to call detention by its name in the case of *Commission v Hungary*, involving immigration detention in transit zones.[101] The Court held that the detention of an applicant for international protection is an autonomous concept of EU law understood as any coercive measure that deprives that applicant of his or her freedom of movement and isolates him or her from the rest of the population, by requiring him or her to remain permanently within a restricted and closed perimeter.[102] The use of autonomous concepts is not only an attempt by the Court to manage legal diversity,[103] but can also be seen as an attempt to uphold the rule of law by bringing practices of detention within the scope of EU law. In another ruling involving border procedures, the Court held

97 Mitsilegas (n 3).

98 Galina Cornelisse and Marcelle Reneman, 'Asylum Procedures at the Borders: European Implementation Assessment' (European Parliament, November 2020) https://www.europarl.europa.eu/RegData/etudes/STUD/2020/654201/EPRS_STU(2020)654201_EN.pdf, accessed 12 October 2024.

99 Ibid.

100 Galina Cornelisse and Marcelle Reneman, 'Border Procedures in the Commission's New Pact on Migration and Asylum: A Case of Politics outplaying Rationality?' (2020) 26 *European Law Journal* 181.

101 Case C-808/2018 *Commission v Hungary* [2020] EU:C:2020:1029.

102 Ibid para 159, by reference to Joined Cases C-924/19 PPU and C-925/19 PPU *FMS v Országos Idegenrendézeti Főigazgatóság Dél-alföldi Regionális Igazgatóság* [2020] EU:C:2020:367, para 223.

103 Valsamis Mitsilegas, 'Autonomous Concepts, Diversity Management and Mutual Trust in Europe's Area of Criminal Justice' (2020) 57 *Common Market Law Review* 45.

that the concept of detention has the same meaning across EU immigration and asylum law,[104] and articulated a number of safeguards underpinning the imposition of immigration detention in EU asylum law.[105] These safeguards include multiple proportionality checks[106] including establishing through an individual assessment that less coercive measures would not be effective.[107] National authorities cannot place an applicant for international protection in detention without having previously determined, on a case-by-case basis, whether such detention is proportionate to the aims which it pursues.[108]

The Court of Justice has elaborated on rule of law safeguards regarding detention in more recent case-law. In a ruling involving claims of instrumentalization,[109] the Court held that EU law precludes legislation of a Member State under which, in the event of a declaration of martial law or of a state of emergency or in the event of a declaration of an emergency due to a mass influx of aliens, an asylum seeker may be placed in detention for the sole reason that he or she is staying illegally on the territory of that Member State.[110] The Court held that the illegal nature of the presence of an applicant for international protection cannot, in itself, be regarded as demonstrating the existence of a sufficiently serious threat affecting a fundamental interest of society and thus it cannot be accepted that such an applicant can, for the sole reason that he or she is staying illegally in a Member State, constitute a threat to national security or public order in that Member State.[111] In a ruling involving the Return Directive,[112] the Court stressed once again the requirement for detention to be subject to the principle of proportionality.[113] The Court reiterated its findings in *Al Chodor* regarding the need for safeguards to address the adverse impact of detention on the right to liberty[114] and the rule of law requirement for protection against state arbitrariness.[115] The Court held that Article 15(1) of the Return Directive does not permit a Member State to order the detention of an illegally staying third-country national solely on the basis of a general criterion based on the risk that the effective enforcement of the removal would be compromised, without satisfying one

---

[104] *FMS v Országos Idegenrendézeti Főigazgatóság Dél-alföldi Regionális Igazgatóság* (n 102).
[105] Ibid. See in particular paras 256–265.
[106] Ibid paras 258 and 264.
[107] Ibid para 258.
[108] Ibid.
[109] *M.A. v Valstybės sienos apsaugos tarnyba* (n 96).
[110] Ibid para 94.
[111] Ibid paras 90–91.
[112] Case C-241/21 *I. L. v Politsei- ja Piirivalveamet* [2022] EU:C:2022:753.
[113] Ibid paras 40, 43.
[114] Ibid para 50.
[115] Ibid para 49.

of the specific grounds for detention provided for and clearly defined by the legislation implementing that provision in national law.[116]

The Court's rule of law parameters on immigration detention are important in assessing the move towards the normalization of detention in the Pact.[117] The 2024 Reception Conditions Directive[118] states that detention must not be punitive in nature,[119] but then goes on to essentially normalize detention by allowing this in order to: determine the applicant's identity or nationality; determine the elements on which the application for international protection is based which could not be obtained in the absence of detention, in particular where there is a risk of absconding; and ensure compliance with legal obligations imposed on the applicant through an individual decision on restriction of movement in cases where the applicant has not complied with such obligations and there continues to be a risk of absconding.[120] The generalization of detention in the Pact risks confirming state practice of turning detention 'from the exception to the rule'.[121]

It is questionable whether these provisions, and the provisions on the length of detention in conjunction with the border procedures and crisis instruments, are compatible with the rule of law requirements set out by the Court of Justice. Firstly, it is clear from the Court's case-law treating detention as a broad, autonomous concept, that EU law is applicable to national detention practices, including *de facto* detention, which may result from the implementation of the new asylum procedures and pre-screening measures,[122] including detention in transit zones and within the territory. Secondly, it is clear that the proportionality test developed by the Court requires an individualized, case-by-case assessment of the necessity of detention – a requirement which appears not to be met by the Pact provisions on generalized detention at the border. Thirdly, detention must be proportionate to the aims pursued by the legislation. While the Court

[116] Ibid para 55.

[117] See Maarten den Heijer, 'The Pitfalls of Border Procedures' (2022) 59 *Common Market Law Review* 641, 663.

[118] Directive (EU) 2024/1346 of the European Parliament and of the Council of 14 May 2024 laying down standards for the reception of applicants for international protection [2024] OJ L 2024/1346.

[119] Ibid art 10(2).

[120] Ibid art 10(4). See also the provisions on detention in Article 5 of the Regulation on the Return Border Procedure.

[121] For the case of Italy see Eleonora Celoria and Virginia Passalacqua, 'Turning the Exception into the Rule' (*Verfassungsblog*, 27 October 2023), https://verfassungsblog.de/turning-the-exception-into-the-rule/, accessed 12 October 2024.

[122] See also Cassarino and Marin (n 19) who note that following the CJEU ruling, it can be argued that the parameters clarified in that decision could also be applied to the case of migrants during the screening phase.

has accepted that detention may be justified for the purposes of identifying asylum seekers, the proportionality test must apply on a case-by-case basis and will not be met when the aims of the legislation are defined in an overtly broad manner – as is the case when legislation is justified under the general aim of preventing entry in the territory and secondary movements.

Moreover, it is questionable whether the grounds of detention enumerated in the Pact are in line with the case-law of the European Court of Human Rights. In *MB v The Netherlands*,[123] the Strasbourg Court reiterated that the detention of asylum seekers under Article 5(1)(f) of the Convention is permitted only to prevent unauthorized entry.[124] The Court noted that although Article 8(3) of the EU Reception Conditions Directive (in force at the time of the proceedings) permitted from an EU law standpoint, detention when national security or protection of public order so requires, this has no bearing on the fact that Article 5(1)(f) of the Convention only allows for immigration detention to prevent unauthorized entry or to effect deportation.[125] Detention which was justified under public order grounds while no removal proceedings were effectively ongoing was arbitrary.[126] This ruling poses questions on the legality, from a European Convention on Human Rights perspective, of a number of the grounds of detention under the Pact, including detention for the purposes of identification and detention on the basis of the assumption of an individual's dangerousness (or 'risk of absconding'), if the link of the latter with the objective of preventing unauthorized entry is not clearly substantiated on a case-by-case basis. A lot will rest on the implementation of the Pact in Member States and on the litigation of such implementation in domestic and European courts.

5 Conclusion

The instruments adopted under the EU Pact on Migration and Asylum present considerable rule of law challenges. They reflect a policy focus on preventing access to territory and negating access to law and rights to third-country nationals. The transformation of the EU external border along these lines reflects what Ayelet Shachar has called 'the shifting border': the distinction between physical entry into the country (which does not count for immigration purposes) and lawful admission through a recognized port of entry (which makes one's presence in the territory permissible, and

[123] *M.B. v The Netherlands* App no 71008/16 (ECHR, 23 April 2024).

[124] Ibid para 64.

[125] Ibid para 72. The Court reiterated the requirement for a close connection between the ground justifying detention and the prevention of unauthorised entry in *B.A. v Cyprus* App no 24607/20 (ECHR, 2 July 2024).

[126] Ibid.

therefore visible, in the eyes of the regulatory state).[127] In this process, viewed holistically, the Pact presents a two-fold fundamental rule of law deficit vis-à-vis migrants. On the one hand, under the fiction of non-entry, access to the territory is not accompanied by full access to rights, with exceptions to the asylum process (such as border procedures) becoming the norm and with key safeguards under EU law being disapplied. On the other hand, and notwithstanding the new instrument's insistence that being part of the asylum procedure does not amount to access to the territory, EU secondary law permits Member States to double down on detention, and to impose detention as a rule to those who are not deemed to be 'within the territory'. This double rule of law deficit is exacerbated by the infiltration into EU secondary law of the extremely problematic, from a rule of law perspective, concept of the instrumentalization of migration. This is a legal translation of a contested, political discourse on so-called 'hybrid' threats and the outcome of a securitization discourse treating migration as an existential threat to national security. The concept of instrumentalization as such does not meet the legality criteria under EU law and is hostage to fortune in terms of its abuse by Member States leading to state arbitrariness. This is extremely problematic from a rule of law perspective as the acceptance of instrumentalization effectively leads to the exception becoming the rule in EU asylum law, with all asylum applications potentially being examined at the border under procedures granting limited rights and under detention. The challenges that this landscape poses to access to asylum, to the right to asylum and to the rule of law are considerable and will be subject to extensive litigation when the Pact is implemented.

[127] Ayelet Shachar, *The Shifting Border: Ayelet Shachar in Dialogue* (Manchester University Press 2020) 3, 23–24.

3

Border Control through the Hostile Environment

1 Introduction

A central element in state border control strategies in recent years has been the generation of a hostile environment,[1] targeting those who assist migrants in their journeys, primarily civil society and non-governmental organizations (NGOs) who conduct search and rescue at sea, and the legal profession providing legal advice to migrants. Civil society is targeted as it is viewed as a threat to state sovereignty, in attempting to resist state practices undermining the rule of law and human rights in the field of immigration control.[2] The creation of a hostile environment has profound implications in a democratic society, in directly undermining the rule of law and the protection of the rights of migrants, by stigmatizing and criminalizing those who help migrants in following their constitutional duties and in addressing the rule of law deficit in state border control.[3] This chapter addresses the rule of law challenges arising from the creation of such a hostile environment by focusing on the use of criminal and administrative law by the state to target those who help migrants. The analysis culminates in addressing directly the undermining of the rule of law through state efforts to stigmatize and criminalize the provision of

---

1 For an analysis of the evolution of the hostile environment terminology and policies in the UK, see Sheona York, 'The "Hostile Environment": How Home Office Immigration Policies and Practices Create and Perpetuate' (2018) 32(4) *Journal of Immigration, Asylum and Nationality Law*.

2 Valsamis Mitsilegas, 'Contested Sovereignty in Preventive Border Control: Civil Society, the "Hostile Environment" and the Rule of Law' in Mary Bosworth and Lucia Zedner (eds), *Privatising Border Control: Law at the Limits of the Sovereign State* (Oxford University Press 2022) 36–56.

3 See Chapters 1 and 2.

legal assistance and legal advice to migrants, through attempts to target the legal professions.

2 The criminal law of the hostile environment: the criminalization of facilitation of unauthorized entry and beyond

A key use of criminal law to generate a hostile environment towards NGOs who perform search and rescue at sea and assist migrants in the context of extraterritorial immigration control has been to prosecute civil society actors on the basis of broad offences of migrant smuggling/facilitation of unauthorized entry. The criminal law of the facilitation of unauthorized entry in Europe is problematic from a rule of law perspective in a two-fold manner. Firstly, it is based on very broad justifications which fail to account directly for the harm affected by the offences. Unlike international law in the field (the Palermo Convention on Transnational Organized Crime and its Smuggling Protocol), which criminalizes migrant smuggling strictly for the purposes of fighting organized crime, European Union (EU) law, and the national law of many Member States, criminalizes facilitation of entry as a migration management tool, with the primary purpose of preventing access of migrants to the territory and the jurisdiction of states.[4] Secondly, EU criminal law on facilitation is problematic from a rule of law perspective in that it introduces overtly broad and vague facilitation offences, which do not comply with the principle of legality in criminal law and result in overcriminalization and in enabling abusive prosecutions against civil society at national level.

EU law has introduced a broad criminalization of the facilitation of unauthorized entry. The relevant EU legal framework is set out by the so-called EU 'facilitators' package', consisting of a (then) first pillar Directive on the facilitation of unauthorized entry, transit and residence,[5] accompanied by a (then) third pillar Framework Decision on the strengthening of the penal framework to prevent the facilitation of unauthorized entry, transit and

4 For a comparison between international and EU law see Valsamis Mitsilegas, 'The Normative Foundations of the Criminalisation of Human Smuggling. Exploring the Fault Lines between European and International Law' (2019) 10 *New Journal of European Criminal Law* 68. See also Valsamis Mitsilegas, 'The Criminalisation of Migration in the Law of the European Union. Challenging the Preventive Paradigm' in Gian Luigi Gatta, Valsamis Mitsilegas and Stefano Zirulia (eds), *Controlling Immigration Through Criminal Law: European and Comparative Perspectives on 'Crimmigration'* (Hart 2021).

5 Council Directive 2002/90/EC of 28 November 2002 defining the facilitation of unauthorised entry, transit and residence [2002] OJ L 328/4 (Facilitation Directive).

residence confirming that the conduct defined as facilitation in the Directive will be treated as a criminal offence by EU Member States.[6]

The criminalization of facilitation in EU law is very broad. In terms of the facilitation of irregular entry or transit, criminal sanctions will be imposed on any person who intentionally assists a person who is not a national of a Member State to enter, or transit across, the territory of a Member State in breach of the laws of the state concerned on the entry or transit of aliens.[7] Unlike the smuggling Protocol in the Palermo Convention, EU law does not include the requirement of financial gain for criminalization of facilitation to be established. EU law rather grants Member States the discretion not to impose sanctions for facilitation and instead apply their national law and practice for cases where the aim of the behaviour is to provide humanitarian assistance to the person concerned.[8] However, this provision is discretionary and its value in redressing the balance set out by the broad definition and criminalization of facilitation under EU law is questionable. According to a 2017 Commission Report, only seven Member States specifically include in domestic law an exemption from punishment for facilitation for humanitarian assistance.[9]

The overcriminalization of facilitation of entry in EU law on the basis of a preventive paradigm has allowed Member States to use domestic criminal law in order to prosecute a wide range of elements of assistance to migrants, which are not motivated by, and do not involve, any financial benefit. Facilitation offences have been used to prosecute NGOs who are addressing state inaction in saving lives at sea,[10] as part of a broader strategy of generating a hostile environment targeting civil society.[11] In addition to targeting of civil society, the overcriminalization of the facilitation of unauthorized entry has further resulted in the prosecution of citizens assisting migrants.[12] It has

6 Council Framework Decision 2002/946/JHA of 28 November 2002 on the strengthening of the penal framework to prevent the facilitation of unauthorised entry, transit and residence [2002] OJ L 328/1 (Facilitation Framework Decision).

7 Facilitation Directive, art 1(1)(a), combined with art 1(1) of the Facilitation Framework Decision.

8 Facilitation Directive, art 1(2).

9 Commission, 'Staff Working Document: REFIT Evaluation of the EU Legal Framework against Facilitation of Unauthorised Entry, Transit and Residence' SWD(2017) 117 final, 14.

10 For a recent overview see PICUM, 'Cases of Criminalisation of Migration and Solidarity in the EU in 2023' (2024), https://picum.org/wp-content/uploads/2024/04/Cases-of-criminalisation-of-migration-and-solidarity-in-the-EU-in-2023.pdf, accessed 12 October 2024.

11 Mitsilegas, 'Contested Sovereignty' (n 2).

12 For examples in Greece, see Nikolaos Chatzinikolaou, 'Crimmigration in Greece: A Study of Exceptional Derogations from the Rule of Law within a Permanent Situation of Emergency' in Gian Luigi Gatta, Valsamis Mitsilegas and Stefano Zirulia (eds), *Controlling*

also resulted in the prosecution of migrants for assisting other migrants,[13] a practice which would be contrary to international law and which is currently subject to litigation before the Court of Justice of the European Union (CJEU).[14] By using the threat of criminal sanctions, the EU measures on facilitation essentially aim at deterring individuals and organizations from coming into contact and assisting any third-country national wishing to enter the territory of EU Member States, generating thus a hostile environment and a chilling effect towards assistance to migrants. As has been noted in an Issue Paper published by the Council of Europe Commissioner for Human Rights, 'the message which is sent is that contact with foreigners can be risky as it may result in criminal charges'.[15]

Notwithstanding the concerns raised regarding the overcriminalization of facilitation in EU law and its negative impact on humanitarian assistance, the Commission initially appeared reluctant to revise the outdated pre-Lisbon EU legislative framework in the field. In an evaluation conducted in 2017, the Commission declined to take up the opportunity to reform the facilitators' package. The evaluation defended resolutely the status quo.[16] The Commission stated that 'there is no sufficient evidence to draw firm conclusions about the need for a revision of the Facilitators package at this point in time'.[17] The Commission changed its approach more recently. It tabled, in November 2023, a new Directive[18] aimed at replacing the facilitators' package.[19] The Directive introduces the following criminal offences: intentionally assisting a third-country national to enter, or transit across, or stay within the territory of any Member State in breach of relevant Union law or the laws of the Member State concerned on the entry, transit and stay of third-country nationals where the person who carries out the

Immigration through Criminal Law: European and Comparative Perspectives on 'Crimmigration' (Hart 2021).

13 Flavia Patanè Maarten P Bolhuis, Joris van Wijk and Helena Kreiensiek, 'Asylum-Seekers Prosecuted for Human Smuggling: A Case Study of Scafisti in Italy' (2020) 39(2) *Refugee Survey Quarterly* 123.

14 See the *Kinsa* litigation below – It's in the next 2 pages and the sub-section does not change.

15 Council of Europe Commissioner for Human Rights, 'Criminalisation of Migration in Europe: Human Rights Implications' (Issue Paper prepared by Elspeth Guild, 2010).

16 Commission, 'Staff Working Document' (n 9).

17 Ibid 35; see Mitsilegas (n 4).

18 Commission, 'Proposal for a Directive of the European Parliament and of the Council laying down minimum rules to prevent and counter the facilitation of unauthorised entry, transit and stay in the Union, and replacing Council Directive 2002/90/EC and Council Framework Decision 2002/946 JHA' COM(2023) 755 final (Facilitation Directive proposal).

19 Ibid art 18. For an analysis see Valsamis Mitsilegas 'Reforming EU Criminal Law on the Facilitation of Unauthorised Entry: The New Commission Proposal in the Light of the Kinshasa Litigation' (2024) 15 *New Journal of European Criminal Law* 3.

conduct requests, receives or accepts, directly or indirectly, a financial or material benefit, or a promise thereof, or carries out the conduct in order to obtain such a benefit;[20] intentionally assisting a third-country national to enter, or transit across, or stay within the territory of any Member State in breach of relevant Union law or the laws of the Member State concerned on the entry, transit and stay of third-country nationals where there is a high likelihood of causing serious harm to a person;[21] and publicly instigating third-country nationals to enter, or transit across, or stay within the territory of any Member State in breach of relevant Union law or the laws of the Member State concerned on the entry, transit and stay of third-country nationals.[22]

The new Directive does little to address the current concerns regarding the overcriminalization of the facilitation of entry in EU law.[23] Criminal law continues to be used to address what could be dealt with under administrative law, and criminalization is framed from a perspective of breach of regulations: facilitation is defined as intentionally assisting a third-country national to enter, or transit across, or stay within the territory of any Member State in breach of relevant EU law or the laws of the Member State concerned. The Directive is broader than international law, in continuing to disassociate between facilitation and organized crime – as the new Directive criminalizes not only facilitation for financial gain, but also facilitation where there is a high likelihood of causing serious harm to a person.

In spite of claims of addressing the criminalization of humanitarianism, it is notable that the Commission proposal does not include an express, unequivocal humanitarian exception to the criminalization of the facilitation of unauthorized entry in the operative part of the text.[24] The criminalization of facilitation where there is a high likelihood of causing serious harm to a person risks maintaining the current paradigm of overcriminalization and perpetuating the hostile environment against those who assist migrants, in particular through search and rescue operations. Moreover, the definition of facilitation where there is a high likelihood of causing serious harm to a person does not meet the requirement of legal certainty; it is not clear how Member States will implement this provision which in essence may serve to perpetuate the criminalization of humanitarianism resulting from the current facilitators' package. The potential use of the offence of the criminalization of facilitation where there is a high likelihood of causing serious harm to a

[20] Commission, 'Facilitation Directive proposal' (n 18) art 3(1)(a).

[21] Ibid art 3(1)(b).

[22] Ibid art 3(2).

[23] Mitsilegas (n 19).

[24] Commission, 'Facilitation Directive proposal' (n 18) recital 7.

person to exacerbate the hostile environment against humanitarian assistance is also clear from the high level of penalties envisaged for this offence, including attempts to commit it – both are punishable by a maximum term of imprisonment of at least 15 years.[25]

The current litigation pending before the Court of Justice constitutes an opportunity for reform. The litigation is the result of a reference for a preliminary ruling to the Court of Justice by the Tribunale di Bologna in Italy. In the *Kinshasa* reference[26] (now renamed as *Kinsa*), lodged on 21 July 2023, the referring Court has asked the CJEU whether the criminalization of the facilitation of unauthorized entry in EU law and in national law even where the conduct is carried out on a non-profit-making basis, without providing, at the same time, an obligation on Member States to exclude from criminalization conduct facilitating unauthorized entry aimed at providing humanitarian assistance is compatible with the Charter. The *Kinsa* litigation is an opportunity for the Court of Justice to address the rule of law deficit generated by the overcriminalization of facilitation in EU law, through an emphasis on the protection of human rights (including the right to asylum) in the Charter, upholding the principle of legality and interpreting EU law in conformity with international law, including the smuggling Protocol and its narrow objectives, international refugee law and international law of the sea, with the search and rescue obligations the latter entails.[27]

The facts in *Kinsa* lay bare the shaky normative foundations and adverse effects of overcriminalization of facilitation of unauthorized entry in EU and Italian law.[28] They involve the prosecution of a Congolese woman arriving at the air border of Bologna for the facilitation of the unauthorized entry of her minor daughter and niece.[29] Prosecution in this case is blatantly inconsistent with the framing of migrants smuggling in international law – the case does not involve the operations of criminal organizations but the arrival of a mother with her daughter and niece at the border. The distance between the two approaches is further highlighted if one is reminded of the ruling of the Canadian Supreme Court in the case of *Appulonappa*.[30] In this ruling,

25 Ibid art 6(4).

26 Case C-460/23, *Kinshasa*, Request for a preliminary ruling from the Tribunale di Bologna (Italy) lodged on 21 July 2023, OJ C 338 (25 September 2023) 12, https://eur-lex.europa.eu/legal-content/EN/TXT/?uri=CELEX%3A62023CN0460, accessed 12 October 2024.

27 Valsamis Mitsilegas, 'Reforming the Facilitators' Package through the *Kinsa* Litigation: Legality, Effectiveness and Taking International Law into Account' (*Eurojus*, August 2024), https://rivista.eurojus.it/wp-content/uploads/pdf/Eurojus-Kinsa-Editorial-July-2024.pdf, accessed 12 October 2024.

28 Mitsilegas (n 19).

29 *Kinshasa* (n 26) paras 1–5.

30 *R. v Appulonappa* [2015] 3 R.C.S. 754.

the Canadian Supreme Court rejected the broad criminalization advocated by the Canadian government by interpreting domestic law in conformity with international law, in particular with the smuggling Protocol. The Court stressed the requirement of the Protocol to criminalize smuggling for financial or other material benefit and noted that it would depart from the balance struck in the Protocol to allow prosecution for mutual assistance among refugees, family support and reunification, and humanitarian aid.[31] According to the Court, Canada's international commitments support the view that the purpose of domestic criminal law is to permit the robust fight against people smuggling in the context of organized crime, which excluded criminalizing conduct that amounted solely to humanitarian, mutual or family aid.[32] While the security goals of domestic law are important, the Court held that these did not supplant Canada's commitment to humanitarian aid and family unity.[33] The Court noted that under the Crown's interpretation, 'a father offering a blanket to a shivering child, or friends sharing food aboard a migrant vessel, could be subject to prosecution'.[34]

In addition to criminalization and prosecution under facilitation offences, states have used criminal law to generate a hostile environment through the prosecution of civil society under a wide variety of offences, ranging from organized crime to offences of collusion with smugglers to 'crimes of disobedience', namely prosecutions for not complying with state orders in managing migration flows.[35] A key example of the latter trend has been the *Rackete* litigation before the Italian *Corte di Cassazione* in the well-publicized prosecution of Carola Rackete, the captain of *Sea-Watch 3*.[36] The case involved prosecution on the grounds of resistance to public officials and resistance and violence against warships. In a significant ruling, the *Cassazione* rejected the appeal to uphold the charges by essentially giving precedence to the duty of rescue as enshrined in international law and to obligations under international refugee law, and rejecting the argument that a ship constitutes a safe place for the purposes of rescue at sea. The Court has thus accepted that bringing migrants recovered in the context of rescue activities in international waters, also in the face of an express ban on entry into territorial waters and/or in the absence of authorization to dock,

31 Ibid para 44.
32 Ibid para 45.
33 Ibid para 57.
34 Ibid para 57.
35 Marta Minetti, 'The Facilitators Package, Penal Populism and the Rule of Law: Lessons from Italy' (2020) 11 *New Journal of European Criminal Law* 335; see also Mitsilegas (n 2).
36 Rackete Case, Cass. pen. section III, 16 January 2020 (dep. 20 February 2020) no 6626, Pres. Lapalorcia.

constitutes fulfillment of the duty of rescue at sea.[37] It has been noted that the ruling by the *Cassazione* can be read as enshrining a 'right of resistance' against state action in breach of hierarchically higher legal principles.[38] By recourse to international law, the *Cassazione* built a line of defence for humanitarian action against the hostile environment generated by the state.

3 The hostile environment through the use of administrative law

In parallel with the use of criminal law, states have been generating a hostile environment through the use of a variety of administrative sanctions against NGOs saving lives at sea. These measures range from disembarkation bans to bans from leaving the port to the imposition of sanctions for breaches of administrative rules such as environmental protection and health and safety regulations. The imposition of administrative sanctions aimed primarily to neutralize, and effectively stop, the humanitarian assistance provided by civil society, undermines the rule of law as it consists in many cases of abuse of law based on state arbitrariness.

A key example of the latter has been the imposition of administrative sanctions to the *Sea-Watch* vessel, resulting in litigation before the Court of Justice.[39] The *Sea-Watch* case involved the conduct of health and safety inspections on, and the subsequent detention of, Sea-Watch vessels which had conducted search and rescue activities at sea. The detention was ordered on the grounds of breaches of health and safety regulations.[40] Sea-Watch, whose vessels had been certified to operate from the German authorities, brought legal action before the Italian courts challenging the legality of state action, arguing inter alia that the latter constituted in fact a roundabout means of attaining an objective of frustrating the search and rescue operations organized by Sea-Watch in the Mediterranean Sea.[41] These actions generated a reference for a preliminary ruling by the Regional Administrative Court of Sicily asking the Luxembourg Court a number of questions including on the applicability of EU transport law on NGOs conducting search and

---

[37] Stefano Zirulia, 'La Cassazione sul caso Sea Watch: le motivazioni sul l'illegitimita dell arresto di Carola Rackete' (*Sistema Penale*, 20 February 2020), https://air.unimi.it/retrieve/dfa8b9a1-cd62-748b-e053-3a05fe0a3a96/Cassazione%20Sea%20Watch_%20illegittimo%20l%27arresto%20di%20Carola%20Rackete%20_%20Sistema%20Penale%20_%20SP.pdf, accessed 12 October 2024.

[38] Ibid point 7.

[39] Joined Cases C-14/21 and C-15/21 *Sea-Watch eV v Ministero delle Infrastrutture e dei Trasporti and Others* [2022] EU:C:2022:604.

[40] Ibid paras 46–49.

[41] Ibid para 49.

rescue at sea, on the relationship between the law of the flag state which has certified the vessels with the flag state imposing inspections and sanctions and on the scope of the powers exercised in this context by the port state.

The Court placed its ruling firmly within the parameters of international law. The Court held that it was necessary to take account of the International Convention for the Safety of Life at Sea (SOLAS Convention), to which all the Member States are parties, when interpreting EU law,[42] and reiterated that provisions of EU secondary legislation must be interpreted, to the greatest extent possible, in conformity both with the international conventions which are binding on the EU and with the relevant rules and principles of general international law.[43] EU law must be interpreted, having regard to its objective and its content, by taking account not only of the SOLAS Convention but also of the Convention on the Law of the Sea[44] which is binding on the EU and its provisions form an integral part of the EU legal order.[45] The CJEU continued by interpreting the objective of the Convention of the Law of the Sea,[46] and examined in some detail the Convention provision on the duty to render assistance at sea and the related obligations in particular of the coastal state, considerations taken into account in the development of the Court's answers to the referring court.[47]

A further key feature of the Court's ruling was to establish clear rule of law parameters aimed to address state arbitrariness in the control of NGO ships conducting search and rescue at sea.[48] Throughout the judgment, the Court imposed a number of rule of law requirements permeating all stages of intervention of the port state. Firstly, the Court required that the decision to inspect must be fully reasoned and, as to the substance, justified both in law and in fact,[49] with the Court proceeding to give detailed guidance as to the factors to be taken into account in the decision by the port authority.[50] Secondly, the Court only permitted ex post control: additional controls by the port state are only permitted after ships have entered its waters and after all the operations relating to the transhipment or disembarking of persons to whom their respective masters decided to render assistance have been

42 Ibid para 91.
43 Ibid para 92.
44 Ibid para 93.
45 Ibid para 94.
46 Ibid para 96.
47 Ibid paras 105–109.
48 Valsamis Mitsilegas, 'Challenging the Hostile Environment for Search and Rescue at Sea: Reflections from the *Sea Watch* Litigation' in Vincenzo Militello and Alessandro Spena (eds), *The Challenges of Illegal Trafficking in the Mediterranean Area* (Springer 2023) 141.
49 *Sea-Watch* (n 39) para 120.
50 Ibid para 121.

completed if that state has established, on the basis of detailed legal and factual evidence, that there are serious indications capable of proving that there is a danger to health, safety, on-board working conditions or the environment, having regard to the conditions under which those ships operate.[51] Thirdly, the Court held that, while the port state is required to ensure that all the deficiencies which have been confirmed or revealed by an inspection have been or will be rectified in accordance with the international conventions whose effectiveness that directive is intended to increase, they may not, by contrast, detain a ship unless such deficiencies pose a clear threat to safety, health or the environment.[52]

The detention of a ship could not be ordered merely on the ground that an inspection carried out under EU law enabled the port state to establish, with precision, that a ship had been operated in a manner posing a danger to persons, property or the environment. It was also necessary for that state to establish in a given case, first, that such a danger or future risk is a clear hazard and, second, that the deficiencies giving rise to that danger or risk, either individually or together, make the ship concerned unseaworthy.[53] The port state may not make the non-detention of those ships or the lifting of such detention subject to demands that ships subject to its jurisdiction hold certificates other than those with which they were issued by the flag state or that they comply with all the requirements applicable to ships covered by a classification other than their own.[54] Finally, the Court held that the corrective measures which may thus be adopted by the port state in a given case must, in any event, be not only suitable and necessary to rectify the deficiencies which are clearly hazardous to safety, health or the environment and which make the ship unseaworthy on which that detention was based, but also proportionate to that end.[55] In this manner, the Court addressed the rule of law deficit consisting of state arbitrariness in targeting civil society by placing state enforcement action under strict conditions of giving reasons and justification, and placed decisions limiting the rights of ships under a clear necessity and proportionality test.

4 Targeting the legal profession

In addition to targeting civil society, the hostile environment against those who help migrants has also more recently taken the form of targeting the

[51] Ibid para 126.
[52] Ibid para 144.
[53] Ibid para 147.
[54] Ibid paras 150–151.
[55] Ibid para 153. The Court further developed an unseaworthiness test in para 148.

legal profession, and the provision of legal assistance and legal advice to migrants. The UK witnessed direct attacks on the legal profession by the judiciary, in the context of the adoption of restrictive domestic immigration legislation and of the development of the UK–Rwanda arrangements.[56] The then Home Secretary used loaded language with regard to the legal profession in this context, transferring the illegitimacy of human trafficking to immigration lawyering and framing legal representation as unwanted 'activism'.[57] Attacks on lawyers have continued, also during discussions on the passage of the Illegal Immigration Bill.[58] These attacks were condemned by representatives of the legal profession,[59] but it was clear that state discourse aimed at transforming the legal profession from defenders of the rule of law to 'bad faith' citizens who are not to be trusted – in the same category with traffickers and ultimately migrants themselves.[60] The direct undermining of the rule of law by stigmatizing lawyers has become more alarming recently. The cultivation of this climate of stigmatization and direct targeting has profoundly corrosive consequences for social peace, leading to a threatening environment against the legal profession and to a chilling effect for the provision of legal representation and advice to migrants. This climate has culminated recently, in the context of riots erupting in the UK after the murder incident in Southport, in direct threats of violence against the legal profession and those who assist and represent migrants.[61] These attacks, aiming to intimidate, are unacceptable in a democratic society and

---

56 JUSTICE, 'The UK's Longstanding Commitment to the Rule of Law is under Grave Threat according to Landmark Report from JUSTICE' (September 2023), https://justice.org.uk/the-uks-longstanding-commitment-to-the-rule-of-law-is-under-grave-threat-according-to-landmark-report-from-justice/, accessed 12 October 2024.

57 Quote from Priti Patel: 'Those defending the broken system – the traffickers, the do-gooders, the leftie lawyers, the Labour Party – they are defending the indefensible', she said. 'Our broken system is enabling this international criminal trade. It is disregarding the most vulnerable, elbowing women and children in need to the side.' In Catherine Baksi, 'Lawyers Fight back over Priti Patels Dangerous Asylum Claims' (*The Times*, 8 October 2020), https://www.thetimes.co.uk/edition/law/lawyers-fight-back-over-priti-patels-dangerous-asylum-claims-8pg3tbjzt, accessed 12 October 2024.

58 'Sunak Attacks "Lefty Lawyers" amid Criticism of Small Boats Strategy' (*Financial Times*, 8 March 2023), https://www.ft.com/content/246232b7-2f83-4698-a2bd-368e396913fe, accessed 12 October 2024.

59 Rowena Mason, 'Tony Attacks on "Lefty Lawyers" Could Fuel Abuse, Barristers Warn' (*The Guardian*, 16 August 2023), https://www.theguardian.com/law/2023/aug/16/attacks-lefty-lawyers-abuse-bar-council-chair, accessed 12 October 2024.

60 Mitsilegas (n 2).

61 Rowena Mason, Vikram Dodd and Aletha Adu, 'Immigration Lawyers "at Risk" amid Far-Right Threats to Target Advice Centres' (*The Guardian*, 6 August 2024), https://www.theguardian.com/uk-news/article/2024/aug/06/lawyers-urge-starmer-to-ensure-safety-of-advice-centres-over-far-right-threat, accessed 12 October 2024.

risk having a chilling effect on legal representation, one of the foundations of the rule of law.

Attacks on the legal profession providing immigration advice have occurred elsewhere in Europe. The criminalization of the provision of legal advice to asylum seekers has ended in litigation before the Court of Justice. In a ruling delivered in 2021,[62] the Court held that the relevant provisions of EU asylum law in force at the time[63] did not exclude assistance given to an applicant for international protection from the respective scope of these provisions, even if the person providing such assistance was aware that the application was unsuccessful.[64] The Court added that the production of criminal penalties undeniably has a very significant deterrent effect, which may lead persons wishing to assist third-country nationals or stateless persons wishing to obtain refugee status in Hungary to refrain from participating in the assistance activities which are the subject of the relevant provisions of EU asylum law.[65] The Court devoted a substantial part of its analysis on rebuffing the argument that targeting legal advice constituted part of the fight against the assistance of misuse of the asylum procedure. The Court held unequivocally that a lawyer must actually be able to carry out satisfactorily his or her task of advising, defending and representing his or her client, failing which that client would be deprived of the rights conferred on him or her by Article 47 of the Charter of Fundamental Rights.[66]

The Court held further that the national law at stake was capable of preventing lawyers from effectively defending the interests of applicants who consult them by discouraging them from advising such applicants to make or lodge an application for asylum in Hungary for the purpose of subsequently challenging the relevant national provisions which appear to them to be contrary to EU law.[67] It would be contrary to Article 47 of the Charter if, for the purpose of accessing a court or tribunal with the power to ensure respect for the rights guaranteed to that person by EU law, a person were compelled to infringe a legal rule or obligation or to be subject to a penalty corresponding to that offence.[68] National law criminalized behaviour which per se cannot in any

---

62 Case C-821/19 *Commission v Hungary* [2022] EU:C:2021:930.

63 Directive 2013/32/EU of the European Parliament and of the Council of 26 June 2013 on common procedures for granting and withdrawing international protection (recast) [2013] OJ L 180/60, art 8(2) and art 22(1); Directive 2013/33/EU of the European Parliament and of the Council of 26 June 2013 laying down standards for the reception of applicants for international protection (recast) [2013] OJ L 180/96, art 10(4).

64 *Commission v Hungary* (n 62) para 92.

65 Ibid para 98.

66 Ibid para 121.

67 Ibid para 122.

68 Ibid para 124.

circumstances be regarded as fraudulent or abusive practice, and thus infringes the rights guaranteed by EU law.[69] The Court noted that that provision was capable of strongly discouraging any person wishing to provide any assistance whatsoever for the purposes of making or lodging an application for asylum, irrespective of the capacity in which that person is involved, despite the fact that the assistance is intended solely to enable a third-country national or stateless person to exercise the fundamental right to apply for asylum in a Member State, as guaranteed in Article 18 of the Charter.[70]

5 Conclusion

This chapter highlighted the rule of law deficit arising from the generation of a hostile environment targeting those who assist migrants, ranging from NGOs, to the legal profession, to migrants themselves. The chapter analysed three key avenues of the generation of such a hostile environment, which aims to prevent migrants from reaching the border and to undermine assistance to migrants who have reached the border: the use of criminal law, via the criminalization of unauthorized entry and prosecution of those who help migrants under this offence but also under other offences including offences of disobedience to the state; the use of administrative law, including the imposition of sanctions for alleged breaches of environmental or health and safety regulations, with the aim to stop NGO boats to conduct search and rescue operations at sea; and the targeting of the legal profession, not only through criminalizing legal advice, but also through the use of a stigmatizing discourse resulting ultimately in intimidation, threats of violence and ultimately, potentially, the commission of violent attacks against lawyers. This multi-faceted hostile environment is a direct challenge not only to the rights of migrants and to international law obligations, but also to the rule of law from many perspectives: through the adoption of overtly broad criminal offences, which are based on shaky normative foundations and which do not meet the requirements of the principle of legality, including foreseeability and legal certainty; the abuse of power by the state by resorting to abusive prosecutions through a variety of legal bases and by taking arbitrary actions against civil society; and through the direct targeting of the legal profession, in a blatant direct attack on the rule of law. Litigation and judicial intervention appear currently to be the main way forward to address this rule of law deficit, with both national courts and the CJEU intervening to uphold human rights and the rule of law and push back against the hostile environment in immigration control.

[69] Ibid para 126.

[70] Ibid para 132.

PART II

Border Violence and Rule of Law: Examining the Role of Frontex in Lawless Border Control

4

Borders, Power and Accountability: The Case of Frontex

1 Introduction

Frontex was established on 1 May 2005 by Council Regulation (EC) No 2007/2004.[1] The latter was amended in 2007,[2] 2011,[3] 2013[4] and 2014,[5] before being replaced in 2016[6] and then again in 2019 via Regulation 2019/

[1] Council Regulation (EC) No 2007/2004 of 26 October 2004 establishing a European Agency for the Management of Operational Cooperation at the External Borders of the Member States of the European Union [2004] OJ L349/1 (2004 Frontex Regulation).

[2] Regulation (EC) No 863/2007 of the European Parliament and of the Council of 11 July 2007 establishing a mechanism for the creation of Rapid Border Intervention Teams and amending Council Regulation (EC) No 2007/2004 as regards that mechanism and regulating the tasks and powers of guest officers [2007] OJ L199/30.

[3] Regulation (EU) No 1168/2011 of the European Parliament and of the Council of 25 October 2011 amending Council Regulation (EC) No 2007/2004 establishing a European Agency for the Management of Operational Cooperation at the External Borders of the Member States of the European Union [2011] OJ L304/1.

[4] Regulation (EU) No 1052/2013 of the European Parliament and of the Council of 22 October 2013 establishing the European Border Surveillance System (Eurosur) [2013] OJ L 295/11.

[5] Regulation (EU) No 656/2014 of the European Parliament and of the Council of 15 May 2014 establishing rules for the surveillance of the external sea borders in the context of operational cooperation coordinated by the European Agency for the Management of Operational Cooperation at the External Borders of the Member States of the European Union [2014] OJ L189/93.

[6] Regulation (EU) 2016/1624 of the European Parliament and of the Council of 14 September 2016 on the European Border and Coast Guard and amending Regulation (EU) 2016/399 of the European Parliament and of the Council and repealing Regulation (EC) No 863/2007 of the European Parliament and of the Council, Council Regulation (EC) No 2007/2004 and Council Decision 2005/267/EC [2016] OJ L251/1 (2016 Frontex Regulation).

1896 which is still in force at the time of writing.[7] One could not say that the agency has had a quiet legislative life. Nor has Frontex been out of the limelight, from international media coverage about its assistance in border control activities of questionable human rights compliance, academic critique of its fundamental rights record, concern by international organizations and European regional ones about compliance with international law, the list is extensive.[8] In its development, Frontex has moved from a coordination mechanism for Member States border authorities to an independent agency with a standing corps of 10,000 to be in place by 2027, a ring-fenced budget and power to carry out activities even in the absence of Member State request or approval.[9] It has further been granted powers to use force in its operations.[10] However, in the process of the development of Frontex and its powers, there has been almost no coordination with EU law on border crossing, particularly the Regulation (EU) 2016/399 (Schengen Borders Code),[11] to which reference is made in very specific and limited ways in the Frontex Regulation. The European Union (EU) created a border control agency which is not entrusted with carrying out the organization's own border control law.

This chapter examines Frontex with a view to understanding the institutional structure which the EU legislator has designed over almost 20 years to provide powers and oversight for the first EU agency to be granted

7 Regulation (EU) 2019/1896 of the European Parliament and of the Council of 13 November 2019 on the European Border and Coast Guard and repealing Regulations (EU) No 1052/2013 and (EU) 2016/1624 [2019] OJ L 295/1 (2019 Frontex Regulation).

8 For an overview of Frontex and the Greek border see European Center for Constitutional and Human Rights analysing Greek Pushbacks (ECCHR), 'Over 20 Years of Concealed State Policy Without Accountability' (February 2022), https://www.ecchr.eu/fileadmin/user_upload/Analyzing_Greek_Pushbacks-_Over_20_years_of_concealed_state_policy_without_accountability.pdf, accessed 12 October 2024. See Patrick Kingsley and Karam Shoumali, 'Taking Hard Line, Greece Turns Back Migrants by Abandoning them at Sea' (*New York Times*, 14 August 2020), https://www.nytimes.com/2020/08/14/world/europe/greece-migrants-abandoning-sea.html, accessed 12 October 2024; and Izabella Majcher, 'Human Rights Violations During EU Border Surveillance and Return Operations: Frontex's Shared Responsibility or Complicity?' (2015) 7 *Silesian Journal of Legal Studies* 45.

9 Yasha Maccanico, 'Immigration Policy and State Power' (2021) 11(4) *Societies* 128.

10 Artur Gruszczak, 'The Use of Force by the Frontex Agency: International Legal Aspects' (2021) 4(88) *Studia Prawnicze KUL*; Luisa Marin, 'Policing the EU's External Borders: A Challenge for the Rule of Law and Fundamental Rights in the Area of Freedom, Security and Justice? An Analysis of Frontex Joint Operations at the Southern Maritime Border' (2015) 7(4) *Journal of Contemporary European Research* 468.

11 Regulation (EU) 2016/399 of the European Parliament and of the Council of 9 March 2016 on a Union Code on the rules governing the movement of persons across borders (Schengen Borders Code) (codification) [2016] OJ L77/1 (Schengen Borders Code).

coercive powers. Until the EU decision to create a border agency, the control of EU external borders was a competence of the Member States. The EU legislator cautiously established an agency responsible for coordination of external border control activities, providing it with only limited powers to work with Member States to achieve the objective of a common approach to external border control. The experiment met with substantial support from the Member States resulting in six changes to the legislation, in each case extending the powers to Frontex (eventually to include operational activities). However, at the same time, increasing concern was expressed by academics and civil society actors regarding the development of Frontex as a tool to increase the use of force against persons crossing the external borders.[12] Additionally, they highlighted the problem of the lack of remedies for individuals adversely affected by Frontex coordinated action and the weakness of the system of oversight built into the system. These concerns were taken seriously by the legislator which sought to include an increasing number of control mechanisms. Yet, as will be seen in the next chapter, these efforts were met with strong resistance from the direction of the institution which sought to avoid any limits or examination of its practices. First we will set out here the development of the agency and its oversight mechanisms.

2 Institutional powers

2.1 Shared responsibility

According to Recital 1 of the 2019 Frontex Regulation, the objective of the agency is to develop and implement European *integrated border management* at national and EU level, which is a necessary corollary to the free movement of persons within the Union and stated to be a fundamental component of an area of freedom, security and justice. It is, of course, a contested point whether integrated border management is indeed a necessary corollary of free movement of persons in the EU. Free movement was an objective of the 1957 European Economic Community Treaty with a deadline of 1968 for free movement of workers, self-employed and service providers which was achieved successfully. It was expanded in the Single European Act of 1987 to include the abolition of border controls among the Member States. It was achieved on 25 March 1995 when the original five Schengen states – France, Germany, Belgium, Luxembourg and the Netherlands – abolished controls on the movement of persons across the whole area. By 1999, when

12 Julien Jeandesboz, 'Reinforcing the Surveillance of EU Borders the Future Development of FRONTEX' (CEPS, 2008); Elspeth Guild and Didier Didier, 'The Transformation of European Border Controls' in Bernard Ryan and Valsamis Mitsilegas (eds), *Extraterritorial Immigration Control* (Brill Nijhoff 2010).

the system was integrated into EU law, most EU Member States were already part of the system.[13] Integrated border management was adopted as a policy field only in 2006 by a Justice and Home Affairs Council meeting. So, free movement of persons was achieved without integrated border management for the majority of its existence within the EU. Nonetheless, the Frontex Regulation states that the two are inherently and intrinsically inter-related notwithstanding all evidence to the contrary.

Integrated border management is defined in the 2016 Frontex Regulation. The Commission states that this means national and international coordination and cooperation among all relevant authorities and agencies involved in border security and trade facilitation to establish effective, efficient and coordinated border management at the external EU borders.[14] However, the article which the Commission relies on for this definition is actually far more oriented towards coercive again against irregular border crossing than trade facilitation, which in fact is not mentioned at all.[15] The purpose is to reach the objective of open, but well controlled and secure, borders.[16] There are two distinct but inter-related dimensions to integrated border management: the internal management among Member States of their common external borders and the external management with third countries of common (for the EU only, external) borders. The question is integration with whom and in respect of what activities. The most revelatory example of what integrated border management means in the context of cooperation with third countries is as regards Moldova and Ukraine. There is a separate EU agency which is devoted exclusively to integrated border management with two neighbouring countries of the EU, Moldova and Ukraine, the EU Border Assistance Mission to

---

13 Eckart Wagner, 'The Integration of Schengen into the Framework of the European Union' (1998) 25(2) *Legal Issues of Economic Integration*; David O'Keeffe, 'The Schengen Convention: A Suitable Model for European Integration?' (1991) 11(1) *Yearbook of European Law* 185; Elspeth Guild, Evelien Brouwer, Kees Groenendijk and Sergio Carrera, 'What is Happening to the Schengen Borders?' (CEPS Paper in Liberty and Security in Europe 86, 2015); Elspeth Guild, 'Schengen Borders and Multiple National States of Emergency: from Refugees to Terrorism to COVID-19' (2021) 23(4) *European Journal of Migration and Law* 385.

14 Commission, 'European Integrated Border Management', https://home-affairs.ec.europa.eu/networks/european-migration-network-emn/emn-asylum-and-migration-glossary/glossary/european-integrated-border-management_en, accessed 12 October 2024.

15 2016 Frontex Regulation, art 4.

16 Mariana Gkliati and Salvatore Fabio Nicolosi, 'External Solidarity in Integrated Border Management: The Role of EU Migration Agencies' in Eva Kassoti and Narin Idriz (eds), *The Principle of Solidarity: International and EU Law Perspectives* (TMC Asser Press 2023); Jörg Monar, 'The European Union's "Integrated Management" of External Borders' in Jörg Monar (ed), *Soft or Hard Borders?* (Routledge 2017).

Moldova and Ukraine (EUBAM). To understand what integrated border management actually entails it is worth briefly looking at EUBAM's mission as regards the practices it promotes. Its mission to achieve integrated border management is to:

1. promote European Union border management standards and procedures for a quicker crossing of people and goods;
2. enhance the professional capacities of the Moldovan and Ukrainian Customs and Border Authorities;
3. assist Moldovan and Ukrainian authorities in combating cross-border crime more efficiently;
4. act as a catalyst and bring together key stakeholders to strengthen cross-border cooperation between the border authorities and law enforcement agencies;
5. contribute to the peaceful settlement of the Transnistrian conflict.

This codification of integrated border management objectives bears attention as the starting place is how to get people and goods moving rapidly across borders. It then focuses on cross-border crime, recommending more integration of two types of law enforcement agencies – those responsible for border controls and those of criminal justice. What is obscured from this definition is that EU laws and objectives on border crossing, let alone criminal justice, do not necessarily converge with those of third countries, even Moldova and Ukraine, countries in receipt of enormous amounts of EU aid (even before the full invasion of Ukraine by Russia).[17] What the EU might classify as cross-border crime is not necessarily the same as that of a third country and certainly subject to very different procedures and penalties. Crossing an international border for the purpose of having an abortion or euthanasia are just two examples which reveal the complexity of the question.

Returning then to the intra-EU meaning of integrated border management, the allocation of powers gives some clarity as to what this is intended to do. In order to achieve Frontex's specific integrated border management objective, it is given the following powers:

[17] Julien Jeandesboz, 'Intervention and Subversion: The EU Border Assistance Mission to Moldova and Ukraine' (2015) 9(4) *Journal of Intervention and Statebuilding* 442; Coralie A Ballieu and René Schwok, 'European Integration in Belarus, Moldova and Ukraine: Assessing the Role and Strategies of the European Union in the Eastern Neighbours Compared with the Western Balkans' (2023) 118 *Global Studies Institute de L'université de Genève Collection*.

1. to establish a technical and operational strategy as part of the implementation of the multiannual strategic policy cycle for European integrated border management;
2. to oversee the effective functioning of border control at the external borders;
3. to carry out risk analysis and vulnerability assessments; to provide increased technical and operational assistance to Member States and third countries through joint operations and rapid border interventions;
4. to ensure the practical execution of measures in a situation requiring urgent action at the external borders; to provide technical and operational assistance in the support of search and rescue operations for persons in distress at sea; and
5. to organize, coordinate and conduct return operations and return interventions.[18]

Integrated border management is stated to be a shared responsibility of Frontex and the national authorities responsible for border management, including coast guards to the extent that they carry out maritime border surveillance operations and any other border control tasks, as well as the national authorities responsible for return. Member States have the primary responsibility for the management of their external borders in their interest and in the interest of all Member States (including issuing return decisions).[19] Frontex's job is to support the application of Union measures related to the management of the external borders and return by reinforcing, assessing and coordinating the actions of the Member States which implement those measures. The activities of the agency should complement the efforts of the Member States.[20]

The idea of a shared responsibility runs through the whole Regulation and is often intertwined with the EU concept of shared competence.[21] However, the strict meaning of shared competence is where Member States are allowed to pass laws in fields covered by the treaties (such as border controls) because the EU has not already proposed laws or has decided that it will not.[22] This is not the same thing as shared responsibility, where

18 2019 Frontex Regulation, recital 3.

19 Ibid art 7.

20 Ibid recital 12.

21 Natalia Barszcz, 'Exercising Shared Competence on the EU's External Borders of Poland, Latvia, and Lithuania Amidst the Recently Increased Irregular Migration on the Border with Belarus' (2022) 1 *Amsterdam Review of European Affairs* 89.

22 Commission, Areas of EU Action, https://commission.europa.eu/about-european-commission/what-european-commission-does/law/areas-eu-action_en, accessed 12 October 2024.

in this area, Frontex and Member State authorities are responsible for achieving an EU objective – integrated border management – and therefore work together. To clarify the difference, Article 7 of the 2019 Frontex Regulation is devoted to explaining the definition of shared responsibility. According to it, Member States retain primary responsibility. However, Frontex provides technical and operational assistance in the implementation of measures either on request of a Member State or without a request, on its own initiative but with the agreement of the Member State. Frontex is specifically excluded from all measures regarding intra-Member State border controls. According to the article, Frontex is fully responsible and accountable for any decision it takes and for any activity for which it is solely responsible under the Regulation. But the Regulation is designed in a way that it will always be difficult, if not impossible, to determine whether Frontex has sole responsibility. The issue of shared responsibility is evidently one which makes the allocation of legal liability particularly confused. In the section on direct action against Frontex heard by the Court of Justice of the European Union (CJEU), the operation of shared responsibility as a mechanism to avoid legal liability has been relatively successful for the moment. There has been a great amount of buck-passing and shadow dancing regarding which body is responsible for actions when things go wrong.[23] This was central to the defence of Frontex's former executive director who resigned on 28 April 2022[24] after a damning report by the European Anti-fraud Office (OLAF) regarding the marginalization of the Frontex Fundamental Rights Officer (FRO) to prevent the investigation of fundamental rights abuse allegations.[25] This is discussed in some depth in the next chapter.

2.2 Schengen or the European Union?

One of the startling anomalies of Frontex's powers is that while they are supervisory on national border police, as well as operational, the territorial scope of the powers is neither inclusive of all EU Member States, nor limited to

[23] See, for instance, Laura Salzano, 'Lost at Sea: That Time Frontex Tried to Redefine the Notion of Distress' (*Refugee Law Initiative Blog*, 26 October 2023), https://rli.blogs.sas.ac.uk/2023/10/26/lost-at-sea-that-time-frontex-tried-to-redefine-the-notion-of-distress/, accessed 12 October 2024; see also Case T-600/21 *WS v European Coast Guard Agency* [2021] EU:T:2023:492.

[24] See https://twitter.com/g_christides/status/1519967913066782720, accessed 9 January 2024.

[25] OLAF, 'Final Report on Frontex, Case no OC/2021/0451/A1' (3 May 2021), https://fragdenstaat.de/dokumente/233972-olaf-final-report-on-frontex/, accessed 12 October 2024.

Member States. Because Frontex's legal status is a continuation of the Schengen *acquis*, the territorial scope is that of the *acquis*, not the EU. As part of the Schengen *acquis*,[26] a body of rules and conventions which developed on an intergovernmental level from 1985 to 1999, while regulated by EU law, it is not limited to the EU. While an obligation to abolish intra-Member State border controls on persons was inserted into EU law in 1987 by the Single European Act,[27] this was never realized. Instead, the Schengen intergovernmental system expanded resulting in the abolition of border controls among its members. When finally incorporated into EU law in 1999, there were already four non-EU states participating which continued to do so (Iceland, Liechtenstein, Norway and Switzerland) and which did not accept to be ousted from the system. So, Schengen came into the EU with non-EU states. Two (then) EU states, Ireland and the UK, refused to join Schengen. The UK subsequently left the EU but Ireland remains outside. In the big enlargement of 2004, the enlargement treaties required the acceding states to join Schengen when the existing Schengen states considered they were ready. The same provision was included in subsequent accession agreements. In the meantime, the institutions gradually adopted EU legislation to replace most of the Schengen rules.

Iceland, Liechtenstein, Norway and Switzerland's continued participation was regularized when the Schengen system was inserted into EU law by agreements between these countries and the EU. This is acknowledged in the recitals of the regulation, with separate arrangements for Iceland and Norway different from those for Liechtenstein and Switzerland. Denmark participates on the same international law basis as these states, a consequence of its Protocol (22) to the Treaty on the Functioning of the European Union (TFEU) also recognized in the recitals (but not as part of EU law). Ireland remains completely out by choice (Protocol 19 TFEU). Cyprus has yet to be admitted to the Schengen area, though it both wishes to be part of it and is required to do so as soon as the existing Schengen states consider that it is ready. The problem of the division of the island is the issue which prevents its entry into the system. The situation of Bulgaria and Romania is more baroque in that from 24 March 2024, the Schengen free movement rules apply to passengers coming to and going from these countries to and from other Schengen states by air or sea but not by land. The regulation of land borders apparently will be negotiated in the future.[28]

---

[26] TFEU Protocol (No 19) on the Schengen *acquis* integrated into the framework of the European Union [2012] OJ C326/290.

[27] Treaty establishing the European Community (Consolidated version 2002) [2002] OJ C 325 (TEC) Art 62; now art 77(2)(b) and (e) TFEU.

[28] Commission, 'EU Will lift Checks at Air and Sea Borders with Bulgaria and Romania in March' (8 January 2024), https://commission.europa.eu/news/eu-will-lift-border-checks-air-and-sea-borders-bulgaria-and-romania-march-2024-01-08_en, accessed 9 January 2024.

A further anomaly is that Frontex's responsibilities are not connected to the EU law on border control, the Schengen Borders Code which sets out the law on who and under what conditions third-country nationals may cross the external Schengen borders into the EU.[29] The only link in the Frontex Regulation with EU law on border crossing is via Council Regulation (EU) No 1053/2013 on the Schengen Evaluation Mechanism Regulation, which states at Article 4 that evaluation shall cover all aspects of the Schengen *acquis*, including the effective and efficient application by the Member States of accompanying measures in the areas of external borders and visa policy.[30] The latter two are specifically covered by EU law. As the recital to the Schengen evaluation mechanism regulation states, while the evaluation mechanism is the primary method for evaluating the implementation of and compliance with Union law in the Member States (which must include the Schengen Borders Code which is the main EU legal instrument regulating the crossing of Schengen external borders together with the Visa Code[31]), it is not the only one. The recital rather opaquely refers to synergies between the Frontex border vulnerability assessment and the Schengen evaluation mechanism, which 'should be maximised with a view to establishing an improved situational picture of the functioning of the Schengen area, avoiding, to the extent possible, duplication of efforts and ensuring the better-coordinated use of the relevant Union financial instruments supporting the management of the external borders'. This is rather incomprehensible language even for the initiated.

The creation of an increasingly powerful border control agency with operational responsibilities without reference to the applicable law on the crossing of the external borders seems like more than a mere oversight. The consequence is that when carrying out its activities, Frontex is not required to adhere to any of the rules set out in the Borders and Visa Codes

[29] Regulation (EU) 2016/399 of the European Parliament and of the Council of 9 March 2016 on a Union Code on the rules governing the movement of persons across borders (Schengen Borders Code) (codification) [2016] OJ L 77/1.

[30] Council Regulation (EU) No 1053/2013 of 7 October 2013 establishing an evaluation and monitoring mechanism to verify the application of the Schengen acquis and repealing the Decision of the Executive Committee of 16 September 1998 setting up a Standing Committee on the evaluation and implementation of Schengen [2013] OJ L 295/27, as amended by Council Regulation (EU) 2022/922 of 9 June 2022 on the establishment and operation of an evaluation and monitoring mechanism to verify the application of the Schengen acquis, and repealing Regulation (EU) No 1053/2013 [2022] OJ L 160/1.

[31] Regulation (EC) No 810/2009 of the European Parliament and of the Council of 13 July 2009 establishing a Community Code on Visas (Visa Code) [2009] OJ L 243/1.

(both of which are regulations directly applicable to the Schengen states). This is problematic as many provisions of the Codes are directly applicable to border police. The immediate example is Article 7(2) which states that while carrying out border checks, border guards shall not discriminate against persons on grounds of sex, racial or ethnic origin, religion or belief, disability, age or sexual orientation. While Article 43(4) of the Frontex Regulation prohibits discrimination,[32] this is a duty of national authorities to ensure, as clarified in Article 43(5), that the 'Member State shall provide for appropriate disciplinary or other measures in accordance with its national law regarding violations of fundamental rights or international protection obligations in the course of any operational activity by the Agency'. This is also a practical example of the weakening effect as regards coherent and consistent supervision which is a result of the shared competence approach to border control. For the individual who has suffered personal injury at the hands of border guards in the context of a Frontex coordinated joint action or made possible through the use of Frontex assets by national border guards, the question of who is legally liable for that injury is by no means evident.

3 Legal existence and responsibility

From its establishment, Frontex has had legal personality.[33] In the various iterations of the Frontex rules, this aspect has been subject only to marginal change. As regards responsibility, Frontex is accountable to the European Parliament and the Council. But the day to day supervision of Frontex is by the Commission which is its effective (or ineffective) boss (Directorate General [DG] HOME is its 'parent' DG). One of the most powerful tools which the 2019 Frontex Regulation gave to the European Parliament has been the power to endorse or not Frontex's budget.[34] In the changes to the 2004 Frontex Regulation, there has been a proliferation of references to

[32] It states: 'Members of the teams shall, in the performance of their tasks and in the exercise of their powers, fully respect fundamental rights, including access to asylum procedures and human dignity, and shall pay particular attention to vulnerable persons. Any measures taken in the performance of their tasks and in the exercise of their powers shall be proportionate to the objectives pursued by such measures. While performing their tasks and exercising their powers, they shall not discriminate against persons on the basis of any grounds such as sex, race, colour, ethnic or social origin, genetic features, language, religion or belief, political or any other opinion, membership of a national minority, property, birth, disability, age or sexual orientation in line with Article 21 of the Charter.'

[33] 2004 Frontex Regulation, art 15.

[34] 2019 Frontex Regulation, art 116.

fundamental rights.[35] This increase in reference has mainly been driven by the European Parliament. Its responsibility for fundamental rights includes contributing to the continuous and uniform application of EU law, of which the EU *acquis* on fundamental rights is an essential element, in particular the EU Charter, at external borders. Its contribution must include the exchange of good practices.[36] Two mechanisms for the reporting of fundamental rights violations are included in the Regulation. The first – and newest – is a complaints mechanism.[37] Under this system, an aggrieved individual can submit a complaint to the agency which is examined by the FRO. As mentioned earlier, in February 2022, an OLAF report[38] regarding misconduct of several individuals employed by the agency in relation to Frontex operational activities, and which resulted in the departure of the then executive director, highlighted the hostility of the executive director to the dissemination of information about the complaints mechanism and noted the obstacles which he placed in the way of its operation (see further on this mechanism in the next chapter).

Apart from the individual complaints system, which has not had substantial uptake, the main mechanism by which allegations of fundamental rights violations are signalled within Frontex is through an internal reporting mechanism driven by the reports of border guards themselves in the pursuance of their operational activities. The key tool is incident reporting which is the main way in which fundamental rights problems are brought to the attention of the Frontex hierarchy. It is open to border guards and cannot be used by other internal instances within Frontex, such as the FRO or the Consultative Forum, which is examined in this chapter, which may investigate allegations of violations but neither the allegations nor the investigations are institutionalized within the Frontex system.

Annex 14 of the Frontex Code of Conduct[39] and Standard Operating Procedures establish rules on serious incident reporting

---

35 Nicolette Busuttil, 'The EU Legislator, Frontex and Fundamental Rights' in Elspeth Guild (ed), *Monitoring Border Violence in the EU* (Routledge 2023).

36 2019 Frontex Regulation, art 5(4).

37 See Frontex's explanation of the mechanism in Frontex, 'Complaints Mechanism', https://www.frontex.europa.eu/fundamental-rights/complaints-mechanism/, accessed 12 October 2024.

38 OLAF (n 25). This version is heavily redacted and not official. However, Frontex has acknowledged its existence and impact in Frontex, 'Statement of Frontex Executive Management Following Publication of OLAF Report' (14 October 2022), https://www.frontex.europa.eu/media-centre/news/news-release/statement-of-frontex-executive-management-following-publication-of-olaf-report-amARYy, accessed 12 October 2024.

39 Frontex, Code of Conduct Applicable to All Persons participating in Frontex Operational Activities, https://www.frontex.europa.eu/assets/Key_Documents/Code_of_Conduct/Code_of_conduct_applicable_to_all_persons_particiating_in_Frontex_operational_activities.pdf, accessed 12 October 2024.

(SIR).[40] These set out how issues of fundamental rights should be addressed by all Frontex staff. It is founded on a system of serious incident reports (SIRs) by which officers on the ground are required to report to Frontex management where they have reason to believe that a fundamental right has been violated. SIRs are divided along a scale of seriousness from Category 1 (the most serious),[41] Category 2 (less serious)[42] and Category 3, which includes everything else.[43] As the categories and the system are established by documents which are subject to change at the discretion of the executive director, their stability is always uncertain. For instance, the order of seriousness was reversed at some point from 1–4 with the most serious as a category 4 incident to 1–3 with the most serious being 1. This occurred between the 2014 and 2021 versions and makes a mess of external reports written between those dates which refer to the SIR system. Specific forms for recording incidents by category are included, timelines for submission (as quickly as possible) and an explanation of the procedure which follows the submission of an SIR. The SIR system is the key internal mechanism for registering possible fundamental rights violations from within the organization which automatically opens a series of consequential investigations and actions to be taken by various actors within Frontex, most importantly the FRO. The effectiveness of the SIR system was the subject of substantial negative evaluation in the OLAF report. Among much damning evidence received by OLAF in

[40] Frontex, 'Decision of the Executive Director No R-ED-2021-51 Standard Operating Procedure (SOP) – Serious Incident Reporting' (19 April 2021), https://prd.frontex.europa.eu/document/frontex-executive-director-decision-on-standard-operating-procedure-serious-incident-reporting/, accessed 12 October 2024.

[41] 'Situations of potential violation of Fundamental Rights or international protection obligations: Potential violations of Fundamental Rights enshrined in the Charter of Fundamental Rights of the European Union or other relevant international law as described under Annex 6; Lack of safeguards of Fundamental Rights protection either by action or failure to act (Article 80(1) of the Regulation); Witnessed potential violations of Fundamental Rights, in particular against human dignity'.

[42] 'Situations of potential violations of Codes of Conduct provisions; Potential violation of the Frontex Codes of Conduct, except for cases which are also related to potential violations of Fundamental Rights and/or the obligations on international protection (Category 1)'.

[43] 'Situations with serious actual or potential negative implications on Frontex core tasks; Serious accidents with the involvement of persons or means during Frontex activities; Serious/severe contagious disease or severe/life-threatening injury of participants; Death of Frontex staff/SNEs/other SC member during Frontex activities; Arrest, detention or criminal proceedings against Frontex staff, SNEs, SC Category 2–4 (except for issues related to Code(s) of Conduct/violation of FR); Any other serious incident which does not fall under SI Category 1 and 2'.

its inquiry was that from national border guards seconded to a Frontex-managed mission in Greece. They feared retaliation from the national border guards (who, it may be surmised, had been involved in serious incidents) including threats against their physical integrity if the seconded border guards sought to make a SIR about fundamental rights violations which they had witnessed.[44]

Frontex operations, however, take place not only through the action of Frontex staff but traditionally through seconded border guards from the Member States. These seconded staff remain integrated into their home institutions which have their own mechanisms for signalling fundamental rights violations. Not infrequently, these seconded staff appear to have more confidence in their national structures than in Frontex ones and reports of potential violations of fundamental rights in Frontex coordinated operations also arrive on the desks of national border guard institutions.[45] In this context, shared responsibility is less of a blessing for Frontex as it also results in responsibility exercised by the hierarchy of national border guard authorities concerned about their exposure through participation in Frontex activities. The original complaint which launched the OLAF investigation came from a Member State delegation which was concerned about allegations of fundamental rights violations which had been brought to its attention. However, as Frontex recruits its standing corps, by 2027 it will have 10,000 border guards directly employed by the agency as staff members and regularly deployed to border guarding missions according to their profile.[46] Consequently, its dependence on seconded border guards will diminish.

There are a number of tools the Frontex executive director has where the conditions to conduct its activities are no longer fulfilled (for instance, as regards the protection of fundamental rights). The first is a duty under Article 46 of the 2019 Frontex Regulation to suspend or to terminate Frontex activities in case of serious or persisting violations of fundamental rights or international protection obligations. The executive director alternatively may decide to withdraw financing and Frontex assets. As regards any of the options, the executive director is required to consult the FRO if the he/she considers that violations are sufficiently serious or are likely to persist. Again, after consultation with the FRO, the executive director may decide not to launch an operation on fundamental rights grounds. The information

44 OLAF (n 25) section 2.2.6.

45 Human Rights Watch (HRW), 'The EU's Dirty Hands: Frontex Involvement in Ill-Treatment of Migrant Detainees in Greece' (2011).

46 Frontex, 'Standing Corps', https://www.frontex.europa.eu/about-frontex/standing-corps/standing-corps/, accessed 12 October 2024.

the executive director must take into account when reaching a decision includes: the number and substance of registered complaints, whether they have been resolved by the national authorities, reports of serious incidents, reports from coordinating officers, relevant international organizations and EU institutions, bodies, offices or agencies. The executive director has only a duty to inform the management board of the decision and reason for it. As the complaints mechanism has been subject to substantial delays, one of the key elements for the director to take into account are the serious incident reports. The difficulties with the submission of serious incident reports are discussed in the next chapter.

4 Consequence of responsibilities

The question of Frontex's compliance with fundamental rights and the consequences for individuals has come before the CJEU three times in direct actions by individuals against the agency for their treatment. At the time of writing, two of the cases are on appeal from the General Court to the CJEU. All three claims of Frontex responsibility have been rejected by the General Court. The procedure to bring a direct action against an EU institution, such as Frontex, before the CJEU, begins with an action to the General Court and is by no means straightforward. In the event of a negative judgment, the aggrieved individual can appeal to the CJEU. In the first effort to hold Frontex accountable for fundamental rights abuses in the Aegean, two individuals, supported by two non-governmental organizations, sought to require Frontex to cease financing and participating in border management operations in the area.[47] They wrote a letter under relevant provision of the TFEU to the executive director inviting him to suspend or terminate Frontex's activities in the Aegean because of allegations of fundamental rights abuses (enumerated in the letter) which were taking place as a result of it. They further noted that the Frontex executive director had not consulted first and foremost with the FRO regarding the incidents where fundamental rights allegations were made. According to the CJEU's summary of the facts, within the relevant time limit, Frontex replied that:

1. the conditions for the adoption of a decision to withdraw financing, to suspend or to terminate its activities in the Aegean Sea, were not satisfied in the present case;
2. after describing the operational plan for its activities in the Aegean Sea region, it noted that only incidents of a certain level of seriousness or likely to persist qualify;

[47] Case T-282/21 *SS & ST v Frontex* [2022] (not yet published).

3. isolated incidents (such as those set out by the applicants) cannot constitute a condition for taking the requested action;
4. a decision to withdraw financing, to suspend or to terminate its activity must be taken in the context of integrated European border management;
5. the incidents complained of had been examined in the final report of the management board's working group on fundamental rights (see further in the next chapter); and
6. none of the incidents were capable of demonstrating the existence of infringements of fundamental rights, with the result that its activities in the Aegean Sea had not been carried out in strict compliance with the applicable legal framework, including with Frontex's responsibilities stemming from fundamental rights.

The judgment does not specify what the incidents were which occurred in 2020 which were documented by the complainants. However, the eight incidents investigated by OLAF in its report on fundamental rights compliance by Frontex may have taken place over the same period. The OLAF report details the fundamental rights issues which arose and found that there had been a failure of effective investigation and the intentional exclusion of the FRO from information relevant to the investigations and procedural irregularities. Of course, at the time of the judgment, the General Court had not yet had the advantage of reading the OLAF report.

The General Court dismissed the complaint on procedural grounds. It found that the complaint was based on a TFEU article which required the EU body to respond within a time frame but does not require the EU body to act in accordance with the invitation to act. The purpose of the provision relied upon, according to the General Court, is to compel the institution to state its position, nothing more. As Frontex had responded to the complaint (which constituted an invitation to act) it had fulfilled its duty under the relevant provision. But the General Court noted that had the complaint been made under another TFEU provision requesting annulment, the complainants could have disputed the reasons provided by Frontex to justify the decision not to take measures.[48] This reliance on legal technicalities and the inflexibility of the General Court to allow the complainants to add annulment to its request must have been particularly frustrating for the lawyers. Frontex was particularly aggressive in its litigation strategy, as far as is apparent from the judgment. It submitted four separate grounds of inadmissibility of the case to the Court (the Court chose only to examine one of the grounds which it found justified to resolve the case). Another twist which revealed the approach of Frontex related to the publication of

[48] Ibid para 33.

content of its plea of admissibility on a website contrary to the obligation of confidentiality on the parties.[49] The applicants advised the Court that they were not responsible for the publication and had no connection with the website. As a result, they could not put an end to the publication. The Court confirmed the confidentiality requirement regarding proceedings as entitling the parties to defend their interests free from all external influences in particular from members of the public. However, Frontex was not satisfied and argued that the applicants should be ordered to pay Frontex's costs in the matter including because of the breach of confidentiality. The Court held that as the applicants had confirmed that they were not responsible for the breach and Frontex had produced no evidence that they were, there was no proven fault on the part of the applicants. Furthermore, for the purpose of the apportioning of costs, the incident was irrelevant. However, the attempt by Frontex to 'punish' the applicants with a costs order against them based on a confidentiality breach which Frontex was unable to prove against them indicates a certain degree of rancour.

The second effort to engage the Court with the possible responsibility of Frontex for damage to individuals' lives resulted in a General Court judgment on 6 September 2023.[50] The applicants, Syrian nationals, arrived on a Greek island on 9 October 2016 in a group of 114 refugees. They were transferred to another island where they applied for asylum on a form entitled beneficiary notice for international protection request. On 20 October 2016, without any conclusion of their asylum claim (or apparently any expulsion decision which in any event could only be adopted after consideration of their asylum claim), the applicants were expelled to Turkey in a return operation carried out by Frontex and the Greek border authorities. There they were issued with temporary protection documents and a travel permission to go to a reception centre. From there they moved to another village in Turkey, then took refuge in Erbil, Iraq where they reside. The applicants lodged two complaints with the Frontex FRO and a complaint before the European Court of Human Rights, claiming inadequate investigation by the Greek police's internal mechanism resulting in the closure of the complaints with only a confidential internal report. This led to the FRO also closing the complaints without further investigation. In the FRO's final report, the issue of Frontex's role in the expulsion was not addressed at all.

The applicants' claim was basically that if Frontex had not infringed its obligations relating to the protection of fundamental rights in the context of joint operations, in particular the principle of *non-refoulement*, the right to

[49] Ibid paras 37–42.

[50] *WS v European Coast Guard Agency* (n 23).

asylum, the prohibition of collective expulsion, the rights of the child, the prohibition of degrading treatment, the right to good administration and to an effective remedy, they would not have been unlawfully returned to Turkey and they would have obtained the international protection to which they were entitled, given their Syrian nationality and the situation in Syria at the material time meant that almost all Syrians received protection in the EU. They claimed damages in the form of:

1. the amount spent to travel to Greece;
2. the cost of renting a house in Saruj, Turkey, and the cost of purchasing furniture;
3. the expenses incurred in fleeing to Iraq;
4. the rent paid in Iraq;
5. the electricity costs for their home in Iraq;
6. the children's school fees in Iraq;
7. the subsistence costs in Iraq; and
8. the cost of legal aid for assistance with their complaints against Frontex.

Again in this case, Frontex claimed that the action was inadmissible, claiming that it should have been for annulment of the Frontex action (which would have rendered the case out of time because of the time limits on annulment actions). The General Court rejected that ground of inadmissibility stating that as the applicants seek compensation for the material and non-material damage which they claimed to have suffered as a result of Frontex's alleged unlawful conduct before, during and after the return operation, the damage invoked by the applicants, first, is not a consequence a Frontex letter to them and, second, would subsist even after the annulment of the challenged acts. Therefore, the action for damages does not have the same purpose or the same effect as an action for annulment brought against those documents. On this ground the case was not inadmissible. Frontex also argued that the case was inadmissible on the ground that EU courts do not have jurisdiction to make statements of principle.

As regards this ground the General Court considered that it was time to engage with the principles on non-contractual liability and their applicability to the cases against Frontex. It reiterated the general position that to incur non-contractual liability for unlawful conduct of EU institutions or bodies three conditions must be satisfied:

1. the alleged conduct of the institution must be unlawful, the decisive test for finding that a breach is sufficiently serious is whether the EU institution or body concerned manifestly and gravely disregarded the limits on its discretion;
2. actual damage must have been suffered; and

3. there must be a causal link between the alleged conduct and the damage pleaded.[51]

As the applicants were asking the Court to find that Frontex has committed a sufficiently serious breach of its obligations relating to the protection of fundamental rights, a necessary condition for a finding that their claim for compensation is well founded, it fulfilled requirement (1). Requirements (2) and (3) depend on the first condition so Frontex's claim of inadmissibility on this ground was dismissed. Then there was a disagreement about whether a number of key documents submitting for the applicants were admissible on grounds of when they were submitted to the Court and the deadlines applicable.[52] The Court found in favour of Frontex, thereby excluding much of the evidence supporting the applicants' case.

The General Court then held that the damage pleaded must be a sufficiently direct consequence of the conduct complained of, which must be the determining cause of the damage.[53] Further, it is for the applicant to adduce evidence of a causal link between the conduct complained of and the damage suffered. It found that the direct causal link was not made out. Frontex had only provided technical and operational support and did not enter into the merits of a return decision (or apparently the presence or absence of one).[54] Similarly, only Member States determine asylum applications, so Frontex had no competence either for the expulsion decision or any asylum application and its determination.[55] Thus, there is no causal link between Frontex's action and the damage suffered. To this end, the Court clarified that the damage invoked must result directly from the alleged illegality and not from the applicant's choice as to how to react to the allegedly unlawful act, and the mere fact that the unlawful conduct constituted a necessary condition for the damage to arise, in the sense that the damage would not have arisen in the absence of such conduct, is not sufficient to establish a causal link.[56] The judgment has been subject to criticism by academics regarding the consistency of the reasoning in comparison with the General Court's constant case-law on damages in other areas of EU law.[57]

---

[51] Ibid para 35.

[52] Ibid paras 40–51.

[53] Mariana Gkliati, 'Frontex before the Judge: The Road to the Judicial Accountability before the CJEU, the ECtHR and National Courts' in Vasileios Pergantis (ed), *EU Responsibility in the International Legal Order: Human Rights – Comparative Approaches – Special Issues* (Sakkoulas Publishers 2023).

[54] *WS v European Coast Guard Agency* (n 23) para 64.

[55] Ibid para 65.

[56] Ibid para 68.

[57] Fransesca Romana Partipilo, 'The EU General Court's Judgment in the Case of *WS and Others v Frontex*: Human Rights Violations at EU External Borders going Unpunished'

The last judgment (at the date of writing) was delivered by the General Court on 13 December 2023.[58] The (unsuccessful) applicants have also appealed the General Court's judgment to the CJEU. The facts also related to Frontex operations at the Turkish–Greek sea border in 2020 and allegations of illegal expulsion without any opportunity to make an asylum claim or challenge the expulsion (apparently made without any official written decision and not notified to the applicant). A Syrian national claimed to have arrived from Turkey on the Greek island of Samos on 28 April 2020 with 22 other persons. After arriving on a beach they walked into the mountains from where the applicant took photos and a video of himself and sent it immediately to someone in Austria. This behaviour may seem odd to those unfamiliar with the circumstances on the Greek islands in 2020. What the applicant claims he was doing was establishing evidence that he had actually arrived in Greece in case he was subsequently subject to an illegal expulsion back to Turkey (so-called ghost landings).

The Greek border guards' practice of illegal expulsion has been the subject of a number of reports by non-governmental organizations and media (practices which appear to continue in Greece in 2023–2024), indicating that the facts are consistent with reports in the media and by non-governmental organizations at the relevant time and subsequently.[59] The border control operation in the relevant area is coordinated by Frontex under the Poseidon operation.[60]

(*EU Law Analysis*, 23 September 2023), https://eulawanalysis.blogspot.com/2023/09/the-eu-general-courts-judgment-in-case.html%3E, accessed 12 October 2024.

58 Case T-136/22 *Hamoudi v Frontex* [2022] (not yet published).

59 HRW, 'Greece: Investigate Pushbacks, Collective Expulsions' (16 July 2020), https://www.hrw.org/news/2020/07/16/greece-investigate-pushbacks-collective-expulsions, accessed 12 October 2024; 'Video Shows Greece Abandoning Migrants at Sea' (*New York Times*, 19 March 2023), https://www.nytimes.com/2023/05/19/world/europe/greece-migrants-abandoned.html, accessed 12 October 2024; 'Greece Opens Investigation into Illegal Deportations to Turkey' (*InfoMigrants*, 25 May 2023), https://www.infomigrants.net/en/post/49168/greece-opens-investigation-into-illegal-deportations-to-turkey, accessed 12 October 2024.

60 According to Frontex's website: 'Operation Poseidon covers the Greek sea borders with Turkey and the Greek islands. In 2023, the Eastern Mediterranean route continued its post-pandemic upward trend with around 60 000 detections or irregular border crossings. Frontex supports Greece with officers who perform border surveillance, assist in the identification and registration of incoming migrants, as well as debriefing and screening. The operation covers a number of aspects of cross border crime as well as several coast guard functions such as search and rescue, detection of illegal fishing and maritime pollution. Debriefing officers deployed by the agency collect intelligence about people smuggling networks operating in Turkey and migrants' countries of origin. The agency shares this information with the Greek authorities and Europol.' See https://www.frontex.europa.eu/what-we-do/operations/operations/, accessed 12 October 2024.

According to the applicant, the group spent some time asking the residents to call the police so they could make their asylum applications. When the police did arrive, it seems that among the first things they did was to confiscate all the telephones of the group, so no further evidence of the actions alleged were captured by the group. According to the applicant, the group was driven to a beach where a small ship and a small boat were waiting. He stated in written evidence that they were pushed onto a life raft with no means of propulsion and pushed out to sea. In the process they were forced to change boats twice. The pushback took place at night. The boat drifted in the sea until the afternoon of the following day when the Turkish Coast Guard picked them up and took them to Turkey. While the boat was drifting in the sea on 29 April 2020, the applicant states that a private surveillance aeroplane possibly equipped with a camera and operated by Frontex flew over the scene twice. This account is similar to one of the events investigated by OLAF in its report into SIR 11095/2020 of a very similar incident on 18–19 April 2020.[61] The presence of Frontex surveillance aeroplanes is also noted in the OLAF report regarding the earlier incident.

The General Court reiterated the conditions for the EU to incur non-contractual liability, unlawful conduct, actual damage and causal link. Frontex's defence was that the applicant has not demonstrated that the alleged incident on 28 and 29 April 2020 involved either himself or airborne or seaborne assets operated or financed by Frontex. The General Court, on the basis of previous decisions, held that it was for the applicant to adduce conclusive proof as to the existence and extent of the damage he alleges. The applicant had submitted his witness statement, a Bellingcat media article, which included two videos and four photos in which he claimed he appeared. The General Court was not satisfied that the evidence met the required standard, though it refused an oral hearing requested by the applicant to present his version of events. Specifically the General Court found that the applicant's witness statement had little probative value; the witness statement also included several statements which were insufficiently specific regarding the essential points of fact; none of the other people who were part of the group made witness statements or were named; the applicant's identity as a member of the group is not clearly and conclusively apparent from the other evidence produced; the Bellingcat article does not feature the applicant's

[61] OLAF's report (n 25) refers to an incident stating that 'During the night between 18 and 19 April 2020, the FSA METIS detected (and video recorded) the activities of some Hellenic Coast Guard assets while dealing with a rubber boat of migrants intercepted within the Greek Territorial Waters. In particular, the migrants were taken on board one of the HCG vessels only to be subsequently transferred back to the rubber boat. The boat was then towed by an HCG asset to the Turkish Territorial Waters where it was left adrift with no engine at about 6:20 local time.'

name; the photos are screenshots of poor quality of a person wearing a hoodie which covers a large part of his or her head and who is not looking directly at the camera; the screenshots do not permit identification compared to the applicant's passport; the date and location of the screenshots are not specified; the link to the Bellingcat article is not for the Court to check, the Court could only have regard to evidence submitted in the applicant's claim; the videos from the Turkish Coast Guard are discounted as again they do not contain concrete evidence establishing the date, location, temporal and geographic continuity or scope of the events nor the identities of the individuals. As a result, the General Court held that the applicant had not demonstrated the actual damage he alleged and therefore the condition relating to actual damage was not satisfied.

It is difficult not to criticize the General Court's assessment of the evidence and approach to the application as a caricature of justice. No mention is made of the OLAF report. The approach of the General Court is reminiscent of national courts' approaches to the credibility of asylum seekers' claims though in the case of the General Court, the refusal to actually hear the applicant makes the implicit negative credibility assessment even more problematic.[62] Further, the General Court held that the applicant should pay the costs of Frontex as regards the matter. As the applicant subsequently managed to enter the territory of the EU and lodge an application for international protection in Germany, this means that the costs order against him is likely to blight his life for many years to come. The General Court's use of the costs order is likely to have a chilling effect on other applicants who might seek damages from Frontex.

In sum, for the moment Frontex has been successful in fending off all legal claims before the Court of Justice that it is responsible for alleged fundamental rights violations. The General Court has been particularly unconvinced of Frontex's liability and the merits of the cases which have come before it.

5 Conclusion

Among the conundrums of Frontex is the lack of clarity regarding what its purpose is. Among its central problems is that it was created as an agency when there was no law for which it was responsible to ensure correct

[62] Robert Thomas, 'Assessing the Credibility of Asylum Claims: EU and UK Approaches Examined' (2006) 8 *European Journal of Migration and Law* 79; Gregor Noll, 'Salvation by the Grace of State? Explaining Credibility Assessment in the Asylum Procedure' in Gregor Noll (ed), *Proof, Evidentiary Assessment and Credibility in Asylum Procedures* (Brill Nijhoff 2005) 197–214; Liza Schuster, 'The Common European Asylum System: Inconsistent, Incoherent and lacking Credibility' (2018) 1 *This Century's Review Journal for Rational Legal Debate* 40.

implementation, thus it began in a lawless field, characterized by the lack of EU law regarding border crossing. There is still no law to form the foundation of what Frontex is supposed to be doing as part of the Area of Freedom, Security and Justice (AFSJ), let alone the internal market. The whole construction of Frontex and its relationship with the Member States is riddled with incoherence and lack of clarity. This makes it the perfect playground for those seeking to avoid responsibility for fundamental rights violations resulting from action and inaction. For the moment, there has been no effective concerted action to make Frontex responsible for the correct application of EU law (in particular the EU Charter), nor what its role is in ensuring the correct application of international treaties to which the EU is a party. While one European Parliament committee stands out as a beacon of hope, it has not been able to reign in or provide coherence to a system which has developed in such a haphazard manner and where that haphazard nature has become so valuable to many of the internal actors that they have no interest in creating clarity. The consequence of the establishment of an agency with coercive powers but without a legal framework setting out the parameters of law is that the field is effectively an area without law, hence our use of the term lawless. It is an agency built on a deficit of rule of law.

5

Frontex: Management and Internal Oversight

1 Introduction

This chapter provides an overview of Frontex's management structure from the perspective of internal monitoring and accountability systems to ensure fundamental rights compliance. It places oversight in the context of internal, within the agency itself, and external mechanisms, established under European Union (EU) law external to Frontex,[1] but internal to the EU as a whole. These mechanisms are interdependent, but there has been discord among them. Nowhere is this more flagrant than in the differences of assessment between the Commission's Frontex evaluation from 2022[2] and the conclusions of the European Anti-fraud Office (OLAF) investigation of the same year.[3] Chapter 6 develops further on the external mechanisms. Here we examine internal accountability. These two chapters focus on accountability within the EU itself rather than within European or international human rights law and structures. As with Chapter 4, the OLAF report is used to highlight problems in the internal fundamental rights monitoring mechanisms of Frontex, though the report is analysed in more detail in Chapter 6, as OLAF is an external monitoring mechanism.

---

1 However, the Commission, which is responsible together with Frontex for ensuring the effectiveness of European integrated border management by means of a multiannual strategic policy cycle, is also included here.

2 Commission, 'Report from the Commission to the European Parliament and the Council on the evaluation of Regulation (EU) 2019/1896 on the European Border and Coast Guard, including a review of the Standing Corps' COM(2024) 75 final.

3 OLAF, 'Final Report on Frontex, Case no OC/2021/0451/A1' (3 May 2021), https://fragdenstaat.de/dokumente/233972-olaf-final-report-on-frontex/, accessed 12 October 2024.

2 An overview of the oversight mechanisms

The EU legislator has gradually included increasing oversight mechanisms, these include parliamentary, administrative and legal accountability. This was not an organic development but one which resulted from substantial concern expressed by civil society actors and academics.[4] As deaths in the Mediterranean increased from the beginning of the millennium, with more than 28,000 persons missing from 2014 until 2023, and the International Organization for Migration's designation of the Mediterranean as the most dangerous border in the world,[5] public pressure (and that of the international community) grew, pushing the Member States and the EU to take action to protect lives.[6]

As regards the accountability of Frontex in its internal administrative structure, there is a management board which has, among other powers, the power to appoint the executive director. It is composed of officials, usually senior officials in charge of border controls, appointed by each of the 27 EU Member States, four Associate Members of the Schengen area, plus two Commission representatives. The executive director who has executive responsibility for the agency is assisted by deputy directors appointed by the management board. As mentioned in Chapter 4, there exists a Fundamental Rights Office (FRO), as well as an advisory body, and a Consultative Forum which provides advice to the director but to which the latter is not required to respond. The Consultative Forum is composed of independent experts, such as a representative of the EU Fundamental Rights Agency (FRA) and the Council of Europe among others.[7]

From a political perspective, the European Parliament, since 2019, has scrutiny powers over Frontex, to which, together with the Council,

4 Andrew W. Neal, 'Securitization and Risk at the EU Border: The Origins of FRONTEX' (2009) 47(2) *Journal of Common Market Studies* 333; Polly Pallister-Wilkins, 'The Humanitarian Politics of European Border Policing: Frontex and Border Police in Evros' (2015) 9(1) *International Political Sociology* 53; Julien Jeandesboz and Polly Pallister-Wilkins, 'Crisis, Enforcement and Control at the EU Borders' in Anna Lindley (ed), *Crisis and Migration* (Routledge 2014) 115.

5 International Organisation for Migration (IOM), 'Missing Migrants Project', https://missingmigrants.iom.int/, accessed 12 October 2024.

6 Nicolette Busuttil, 'The EU Legislator, Frontex and Fundamental Rights' in Elspeth Guild (ed), *Monitoring Border Violence in the EU: Frontex in Focus* (Routledge 2023) 50–60; Jori Pascal Kalkman, 'Frontex: A Literature Review' (2021) 59(1) *International Migration* 165.

7 Leila Giannetto, 'CSOs and EU Border Management: Cooperation or Resistance? The Case of Frontex Consultative Forum' (2020) 64(4) *American Behavioral Scientist* 501; Leila Giannetto, 'Lobbying EU Agencies from Within: Advocacy Groups in Frontex Consultative Forum on Fundamental Rights' in Doris Dialer and Margarethe Richter (eds), *Lobbying in the European Union: Strategies, Dynamics and Trends* (Springer 2019) 165–184.

Frontex is accountable. Administrative accountability engages both the Parliament and the Council which are entitled to hold Frontex accountable through the authorization of its budget and the required grant of discharge regarding the implementation of the budget.[8] Frontex is also accountable to national parliaments, though in an examination of this form of accountability, Salzano has considered that this is an unexplored opportunity.[9] Further, the Court of Auditors is entitled to audit Frontex activities, a power which it has used, publishing a Special Report in 2021 on Frontex which was highly critical.[10] Similarly as regards administrative scrutiny, OLAF has the power to carry out administrative investigations, including on-the-spot checks and inspections consistent with its mandate to combat fraud, corruption and other illegal activities.[11] These powers were used rather remarkably in 2021 resulting in its report on extensive unlawful activity by senior officials at Frontex and resulting in the departure of the Frontex executive director.[12]

Additionally, the European Public Prosecutor's Office (EPPO) is also mandated to investigate and prosecute fraud and other illegal activities affecting the financial interests of the EU,[13] a power it has yet to exercise notwithstanding the OLAF findings. As regards these powers, the regulation specifically applies for the application of the Court of Auditors, OLAF and EPPO powers to examine working arrangements with third countries and with international organizations, grant agreements, grant decisions and contracts of Frontex. Article 117(5) of the 2019 Frontex Regulation specifies that these must contain provisions expressly empowering the Court of Auditors, OLAF and EPPO to conduct such audits and investigations, in accordance with their respective competences. For the moment, the EPPO has not engaged with Frontex, except in so far as the EPPO's first

---

8 Regulation (EU) 2019/1896 of the European Parliament and of the Council of 13 November 2019 on the European Border and Coast Guard and repealing Regulations (EU) No 1052/2013 and (EU) 2016/1624 [2019] OJ L295/1 (2019 Frontex Regulation), art 116.

9 Laura Salzano, 'Unexploited Monitoring Opportunities: Exercising Oversight on Frontex through National Parliaments' (*Verfassungsblog*, 28 October 2022), https://verfassungsblog.de/unexploited-monitoring-opportunities/, accessed 12 October 2024.

10 2019 Frontex Regulation, arts 116(3) and 117(2). See European Court of Auditors, 'Special Report 08/2021: Frontex's Support to External Border Management: Not Sufficiently Effective to Date' (7 June 2021), https://www.eca.europa.eu/en/publications?did=58564, accessed 12 October 2024.

11 2019 Frontex Regulation, art 117(1) and (3).

12 OLAF (n 3).

13 2019 Frontex Regulation, art 117(4).

Administrative Director appointed on 20 January 2021 previously held the post of Director of Corporate Governance at Frontex.[14]

Also administratively, the European Ombudsman has powers to carry out scrutiny of Frontex according to Article 119, which states that Frontex shall be subject to inquiries of the European Ombudsman. The European Ombudsman has a long history of engaging with Frontex commencing in 2013,[15] though the effectiveness of the recommendations and their implementation is put into question by the OLAF report where very serious misconduct was not picked up by the Ombudsman's office notwithstanding the opening of several inquiries. A 2024 report of the Ombudsman on the 2023 *Adriana* shipwreck off the coast of Greece, which resulted in at least 82 persons dying, and Frontex's fundamental rights obligations of search and rescue in the context of maritime surveillance stands out as possibly evidencing a new more rigorous approach.[16]

Furthermore, Frontex is subject to administrative scrutiny by the European Data Protection Supervisor (EDPS). This has specific pertinence as the 2019 Frontex Regulation modifies very substantially the tasks and powers of the agency as regards the processing of personal data.[17] Its Article 68(5) provides that any working arrangement concluded with international organizations regarding the exchange of personal data is subject to EDPS scrutiny, and the EDPS is entitled to be consulted on the provisions of the status agreement related to the transfer of data to identify whether those provisions differ substantially from the model status agreement under Article 73(3) and (4). These powers have been exercised by the EDPS including as regards arrangements for data sharing with third countries, for instance its 2023 report on data sharing with Niger.[18]

The 2019 Frontex Regulation also establishes a role for the FRA entitling it to consultation regarding the drafting of a model status agreement for

[14] European Public Prosecutor's Office (EPPO), 'EPPO Appoints Administrative Director' (21 January 2021), https://www.eppo.europa.eu/en/media/news/eppo-appoints-administrative-director, accessed 12 October 2024.

[15] European Ombudsman, 'The Agencies' Practices regarding Disclosure of the Names of Selection Board Members, Case OI/4/2013/CK' (12 August 2013), https://www.eppo.europa.eu/enhttps:/www.ombudsman.europa.eu/en/opening-summary/en/51206/media/news/eppo-appoints-administrative-director, accessed 12 October 2024.

[16] European Ombudsman, 'Decision on how the European Border and Coast Guard Agency (Frontex) complies with its fundamental rights obligations with regard to search and rescue in the context of its maritime surveillance activities, in particular the Adriana shipwreck, Case OI/3/2023/MHZ' (26 February 2024), https://www.ombudsman.europa.eu/en/decision/en/182665, accessed 12 October 2024.

[17] For an analysis see Chapter 7.

[18] European Data Protection Supervisor (EDPS), 'Decision on the request for prior authorisation of the Working arrangement establishing operational cooperation between

actions conducted on the territory of third countries, a job which is allocated to the Commission.[19] Further, a FRA representative is entitled to attend meetings of Frontex's management board.[20] No other more substantive role is provided for the FRA, though in its work, it frequently focuses on the role of Frontex such as in the FRA's Annual Forced Return Monitoring, which it commenced in 2014 and which examines the role of Frontex in expulsion operations. A delegate of the FRA sits on the Frontex Consultative Forum.

In light of this, the key mechanisms regarding fundamental rights protection have been the Parliament's Frontex Scrutiny Working Group and OLAF, the roles of which are examined in the Chapter 6. The other EU external mechanisms will only be referred to in passing as their contribution to the struggle for fundamental rights respect in Frontex has been more limited. In addition, legally, Frontex is accountable to CJEU (the General Court and CJEU).[21] Five cases have been brought against Frontex so far, three in direct actions regarding damages were discussed in Chapter 4 and two on the duty to withdraw from joint actions on the basis of fundamental rights concerns are also dealt with in Chapter 6.

Although outside the scope of this chapter, it is noteworthy that Frontex has come to the attention of international judicial bodies, specifically the International Criminal Court. It is the subject of two communications to the Office of the Prosecutor of the International Criminal Court, the first in 2019 and the second in 2021. These were followed by a semi formal call for the Prosecutor to investigate EU and Member State officials for crimes against humanity as regards interception of persons at sea and their return to Libya. In the first communication, submitted by two law professors at Sciences-Po Paris, the authors argue that EU and Member State officials had been involved in crimes against humanity 'committed as part of a premeditated policy to stem migration flows from Africa via the Central Mediterranean route from 2014 to date'.[22] The second, lodged by the Syria Justice and Accountability Centre, argues that:

Frontex and the Republic of Niger' (1 August 2022), https://www.edps.europa.eu/data-protection/our-work/publications/authorisation-decisions-transfers/2022-08-01-edps-request-prior-authorisation-working-arrangement-operational-cooperation-between-frontex-and-republic-niger_en, accessed 12 October 2024.

[19] 2019 Frontex Regulation, art 76.

[20] Ibid art 104(6).

[21] Ibid arts 84 on negligence, 97 (liability), 98 (regarding actions before the court) and 114 (transparency).

[22] Communication to the Office of the Prosecutor of the International Criminal Court Pursuant to the Article 15 of the Rome Statute: EU Migration Policies in the Central Mediterranean and Libya (2014–2019), https://www.statewatch.org/media/documents/news/2019/jun/eu-icc-case-EU-Migration-Policies.pdf, accessed 12 October 2024.

> [T]he combined treatment of refugees in Greece by Greek government officials and their agents, in conjunction with Frontex officials and their agents, since the EU–Turkey Deal's entry into force in March 2016, constitutes a widespread and systematic attack against an identifiable civilian population for the purpose of deterring vulnerable individuals from seeking asylum in Europe, and amounts to crimes against humanity under Article 7 of the Rome Statute.[23]

This second communication was updated in November 2021.[24] The European Center for Constitutional and Human Rights and the non-governmental organization (NGO) Sea-Watch made a request to the International Criminal Court Prosecutor to investigate possible crimes against humanity regarding the interception and return of persons to Libya.[25]

The role of civil society including media and NGOs in holding Frontex to account has been of tremendous importance in pushing those bodies with statutory powers of scrutiny to use them extensively. In the next sections, each of the bodies which engages in scrutiny of Frontex will be examined separately.

3 Frontex's internal oversight mechanisms

3.1 The Commission as an internal fundamental rights monitoring mechanism

Frontex is responsible to the Commission, which is guardian of the Treaties, including competences for external border controls in accordance with Article 77 of the Treaty on the Functioning of the European Union. It is the Commission's responsibility to ensure that its agency complies with the Treaties and the EU Charter. For this reason, the Commission is intrinsically engaged with the supervision of Frontex which frequently has led its commissioner to be required to respond to questioning by the Parliament for actions undertaken by Frontex. As Sarantaki has noted, the Commission

23 Syria Justice and Accountability Centre, 'SJAC Calls on ICC Prosecutor to Investigate Crimes against Humanity Committed by Greece against Refugees' (28 January 2021), https://syriaaccountability.org/sjac-calls-on-icc-prosecutor-to-investigate-crimes-against-humanity-committed-by-greece-against-refugees/, accessed 12 October 2024.

24 Ibid.

25 European Center for Constitutional and Human Rights (ECCHR), 'Interceptions at Sea and Returns of Migrants and Refugees to Libya Constitute a Crime against Humanity: The Hague Must Investigate the Responsibility of EU Officials' (30 November 2022), https://www.ecchr.eu/en/press-release/das-abfangen-auf-see-von-gefluechteten-und-migranten-und-deren-rueckfuehrung-nach-libyen-sind-ein-verbrechen-gegen-die-menschlichkeit/, accessed 12 October 2024.

does not participate in the drafting of Frontex operational plans or its operational activities (including joint operations). She has stressed that while the Commission has two representatives on the management board, these representatives have been outvoted on a number of occasions.[26] As will also be shown in Chapter 6, the OLAF investigation concluded that some senior management officials of Frontex held their Commission counterparts in low esteem and even went so far as to brief members of the management board against the Commission representatives, thereby inhibiting the effectiveness of their interventions.

Nonetheless, two years after the OLAF report in February 2022, the Commission published its evaluation of the Frontex Regulation, as required by the 2019 Frontex Regulation.[27] The object of the report is to assess the impact, effectiveness and efficiency of Frontex. The Commission commenced its report with praise for the agency as 'a true example of European integration in the area of external border management'.[28] It accepted that respect for fundamental rights is an integral part of European integrated border management and as regards compliance it found that the 'Agency's compliance with EU and international law, in particular the fundamental rights framework in place in Frontex, effectively contributes to the prevention of fundamental rights violations in the context of the provision of the support to Member States and third countries'.[29] This is rather far from the conclusion of OLAF that:

> [B]ased on evidence collected during the investigation, the allegations [of serious misconduct] are proven. [Named individuals] within their differing roles and responsibilities, committed serious misconduct and other irregularities. In doing so they hindered the capacity of Frontex to fully comply with its responsibilities, namely monitoring compliance with fundamental rights in its activities at the external borders, and ensuring respect for, protection and promotion of, fundamental rights, as enshrined in particular in the Charter of Fundamental Rights of the EU.[30]

The much rosier assessment by the Commission more than a year later seems somewhat misplaced in light of OLAF's conclusions. It would seem that as far as the Commission was concerned for the purposes of its assessment of

---

26 Antonia-Maria Sarantaki, *Frontex and the Rising of a New Border Control Culture in Europe* (Taylor & Francis 2023).

27 Commission (n 2).

28 Ibid 1.

29 Ibid 5.

30 OLAF (n 3) 3.

Frontex in 2023, the OLAF conclusions were irrelevant. This raises questions about the effectiveness and comprehensiveness of the Commission's oversight of Frontex as regards fundamental rights compliance or the appetite within the Commission to address these issues.

3.2 The executive director and the management board

The executive director is appointed by the management board and is responsible to it.[31] The Board also appoints the FRO.[32] The management board must establish procedures for the executive director to take decisions relating to technical and operational tasks; exercise disciplinary authority over the executive director and, in consultation with the executive director, over the deputy executive directors; adopt internal rules for the prevention and management of conflicts of interest in respect of its members; ensure adequate follow-up to findings and recommendations stemming from the internal or external audit reports and evaluations, as well as from investigations of OLAF.[33] It may advise the executive director on any matter related to the development of operational management of the external borders and training, including activities related to research among other duties.[34] It must forward annually to the Parliament and to the Council any information relevant to the outcome of the evaluation procedures.[35]

Nevertheless, the way the agency has been established and the scope of its mandate creates challenges for effective management by the Board. According to the 2019 Frontex Regulation, responsibility for Frontex's operations rests with the executive director who must report to the management board.[36] At the same time, the agency as a whole, including the executive director and the management board, are responsible to the Parliament and the Council.[37] The extent of the powers of the executive director are notable. Notwithstanding the reporting to the management board, it is the executive director's decision what operations are instigated when, where and for what duration. Through the executive director, Frontex participates in the Schengen Strategy, the implementation of European integrated border management which is guided by the multiannual strategic policy cycle (European Integrated Border Management [EIBM] policy cycle). The cycle is supposed to guide how Frontex should effectively operate as a structure

[31] 2019 Frontex Regulation, art 100(2)(a).
[32] Ibid art 100(2)(z).
[33] Ibid art 100(2).
[34] Ibid art 100(4).
[35] Ibid art 100(6).
[36] Ibid art 106(5).
[37] Ibid art 6. See Chapter 6.

over the following five years and implement European integrated border management. At operational level, this cycle is supposed to give a common framework, steering the daily work of national authorities and Frontex.[38] However, the five-year plan became a ten-year plan in 2020 according to the Commission's evaluation of 2022.[39]

The ten-year plan for strategic risk analysis for European integrated border management, adopted in 2020, identified the following key challenges: cross-border crime, terrorism and threats of a hybrid nature; passenger and cargo flows by improving data collection, risk management and interoperability; digitalization of border crossing (visas, travel authorizations, and so on); cyber and terrorist attacks against international/domestic passengers; increased international migration, secondary (intra-EU) migratory movements and cross-border smuggling activities; the impact of low-cost flight intensity; intensification of illicit smuggling flows affecting the internal and external security; cybercriminals and the shift of previously offline activities online (thus less engagement with border crossing); the benefits for tourism and trade of border control authorities making best use of non-intrusive identification technologies specifically in the online environment (subject to data protection requirements); regarding terrorism and hybrid threats, various challenges are related to the timely sharing of information to improve the checks and rapid response. This is an impressive list of problems to which integrated border management and Frontex are designed to provide solutions. Many of the objectives may be questioned regarding the relevance of border management, for instance the move of formerly illicit cross-border activities to online activities with no border-crossing element (such as the shift to the provision of sex workers' services online).[40] This is also an issue for cybercrime where the cross-border element is a component of the EU's free movement of services and consumer protection rather than the crossing of EU external borders by human beings. Similarly, the issue of so-called secondary movement within the Schengen area from which the 2019 Frontex Regulation excludes Frontex competence. The breadth of the objectives of the ten-year plan provides ample scope for an executive director to make choices about priorities.

Of the 15 components of integrated border management contained in the 2019 Frontex Regulation, 12 encompass: border control, search and rescue in situations that may arise during maritime border surveillance

---

38 Commission, 'Policy document developing a multiannual strategic policy for European integrated border management in accordance with Article 8(4) of Regulation (EU) 2019/1896' COM(2022) 303 final.

39 Ibid.

40 Nick Cowen and Rachela Colosi, 'Sex Work and Online Platforms: What Should Regulation Do?' (2021) 10(2) *Journal of Entrepreneurship and Public Policy* 284.

operations, risk analysis, inter-agency cooperation at national and EU level, cooperation between Member States and Frontex, cooperation with third countries, returns and other measures within the Schengen area, a Schengen quality control mechanism and solidarity mechanisms including EU funding instruments. Again, these components leave substantial choice to the executive director regarding the emphasis placed on them. The components are subject to three overarching requirements: fundamental rights; research and innovation; and education and training. Further they must be designed to ensure that effective border control and return policy are in line with EU and Member States' international obligations and values. The long view is supplemented by the biannual strategic risk analysis which is designed to identify long-term understanding of migratory flows, identify challenges at the external borders and within the Schengen area (again notwithstanding the exclusion of Frontex from intra-Schengen movement of persons) and expulsion of third-country nationals.

The role of the management board in monitoring the activities selected by the executive director includes the need to provide various approvals. However, the rigour of the Board's monitoring of allegations of fundamental rights breaches has been far from comprehensive. The example of the Working Group on Fundamental Rights and Legal Operational Aspects of Operations (WG FRaLO) is indicative.

3.3 A specific management board response to fundamental rights abuses: Working Group on Fundamental Rights and Legal Operational Aspects of Operations

In response to media allegations of fundamental rights abuses, the Frontex management board established the WG FRaLO in November 2020 to investigate whether staff, ships or aircraft working with or financially supported by Frontex had been engaged in human rights violations.[41] It investigated the allegations and produced a report in March 2021 which mainly exonerated Frontex. It examined 13 specific incidents finding no fundamental rights violation in eight of them, closed four out of the five investigations into the remaining incidents while noting that the allegations indicated only a possibility of a violation.[42] In comparison with the detail of the OLAF report and the seriousness of its investigation, the

---

41 Ashleigh Guest, 'Frontex and Its Fundamental Rights Officer' in Elspeth Guild (ed), *Monitoring Border Violence in the EU: Frontex in Focus* (Routledge 2023).

42 Frontex, 'Fundamental Rights and Legal Operational Aspects of Operations in the Aegean Sea: Final Report of the Frontex Management Board Working Group' (1 March 2021), https://www.frontex.europa.eu/assets/Key_Documents/MB_Documents/Agenda_Point_WG_FRaLO_final_report.pdf, accessed 12 October 2024.

management board's efforts look rather weak. The report was received with a degree of derision by human rights NGOs working in the area.[43] It is noteworthy that in the OLAF report, it found that the senior management of Frontex had provided incorrect information to WG FRaLO about the involvement of some Frontex staff in the handling of a serious incident report so the inaccuracies of its report may be due in part at least to reliance on misleading information provided by Frontex senior authorities.

3.4 The Consultative Forum

The Frontex Consultative Forum on fundamental rights was established in 2011 with a mandate to assist the executive director and the management board regarding fundamental rights matters.[44] The management board appoints the members of the forum on the basis of a proposal by the executive director and the board decides on its composition and the working methods and the modalities of the transmission of information to it. At the time of writing, the forum is composed of 13 delegates representing international organizations and European civil society.[45] The forum's access to information and possibilities of operation were widened by the 2019 Frontex Regulation and now include

> effective access in a timely and effective manner to all information concerning the respect for fundamental rights, including by carrying out on-the-spot visits to joint operations or rapid border interventions subject to the agreement of the host Member State or the third country,

---

[43] Eva Cosse, 'Frontex Turns a Blind Eye to Greece's Border Abuses' (*Human Rights Watch*, 10 March 2021), https://www.hrw.org/news/2021/03/10/frontex-turns-blind-eye-greeces-border-abuses, accessed 12 October 2024.

[44] Regulation (EU) No 1168/2011 of the European Parliament and of the Council of 25 October 2011 amending Council Regulation (EC) No 2007/2004 establishing a European Agency for the Management of Operational Cooperation at the External Borders of the Member States of the European Union [2011] OJ L 304/1, art 26a.

[45] The delegates at the time of writing are: (1) Churches' Commission for Migrants in Europe (CCME); (2) Council of Bars and Law Societies of Europe (CCBE); (3) European Union Agency for Asylum (EUAA); (4) European Union Agency for Fundamental Rights (FRA); (5) International Organization for Migration (IOM); (6) Jesuit Refugee Service Europe (JRS) (7) Office for the High Commissioner for Human Rights (UN Human Rights); (8) Organization for Security and Co-operation in Europe – Office for Democratic Institutions and Human Rights (OSCE-ODIHR); (9) Save the Children (SC); (10) The Council of Europe (CoE); (11) The Global Campus for Human Rights; (12) The Rule of Law Institute Foundation; (13) United Nations High Commissioner for Refugees (UNHCR).

as applicable, to hotspot areas and to return operations and return interventions, including in third countries.[46]

It prepares a public annual report on its activities. On at least one occasion, the Consultative Forum has called on the executive director to halt participation in a joint operation on fundamental rights grounds.[47] The executive director only replied after a substantial delay and provided only a cursory letter notifying the forum that their recommendation would not be implemented. The impact of the Consultative Forum is important, not least as it publishes annual reports on its activities, in particular on site visits during joint operations. However, its capacity to influence the operation of Frontex is limited by the absence of any actual duties on the part of the executive director or the management board to respond to or act in respect of recommendations of the Consultative Forum.

3.5 The Fundamental Rights Officer

Regulation (EU) 1168/2011 established the post of the FRO within the structure of Frontex. The tasks of the FRO were expanded in the 2019 Frontex Regulation to include a wide range of investigation and reporting duties. These include: contributing to Frontex's fundamental rights strategy and the corresponding action plan, including by issuing recommendations for improving them; monitoring Frontex's compliance with fundamental rights, including by conducting investigations into any of its activities; promoting Frontex's respect of fundamental rights; advising the executive director where he or she deems it necessary or where requested on any of its activity without delaying those activities; providing opinions on the operational plans drawn up for the operational activities of Frontex, on pilot projects and on technical assistance projects in third countries; providing opinions on working arrangements; carrying out on-the-spot visits to any joint operation, rapid border intervention, pilot project, migration management support team deployment, return operation or return intervention, including in third countries; providing the secretariat of the Consultative Forum; inform the executive director about possible violations of fundamental rights during activities of Frontex; and selecting and managing the fundamental rights monitors.[48] Among the critical tasks of the FRO is to investigate

[46] Frontex Regulation, art 109(5).

[47] Fifth Consultative Forum on Fundamental Rights, 'Fifth Annual Report' (2017) section 4.3.1, https://www.statewatch.org/media/documents/news/2018/may/eu-frontex-consultative-forum-on-fundamental-rights-report-2017.pdf, accessed 12 October 2024.

[48] 2019 Frontex Regulation, art 108(2).

any serious incident report which involved an allegation or indication of fundamental rights violations. The highest level of serious incident reports must be notified to the FRO for action. This will be an issue on which the OLAF investigation focused, in particular regarding the efforts of the senior management to avoid the FRO having responsibility for investigations and pressuring staff to reduce the seriousness indicator of an incident report to fall outside the scope of the FRO's remit. The FRO is also responsible for the good operation of the complaints mechanism and follow up on complaints involving fundamental rights.

The FRO is responsible for recruiting the fundamental rights monitors (of which 40 had to be in place by 5 December 2020, a deadline which was widely missed but achieved by the time of writing).[49] The FRO reports to the executive director and the latter is required to reply to the FRO as to how concerns regarding possible violations of fundamental rights have been addressed. The FRO is an internal mechanism of Frontex integrated into its administrative and management structures including the management board, the executive director and the Consultative Forum. It performs a very important role regarding fundamental rights, not least implementing Frontex's fundamental rights strategy, but it cannot be claimed that the post is independent of Frontex.

On 8 October 2020, OLAF received information by post regarding irregularities at Frontex, including the exclusion of the FRO from the reporting line. On the basis of the information provided, it opened an investigation which included as one of the issues 'possible irregularities concerning the working relationship between persons concerned and the fundamental rights officer, and more generally, the FRO office'. OLAF examined eight specific cases of alleged fundamental rights abuses at sea, mainly regarding failure to rescue, pushing people on little boats into the waters of another country (Turkey) and failure to investigate. These include both incidents where a serious incident report was filed and some where there was none, notwithstanding information available to Frontex, including so-called ghost landings, such as the circumstances alleged in Case T-136/22 *Hamoudi v Frontex*,[50] discussed in Chapter 4.[51] The issue of a serious incident report at the highest alert level should automatically engage the FRO in an investigation. In respect of those cases where serious incident reports were issued, OLAF found that the senior hierarchy within Frontex went to substantial lengths to exclude the FRO from accessing information relating to the reports. In one case OLAF found that rather

[49] Ibid art 110(6).

[50] Case T-136/22 *Hamoudi v Frontex* [2022] (not yet reported).

[51] See Chapter 4, Section 4.

than inform the FRO of a serious incident report of the highest alert level, the executive director chose to appoint a different internal colleague to investigate it. According to one witness interviewed by OLAF and cited in the report: '[T]his also increased my stress level in dealing with situations that I consider to be illegal but which the [redacted name] in consideration of the geopolitical dimension, wanted to cover and [t]o not allow the FRO to investigate.'[52] In respect of another incident, the Frontex hierarchy chose to classify the information to prevent access by the FRO among others even though it related to a serious incident of a high enough category to require the FRO to investigate. The OLAF witness stated (as set out in the report) '[name redacted] had made it clear that it was an [redacted] to classify the operational video footages so to avoid FRO office having access to them'.[53] The Frontex hierarchy also excluded the FRO from access to Eurosur, the surveillance system,[54] altogether. This meant that FRO had no possibility to check information from surveillance sources regarding serious incidents which the office was investigating.

From the WhatsApp messages among the most senior Frontex officials, to which OLAF had access, there are highly derogatory references to the FRO and the FRO's team as constituting a danger to operations, implementing a reign of terror within the agency. OLAF also cited another witness who stated that the FRO Office colleagues were 'an independent group and not real Frontex colleagues acting against the interests of the Agency supported by leftist parties in the EU Parliament'.[55] In a compilation in the OLAF report of comments made by witnesses regarding the relationship of the executive director and the FRO, it cited the following:

> On the [fundamental rights] matter in general, I can say that my personal perception is that the fundamental rights issue is perceived by [redacted] as a gimmick, a kind of gadget with no real use and need, less essential to the mission of the Agency than deployment of EU border guards.[56]

The functional assessment of the witnesses was complemented by comments regarding the relationship of the individuals holding the two key posts, the executive director and the FRO, which was strained. However, the matter was not simply personal, it went to the heart of the ability of the FRO to

52 OLAF (n 3) 28–29.
53 Ibid 33.
54 For an analysis on Eurosur, see Chapter 7.
55 OLAF (n 3) 56.
56 Ibid 60.

carry out their activities. In short, the OLAF investigation found that senior Frontex officials intentionally thwarted the FRO from carrying out her tasks as required by the 2019 Frontex Regulation and disparaged the importance of fundamental rights protection in external border control operations.

On 26 February 2024, the EU Ombudsman's Office published its decision on the shipwreck of the *Adriana*.[57] The own initiative inquiry examined how Frontex complies with its fundamental rights obligations with regard to search and rescue in the context of its maritime surveillance activities. By the time of the specific events covered by the decision, both the executive director and the FRO had been changed. As mentioned in Chapter 4, the sinking of the *Adriana* off the Greek coast on 14 June 2023 was the deadliest event of its kind and provoked international outcry. Of the estimated 750 people on board, 104 people were rescued and only 82 bodies recovered. The ship was observed by a Frontex surveillance plane, which sent information to Frontex headquarters which notified the Greek authorities. The Italian Coast Guard had already alerted the Greek Coast Guard to the existence of the ship, travelling in high seas and in difficulties. Although according to the decision, Frontex offered assistance with further surveillance of the ship, the Greek authorities did not take up the offer. The Ombudsman took evidence from senior Frontex management, the FRO and civil society. The FRO provided substantial information, in particular regarding the way in which Frontex makes risk assessments in respect of information received about boats in difficulties at sea and cooperation between Frontex and some Member States (the inquiry also addressed another shipwreck which engaged the Italian authorities). As regards the role of the FRO, the Ombudsman concluded that where the FRO identifies persistent violations of fundamental rights by a Member State in responding to maritime emergencies, Frontex should consider terminating, withdrawing or suspending Frontex's activities with the Member State in question, in line with Article 46 of the 2019 Frontex Regulation.[58] Furthermore, the decision called for a sustained and serious organization-wide reflection, led by its executive director and with the involvement of members of its management board, on how it upholds its fundamental rights obligations in its response to maritime emergencies and search and rescue operations.[59] Finally, it also called for the FRO to introduce practical arrangements to ensure that, where serious maritime

[57] European Ombudsman, 'Decision on how the European Border and Coast Guard Agency (Frontex) complies with its fundamental rights obligations with regard to search and rescue in the context of its maritime surveillance activities, in particular the Adriana shipwreck (OI/3/2023/MHZ)' (2024), https://www.ombudsman.europa.eu/en/decision/en/182665, accessed 12 October 2024.

[58] Ibid para 77 and suggestion A.

[59] Ibid para 78 and suggestion B.

incidents are detected in the context of Frontex's surveillance activities, a fundamental rights monitor is present in European Surveillance Room.[60] If the physical presence of the fundamental rights monitor is not possible, the assigned fundamental rights monitor should be available and able to provide advice on fundamental rights compliance to such incidents in real time.[61]

While the existence of the FRO and its monitors is a key element to internal monitoring of Frontex activity to promote and protect fundamental rights, a culture developed and nourished at the highest levels in Frontex of disregard for the FRO and fundamental rights protection as inconsistent with Frontex's mandate favoured by the senior officials. Notwithstanding statements to the contrary and from Frontex management of tragedies in 2023, it is not clear that there has been a substantial change to this culture.

3.6 The complaints mechanism

An additional internal body for the protection of fundamental rights (though not strictly an oversight mechanism) is the individual complaints mechanism. A complaints mechanism was introduced in Regulation (EU) 2016/1624[62] and is currently foreseen in Article 111 of the 2019 Frontex Regulation. The latter requires the FRO to take the necessary measures to set up and further develop an independent and effective complaints mechanism to ensure respect for fundamental rights in all Frontex activities. The mechanism is to be open to all individuals affected by Frontex operations whether within or outside the EU. The FRO is designated responsible for handling all complaints under this mechanism in a manner that is both independent and effective. However, follow up to a complaint remains the responsibility of the executive director. The complaints mechanism met with some scepticism among civil society actors. The difficulty of persons in such vulnerable situations as those irregularly crossing EU external borders to access such a mechanism is evident. The inability of the mechanism to provide a solution to their urgent and immediate objective to enter the EU somehow, usually related to an international protection claim, makes it rather redundant to the main concern of those suffering border violence.[63]

---

60 Ibid paras 90–91.

61 Ibid suggestion F.

62 Regulation (EU) 2016/1624 of the European Parliament and of the Council of 14 September 2016 on the European Border and Coast Guard and amending Regulation (EU) 2016/399 of the European Parliament and of the Council and repealing Regulation (EC) No 863/2007 of the European Parliament and of the Council, Council Regulation (EC) No 2007/2004 and Council Decision 2005/267/EC [2016] OJ L 251/1, art 72.

63 Markus Jaeger, Apostolis Fotiadis, Elspeth Guild and Lora Vidović, 'Feasibility Study on the Setting up of a Robust and Independent Human Rights Monitoring Mechanism at the External Borders of the European Union' (*Pro Asyl*, 4 May 2022).

It is difficult to imagine how such a complaints mechanism could be independent when its operation is dependent on the FRO who is an internal Frontex body and follow up is the responsibility of the executive director. This problem was noted by the Frontex Scrutiny Working Group in July 2021 but remains unresolved.[64] The Ombudsman carried out an inquiry into Frontex's complaints mechanism which concluded in June 2021. The report is far from complementary regarding the operation of the complaints mechanism and its effectiveness. A substantial number of recommendations were made.[65] In the OLAF report, an attempt by the (then) FRO to increase visibility and effectiveness of the complaints mechanism was blocked for more than ten months by the executive director with no substantive reason for the delay. The conclusion was that this was the result of the antagonism which had developed between the two.[66] However, the assumption that the complaints mechanism is an effective part of fundamental rights monitoring of Frontex action is questionable. In the *WS* case,[67] discussed in Chapter 4,[68] the FRO's management of the complaints of the applicants was inefficient. Not only were the complaints merely passed on to the Greek police internal mechanism which closed the complaints with a confidential internal report and did not inform the complainants, but the FRO made no apparent effort to investigate the complaints. The FRO simply closed the file with a report which did not even address the subject matter of the complaints.

4 Conclusion

This chapter examined the internal monitoring mechanisms of Frontex, which are numerous, uncoordinated and contradictory in their assessments. Notwithstanding very regular reviews and amendments of the Frontex regulation, the capacity of the EU legislator to put in place effective oversight mechanisms has been notable by its failures. This is no doubt the result of numerous causes, not least the complex mechanisms at work in the EU legislative procedure where, from a Commission proposal to the final adoption of the changes, there is substantial opportunities for incoherence to slip in as amendments and political compromises result

[64] Parliament, 'Report on the fact-finding investigation on Frontex concerning alleged fundamental rights violations' (14 July 2021).

[65] European Ombudsman, 'How the European Border and Coast Guard Agency (Frontex) deals with complaints about alleged fundamental rights breaches through its "Complaints Mechanism" – Case OI/5/2020/MHZ', https://www.ombudsman.europa.eu/en/case/en/57955, accessed 12 October 2024.

[66] OLAF (n 3).

[67] Case T-600/21 *WS v European Coast Guard Agency* [2021] EU:T:2023:492.

[68] See Chapter 4, Section 4.

in less than coordinated end results. However, the generally ineffective results from the perspective of the complainant are stark, particularly when considering the civil society pressure on the institutions to rectify the rule of law deficits. A full review of these mechanisms is needed with a view to actually strengthening fundamental rights compliance in EU external border controls.

6

EU External Oversight of Frontex and Border Violence

1 Introduction

As has been set out in Chapter 5, the effectiveness of internal fundamental rights monitoring mechanisms within Frontex regarding European Union (EU) external border controls has proven insufficient to satisfy the concerns of a wide range of EU and international institutions, civil society and the public. From the creation of the Schengen external border system and the establishment of Frontex as the EU body entrusted with assuring external border controls, the question of external oversight has arisen. In this chapter the EU monitoring mechanisms outside of Frontex itself but within the EU are examined, with emphasis being placed on oversight by the Parliament, the European Anti-fraud Office (OLAF) and the Court of Justice of the European Union (CJEU). The establishment of a working group in the European Parliament's Committee on Civil Liberties, Justice and Home Affairs (LIBE Committee) dedicated to follow Frontex was made possible by the amendment of the regulation in 2019 to make the agency also accountable to the Parliament (something which had not been the case before). The members of the working group proved particularly dedicated to their task of seeking to establish effective parliamentary oversight to the agency. This development was not appreciated by the direction of Frontex which was not accustomed to being required to reply to parliamentary questions and critiques. This was evidenced by the rather conflictual relationship between the working group and the (then) director with unaccountable delays in providing information, the insufficiency of information provided and the apparent lack of candour in the (then) director's evidence to the working group regarding some issues.

The OLAF investigation came out of the institutional irregularities with Frontex, in particular the violent marginalization of the Frontex

Fundamental Rights Officer (FRO) by the direction of the agency. The rather flagrant maladministration of the agency, whereby one of its key internal accountability structures was effectively excluded from all information necessary to carry out its role, led OLAF to commence its forensic investigation into the agency to discover what had gone wrong. As an agency which carries out investigations evidence from which must be admissible in criminal courts, the direction of Frontex found itself suddenly under the microscope of an agency with a criminal law manner of working. This was clearly not anticipated by the Frontex management which until then had been able to cover up the direction's antagonism for fundamental rights and oversight constraints. The unfortunate language used by the director and senior staff in their WhatsApp messages indicates that they believed that these could not be accessed in an OLAF investigation, a belief which was incorrect.[1]

The OLAF report was extremely revealing about maladministration in the agency, but OLAF is only an occasional actor in respect of Frontex.[2] Its job is not to review the day-to-day activities of the agency. The final and latest actor to become engaged in the question of the legality of Frontex's external border control activities is the CJEU. It did not go unnoticed by critics of Frontex that the only time the director suspended an operation was when the CJEU held that there were fundamental rights violations taking place within it.[3] The fact that the Consultative Forum had already made such a recommendation to the director indicated that the director was only moved to act when the CJEU held that the operation was problematic.[4] Civil society actors began to assist those persons whose efforts to seek asylum in the EU had been thwarted by Frontex coordinated or facilitated pushbacks to bring direct actions before the CJEU. At the time of writing these have not resulted in a positive outcome for the applicants but a number of the cases are in the appeal process in the CJEU.

---

1 According to the report, some participants in the WhatsApp messages suggested sending information by email, to which another participant recommended not doing so as emails are formal (and therefore of a different forensic quality than WhatsApp).

2 OLAF, 'Final Report on Frontex, Case no OC/2021/0451/A1' (3 May 2021), https://fragdenstaat.de/dokumente/233972-olaf-final-report-on-frontex/, accessed 12 October 2024.

3 Case C-808/18, *Commission v Hungary* [2020] EU:C:2020:1029.

4 Colonel Istvan Kobolka and Lieutenant-Colonel Janor Sallai, 'The Border Guards' Preparedness to the Schengen Regime' Periodical of the Scientific Board of Military Security Office' (2007), https://www.knbsz.gov.hu/hu/letoltes/szsz/2007_1_spec.pdf, accessed 12 October 2024.

2 Parliament: the LIBE Committee and the Frontex Scrutiny Working Group

Frontex was not accountable to the Parliament until Regulation (EU) 2019/1896, Article 6 of which introduced this requirement.[5] This accountability is shared with the Council. Before this specific power, the Parliament still had budgetary power over the agency, a general power in respect of EU agencies, which requires all agencies to obtain from the Parliament budgetary discharge.[6] It was also involved in the appointment of the executive director.[7] The Parliament is entitled to a presentation of the annual report.[8] There is also a practice in the Parliament to link one of its Members to each EU agency with responsibilities to carry out as much scrutiny as possible and report back to the relevant committee and plenary.[9] These mechanisms were in place before the 2019 Frontex Regulation changed the situation by extending Frontex accountability to the Parliament.

Even before the Parliament acquired formal scrutiny powers over Frontex, it was outspoken about fundamental rights compliance in EU external border operations. Particular focus in 2016 and 2018 was on pushbacks,[10] whereby the Parliament condemned in two resolutions in those years.[11] In

---

5 Regulation (EU) 2019/1896 of the European Parliament and of the Council of 13 November 2019 on the European Border and Coast Guard and repealing Regulations (EU) No 1052/2013 and (EU) 2016/1624 [2019] OJ L 295/1 (2019 Frontex Regulation).

6 For a good explanation of the discharge procedure, see in European Parliament's website: https://www.europarl.europa.eu/committees/en/cont/discharge-procedure/practical-information, accessed 12 October 2024.

7 2019 Frontex Regulation, art 107.

8 Ibid art 65.

9 Parliament 'Fact Sheets on the European Union', https://www.europarl.europa.eu/factsheets/en/sheet/23/the-role-of-the-european-parliament, accessed 12 October 2024.

10 This is defined in the Parliament documents as the situation when individuals, who irregularly cross a border, are apprehended and returned to a third country without consideration of their individual circumstances and in violation of the principle of *non-refoulement*, the right to asylum and the prohibition on torture, inhuman or degrading treatment or punishment, see: Anja Radjenovic, 'Pushbacks at the EU's External Borders' (EPRS, March 2021), https://www.europarl.europa.eu/RegData/etudes/BRIE/2021/689368/EPRS_BRI(2021)689368_EN.pdf, accessed 20 October 2024.

11 Parliament, 'Resolution of 12 April 2016 on the situation in the Mediterranean and the need for a holistic EU approach to migration' (P8 TA (2016)0102), https://www.europarl.europa.eu/doceo/document/TA-8-2016-0102_EN.html, accessed 12 October 2024; 'Resolution of 12 September 2018 on a proposal calling on the Council to determine, pursuant to Article 7(1) of the Treaty on European Union, the existence of a clear risk of a serious breach by Hungary of the values on which the Union is founded' (P8_TA(2018)0340), https://www.europarl.europa.eu/doceo/document/TA-8-2018-0340_EN.html, accessed 12 October 2024.

2021, it adopted a resolution regarding fundamental rights violations in asylum border procedures, in particular automatic refusal of entry, *refoulement* and collective expulsions, all of which are prohibited by the Charter.[12] In addition to the extensive media and non-governmental organization (NGO) evidence regarding Frontex fundamental rights failures, the publication of the report of the UN Special Rapporteur on human rights of migrants in April 2022,[13] which singled out Frontex as complicit in human rights abuses of migrants,[14] spurred the Parliament to use its new powers of scrutiny in a coherent and effective manner through the creation of the Frontex Scrutiny Working Group (FSWG). In 2023, the Parliament once again expressed its concern about activities at the external borders of the EU, including pushbacks, emphasizing the unlawfulness of such actions and the duty of the EU and Member States to counter them.[15]

---

12 Parliament, 'Resolution of 10 February 2021 on the implementation of Article 43 of Directive 2013/32/EU of the European Parliament and of the Council of 26 June 2013 on common procedures for granting and withdrawing international protection' (P9_TA(2021)0042), https://www.europarl.europa.eu/doceo/document/TA-9-2021-0042_EN.html, accessed 12 October 2024.

13 Office of the High Commissioner of Human Rights (OHCHR), 'Human rights violations at international borders: trends, prevention and accountability' (26 April 2022), https://www.ohchr.org/en/documents/thematic-reports/ahrc5031-human-rights-violations-international-borders-trends-prevention, accessed 12 October 2024.

14 Ibid para 53, which reads: 'The Special Rapporteur is concerned that in 2021 over 32,000 migrants were forcibly returned to Libya, where they are at risk of extensive abuses and human rights violations by both State and non-State actors, potentially amounting to crimes against humanity. Migrants are allegedly intercepted by the Libyan Coast Guard in the framework of the renewed deal between Italy, the European Union and the Government of Libya to reduce migrant arrivals to Europe. Frontex has reportedly facilitated these interceptions through drone surveillance and secretive communication practices that prevent private and NGO ships from accessing information regarding boats in distress and undermine their timely and effective involvement in search and rescue.'

15 Parliament, 'Resolution of 18 January 2023 on human rights and democracy in the world and the European Union's policy on the matter – annual report 2022' (P9_TA (2023) 0011) para 92, https://www.europarl.europa.eu/doceo/document/TA-9-2023-0011_EN.html, accessed 12 October 2024, which reads: 'Recalls its commitment to the rights of refugees, as provided by international human rights and refugee laws, in particular the 1951 Convention Relating to the Status of Refugees and the 1967 Protocol thereto; recalls the obligations of states to protect refugees and respect their rights in accordance with the relevant international law; deplores the number of migrant deaths occurring along migration routes and illegal pushbacks in violation of international law; recalls that the EU and its Member States, in their external and extraterritorial actions, agreements and cooperation in the areas of migration, borders and asylum, should respect and protect human rights, notably those enshrined in the Charter, including the right to life, liberty and to seek asylum, through the individual assessment of asylum applications and the principle of non-refoulement; highlights in this regard the importance of the Member States leading by example by strictly upholding their obligations under international

The Parliament's scrutiny powers, as set out in the 2019 Frontex Regulation, are scattered throughout the text and do not constitute a single chapter.[16] From the starting place of Article 6, which rather baldly states that Frontex is accountable to the Parliament, the next parliamentary power is the right to receive and discuss the Commission's multiannual strategic policy for integrated border management.[17] This is mainly a transparency power, as there is no right for the Parliament to reject the policy. However, four years from the presentation of the policy, the Commission must produce an evaluation of implementation which must be provided to the Parliament.[18] Also in the category of transparency, there is a general duty on Frontex to take all necessary measures to facilitate the exchange of information relevant to its tasks with the Parliament.[19] As regards Frontex's biannual strategic risk analysis for integrated border management, this must be submitted to the Parliament.[20] At least once a year, Frontex must transmit its external borders vulnerability assessment to the Parliament.[21] It is also entitled to be informed (without delay) of any substantial additional financial needs.[22] Any situations requiring urgent action as well as measures and decisions taken in response must also be provided to Parliament.[23] The Parliament is entitled to a detailed evaluation report on return operations every six months which is transmitted by the executive director.[24] There is a complicated chain of notifications regarding the composition and the deployment of equipment which is part of the technical equipment pool: the executive director informs the management board, then the management board informs the Commission and finally the Commission informs the Parliament. No time limits apply other than that the executive director must report 'regularly'.[25] The management board is responsible for submitting to the Parliament the annual report.[26] Another transparency requirement applies in the form of

refugee law, and of substantially increasing their assistance to those fleeing repression or war, their hosting capacity and their resettlement pledges.'

16 Micaela Del Monte and Katrien Luyten, 'European Parliament Scrutiny of Frontex' (EPRS, November 2023), https://www.europarl.europa.eu/RegData/etudes/BRIE/2021/698816/EPRS_BRI(2021)698816_EN.pdf, accessed 12 October 2024.

17 2019 Frontex Regulation, art 8(4).

18 Ibid art 8(7).

19 Ibid art 15(1).

20 Ibid art 29(2).

21 Ibid art 32(11).

22 Ibid art 36(4).

23 Ibid art 42(2).

24 Ibid art 50(7).

25 Ibid art 64(13).

26 Ibid art 65(1). This report covers the implementation of Articles 51: the pool of forced return monitors, Article 55: the statutory staff in the standing corps, Article 56: Member States' contribution to the standing corps by seconding operational staff, Article

a duty on Frontex to disseminate the results of its research and innovation activities for integrated border management to the Parliament.[27] In addition, Frontex must inform the Parliament of cooperation with EU or international bodies[28] and of technical and operational assistance activities with third countries, the deployment of liaison officers and compliance in this regard with fundamental rights.[29] The Parliament must be provided with detailed information before any working arrangement with third countries is concluded which information must at least include the parties and envisaged content of the arrangement.[30] All decisions to deploy liaison officers to third countries must be reported to the Parliament.[31] The management board is responsible for sending to the Parliament the annual activity report, multiannual programming and work programme for the following year. It must further send the Parliament information about the outcome of evaluation procedures.[32] The Parliament is entitled to consultation on a single programming document but only a positive decision of the Commission is required. Should the Parliament raise any issues with the document in the consultation process, the management board must provide a thorough justification.[33] At the discretion of the management board's chair, an expert from the Parliament may be invited to attend the board's meetings.[34] When requested by the Parliament, the executive director must report on Frontex activities including by way of a statement to the Parliament. Further the executive director must answer in writing any question posed by a member of the Parliament within 15 calendar days from receipt of the question.[35]

The executive director must also report regularly to parliamentary committees and bodies. It is also the executive director's responsibility to ensure that all reports are sent to the Parliament as soon as possible, within

57: Member States' contribution to the standing corps by nominating border guards and other relevant staff, Article 58: contribution to operational staff to the standing corps by means of a reserve for rapid reaction; Article 63: acquisition or lease of technical equipment to be deployed during joint operations, pilot projects, rapid border interventions, activities in the area of return, including return operations and return interventions, migration management support team deployments or technical assistance projects in accordance with the financial rules and Article 64: the composition of the technical equipment pool.

27 Ibid art 66(1).
28 Ibid art 68(2).
29 Ibid art 73(7).
30 Ibid art 76(4).
31 Ibid art 76(5),
32 Ibid art 100(2)(j)–(k) and (6).
33 Ibid art 102(1).
34 Ibid art 104(7).
35 Ibid art 106 (2).

six months, or justify any further delay.[36] The Parliament has a substantive role in the appointment of the executive director and the candidates chosen by the Commission must make a statement before the Parliament after which the Parliament may propose a preferred candidate. When the management board appoints a candidate (which is within its power), if it does not choose the Parliament's recommended one, it must explain the manner in which the opinion of the European Parliament was taken into account.[37] A role for national parliaments is included with that of the European Parliament regarding cooperation to ensure effective scrutiny of Frontex, though as mentioned earlier, this form of scrutiny does not appear to have been much used. The executive director and the chair of the management board are required to attend on request meetings with both the European Parliament and national parliaments.[38] The Parliament is entitled to a provisional draft estimate of Frontex's revenue and expenditure and a provisional establishment plan.[39] There is a complex formula for determining when the final accounts must be submitted, but it is the duty of executive director to send them to the Parliament as well as any follow-up information needed for the purpose of discharge. Where the Council recommends discharge of the accounts, the Parliament is to provide that discharge.[40]

From this outline it becomes apparent that the majority of the powers provided to the Parliament are related to transparency and access to documents. Only rarely there is extension to a power to summon the executive director, though there is a somewhat more substantive role in the director's appointment and the possibility to delay discharge of the accounts. For the Parliament, the issue of fundamental rights compliance has been critical to its struggle for greater scrutiny of powers. Thus, the focus on transparency is understandable. But it is not always evident whether the reports and other documents which must be produced are substantive or will have the effect of burying the Parliament under a weight of inconsequential publications. It is clear that for MEPs, these new powers are far too time-consuming and complex for them to engage fully with the implications of each of the powers and the flood of documents which it may unleash. At the same time, the power of the Parliament is primarily in accessing documents in order to examine compliance with fundamental rights.

The need to address allegations which have been made and continue to be made against Frontex regarding its failure to comply with fundamental rights

---

[36] Ibid art 106(2) and (3): This is no doubt the consequence of the reluctance of a former executive director to inform the Parliament or respond to requests for information.

[37] Ibid art 107.

[38] Ibid art 112(1)–(2).

[39] Ibid art 115(5).

[40] Ibid art 116(3), (7), (10) and (11).

at the external borders together with the new transparency requirements in the regulation, prompted the Parliament to establish the FSWG in July 2020. While originally a time-limited working group, the Parliament then lifted the time limit on its work in January 2021. Its mandate is to monitor all aspects of the functioning of Frontex with specific reference to fundamental rights, transparency and accountability to Parliament. The mandate also includes the correct application of EU law and in addition to examine Frontex's involvement in allegations of fundamental rights violations, it also extends to Frontex's knowledge of the commission of such violations and its action or inaction accordingly. The FSWG has thus taken the leading role in examining the documents and making the calls on what is important to the interests of the Parliament and what is not which are then confirmed by the LIBE Committee, other committees and the plenary.

In its capacity as a parliamentary scrutiny body in respect of Frontex, the FSWG has focused on the issue of pushbacks of small boats carrying persons seeking to arrive in the EU mainly via Greece and Italy to unsafe countries, such as Libya, and the role of Frontex in participating in, supporting or enabling such actions.[41] In the investigation, which began in 2020, the FSWG used all the new powers conferred on it by the 2019 Frontex Regulation. First, the FSWG called the executive director to appear before it in July and December 2020 to question him on Frontex and pushbacks which had been documented by media and NGOs. On both occasions the executive director denied any Frontex involvement. Further questions were posed to the executive director and when that provided little concrete information, the FSWG turned its attention to the Commission, seeking information regarding what Frontex had provided regarding the incidents documented. The FSWG used its transparency powers to request documents regarding statistics from the Commission which were not provided. Following internal discussions, the Parliament's budget committee proposed to the plenary in April 2021 to postpone the discharge of Frontex's budget for the financial year 2019 which was then before it.[42] There were three grounds for this recommendation, first, delays in the recruitment of a FRO and fundamental rights monitors, second, gender imbalance among Frontex staff and, third, the alleged violations of fundamental rights.

In September 2021, the LIBE Committee itself (on the advice of the FSWG) again called on the budget committee not to grant discharge of the

[41] These actions usually have as principal actor national border police but as is made clear in the OLAF report, often the actions of national border police are enabled by Frontex assets such as boats and surveillance information.

[42] Micaela Del Monte and Katrien Luyten, 'European Parliament Scrutiny of Frontex' (European Parliament Research Service, November 2023), https://www.europarl.europa.eu/thinktank/en/document/EPRS_BRI(2021)698816, accessed 12 October 2024.

2019 budget.[43] The discharge was again delayed and ultimately provided on 11 October 2021. However, it also requested that part of the 2022 budget to be frozen until such time as all the fundamental rights monitors had been recruited as well as three deputy directors, improvement in the operation of the reporting of serious incidents and the establishment of a comprehensive fundamental rights monitoring system. This effort was unsuccessful.[44] Instead, the Parliament postponed the discharge of Frontex's 2020 budget on the grounds that Frontex had failed to comply with requests of the Parliament for information and also that the report of the OLAF investigation was not yet available.[45] This prompted Frontex to submit an overview of responses and measures,[46] which prompted a decision of discharge in November 2022.[47] The delay in discharge is a matter classed by the Court of Auditors as one of emphasis in their 2022 audit of EU agencies.[48]

Allegations of fundamental rights violations and Frontex's involvement did not go away and the determination of the FSWG to investigate them using their (then) new powers increased. Between March and July 2021 when it published its report,[49] it met again with the executive director, the Commissioner, the Fundamental Rights Agency, the Ombudsman, NGOs, legal experts, media and national coast guards about allegations of pushbacks

43 Parliament, 'Opinion of the Committee on Civil Liberties, Justice and Home Affairs for the Committee on Budgetary Control on discharge in respect of the implementation of the budget of the European Border and Coast Guard Agency for the financial year 2019' (2020/2167 (DEC), 9 September 2021).

44 Stephane Saurel, 'Frontex under the Budgetary Scrutiny of the European Parliament' (*EU Migration Law Blog*, 31 May 2022), https://eumigrationlawblog.eu/frontex-under-the-budgetary-scrutiny-of-the-european-parliament/, accessed 12 October 2024.

45 Parliament, 'Resolution of 4 May 2022 on discharge in respect of the implementation of the budget of the European Union agencies for the financial year 2020: performance, financial management and control' (P9_TA (2022) 0196), https://www.europarl.europa.eu/doceo/document/TA-9-2022-0196_EN.html, accessed 12 October 2024.

46 Frontex, 'Report on Discharge 2020: European Parliament's Resolution of 4 May 2022 forming an Integral Part of the Decision on Discharge in respect of the Implementation of the Budget of the European Border and Coast Guard Agency for the Financial year 2020' (27 June 2022).

47 Decision (EU) 2023/328 of the European Parliament of 22 November 2022 on the closure of the accounts of the European Border and Coast Guard Agency (Frontex) for the financial year 2020 [2023] OJ L 45/24.

48 European Court of Auditors, '2022 Audit of EU Agencies in Brief' (26 October 2023), https://www.eca.europa.eu/en/publications?ref=SAR-AGENCIES-AIB-2022, accessed 12 October 2014.

49 Parliament, 'Report on Fact-Finding Investigation on Frontex Concerning Alleged Fundamental Rights Violations' (LIBE, 14 July 2021), https://www.europarl.europa.eu/cmsdata/238156/14072021%20Final%20Report%20FSWG_en.pdf, accessed 12 October 2024.

and the failure to recruit fundamental rights monitors. The executive director maintained his position of no knowledge or involvement on the part of Frontex. The report was published on 14 July 2021 where it acknowledged the credibility of allegations of unlawful pushbacks, found that Frontex had failed to take action to prevent or reduce the risk of such unlawful activities which were within its mandate, deplored the failure to recruit fundamental rights monitors whose role it was to carry out this work for Frontex and thus was not acting in accordance with its fundamental rights obligations in the regulation. It further outlined the lack of transparency by Frontex in its dealings with the Parliament contrary to the 2019 Frontex Regulation.[50] This report constituted an important milestone in the investigation of Frontex's activities at the external borders and has been relied on substantially by other institutions in their oversight of the agency. The key findings of the report concerned:

1. reliable actors, such as national and international human rights bodies and organizations, consistently reported human rights violations at the border in a number of Member States, but Frontex generally disregarded these reports;
2. Frontex failed adequately to respond to internal observations about certain cases of probable fundamental rights violations in Member States which were raised by the FRO, Consultative Forum or through incident reports;
3. the FSWG did not find conclusive evidence of the direct performance of pushbacks and/or collective expulsions by Frontex in the serious incident reports it examined;
4. Frontex had found evidence in support of allegations of fundamental rights violations in Member States with which it had joint operations but failed to address and follow up on these violations promptly, vigilantly and effectively. As a result, Frontex did not prevent these violations nor reduce the risk of future fundamental rights violations;
5. there was a lack of cooperation by senior Frontex management to comply with the fundamental rights obligations in the Regulation which led to significant delays in their implementation; and
6. there was a need for the management board to play a more proactive role in acknowledging the serious risk of fundamental rights violations and to take action to ensure that Frontex fulfils its negative and positive fundamental rights obligations.

[50] Parliament, 'LIBE Committee Working Document Report on the Fact-finding Investigation on Frontex concerning alleged Fundamental Rights Violations' (14 July 2021), https://www.europarl.europa.eu/cmsdata/238156/14072021%20Final%20Report%20FSWG_en.pdf, accessed 12 October 2024.

The report sparked a number of exchanges between Frontex's executive director and the FSWG which diminished with the publication of the OLAF report which confirmed the FSWG concerns about Frontex complicity in pushbacks and other fundamental rights violations and the rapid departure of the executive director.[51] A (then) new FRO was appointed, and an interim executive director was confirmed until the new executive director, who was appointed by the management board, taking into account the Parliament's opinion, took up his post on 20 December 2022. The FSWG maintained pressure on Frontex, and the interim director took pains to explain how compliant Frontex was in taking on board its recommendations. However, on 26 February 2023, there was a shipwreck at Steccato di Cutro in Italy of a boat carrying about 200 people seeking to arrive in Europe, from which 62 bodies were recovered.[52] A Lighthouse Report with the support of Amnesty International investigated the tragedy and in the process it became apparent that notwithstanding the high seas and evidence of danger for the passengers, observed by Frontex surveillance assets, the agency sent a law enforcement notification to the Italian authorities which resulted in a police boat attempting to reach the ship (but having to return because of the terrible weather conditions) rather than Frontex immediately notifying the Italian authorities that the situation merited a search and rescue operation which would have meant that Italian boats equipped for search and rescue in high seas would have been sent.[53] This could have made the difference between life and death for many who were on the boat. When the Parliament's LIBE Committee questioned the executive director about the nature of the Frontex notification to the Italian authorities he replied: 'You could argue that a small rubber boat trying to cross an ocean or, in this case, the Mediterranean is always in distress. That is true. But I think our threshold is a bit higher than that'.[54] According to Salzano, 'contrary to the Director's assertion, the notion of distress is not subject to Frontex's review'. In fact, his interpretation openly diverges from that of the International Law Commission, which characterizes it as 'a situation of

[51] OLAF (n 2).

[52] Angela Guiffrida, 'The Beach is like a Cemetery: Italian Village Grapples with Shipwreck Aftermath' (*The Guardian*, 27 February 2023), https://www.theguardian.com/world/2023/feb/27/italy-shipwreck-calabria-migration, accessed 12 October 2024.

[53] Lighthouse Reports, 'The Crotone Cover Up' (2 June 2023), https://www.lighthousereports.com/investigation/the-crotone-cover-up/, accessed 12 October 2024; and Amnesty International, 'Italy: New Investigation Reveals Damning Details about Preventable Drownings' (2 June 2023), https://www.amnesty.eu/news/italy-new-investigation-reveals-damning-details-about-preventable-drownings/, accessed 20 October 2024.

[54] LIBE, 'Parliamentary Committee Meeting 21 March 2023' (min. 17.23).

serious danger ... but not necessarily one that jeopardizes the very existence of the person concerned'.[55]

The (then) new executive director provided assurances to the FSWG in March 2023 that Frontex would provide full transparency on incident reports at EU external borders. Further, the Commission carried out an evaluation including the implementation of fundamental rights under Articles 121 and 59 of the Regulation.[56] Then, on 14 June 2023, the *Adriana* shipwreck took place, whereby 83 bodies were recovered but over 500 persons were lost and 104 were rescued.[57] The Ombudsman opened an investigation on 24 July 2023.[58] However, one of the key issues in the cases of shipwrecks at sea relates to the surveillance capacities of Frontex, through Eurosur, to watch and follow boats in the Mediterranean in real time and the extent of Frontex's duties to pass information to national search and rescue centres to launch an appropriate response. As was revealed in the OLAF report, in the past, the Frontex executive director was complicit in directing the redeployment of surveillance aircraft away from an area where a boat was at risk in order not to be witnesses in the event of fundamental rights violations.[59]

A further report by the FSWG was adopted by the LIBE Committee in October 2023, following the *Adriana* tragedy, which again called for greater transparency and for Frontex to uphold fundamental rights standards.[60] This was followed by a LIBE Committee resolution calling for Frontex to scale down its operations to monitoring and presence on the ground in cases where a Member State is unable to respect EU principles and values (particularly the case of Italy and Hungary).[61] The substantial increase in transparency powers for the Parliament and the explicit commitment of the

---

55 Laura Salzano, 'Lost at Sea: That Time Frontex Tried to Redefine the Notion of Distress' (*Refugee Law Initiative Blog*, 26 October 2023), https://rli.blogs.sas.ac.uk/2023/10/26/lost-at-sea-that-time-frontex-tried-to-redefine-the-notion-of-distress/, accessed 12 October 2024.

56 Commission, 'Report from the Commission to the European Parliament and the Council on the evaluation in accordance with Article 121 of Regulation (EU) 2019/1896 including review of the standing corps' COM(2024) 75 final.

57 Matina Stevis-Grindeff and Karam Shoumali, 'Everyone Knew the Migrant Ship was Doomed' (*New York Times*, 3 July 2023), https://www.nytimes.com/2023/07/01/world/europe/greece-migrant-ship.html, accessed 12 October 2024.

58 European Ombudsman, 'The Role of the European Border and Coast Guard Agency (Frontex) in the Context of Search and Rescue (SAR) Operations' (Case OI/3/2023/MHZ, 26 February 2024), https://www.ombudsman.europa.eu/en/doc/correspondence/en/176666, accessed 12 October 2024.

59 OLAF (n 2).

60 Ibid.

61 European Parliament, 'Resolution of 14 December 2023 on Frontex building on the fact-finding investigation of the LIBE Working Group for Frontex Scrutiny' (P9_TA

Frontex executive director to ensure full compliance with these transparency powers has not resulted in the Parliament being kept in the loop on situations where fundamental rights violations are at risk or have occurred. The culture of secrecy in Frontex appears to have survived the negative reports by the Parliament and OLAF.

3 European Anti-fraud Office

OLAF was created in 1999 as part of the Commission, replacing the then Task Force for Coordination of Fraud Prevention.[62] Its mandate is to carry out external administrative investigations for the purpose of strengthening the fight against fraud, corruption and any other illegal activity adversely affecting the EU's financial interests, as well as any other act or activity by operators in breach of EU provisions.[63] It is also charged with the investigation of serious facts linked to the performance of professional activities which may constitute a breach of obligations by EU officials likely to lead to disciplinary and, in appropriate cases, criminal proceedings or an analogous breach of obligations by members of the institutions and bodies, heads of the bodies or members of staff of the institutions and bodies.[64] Its complete independence was safeguarded by the decision.[65]

The jurisdiction of OLAF over Frontex was given effect by the latter joining the Interinstitutional Agreement of 25 May 1999 between the Parliament, the Council and the Commission concerning internal investigations by OLAF.[66] This is the standard mechanism referred to in the 2019 Frontex Regulation.[67] The Frontex management board is charged with ensuring adequate follow-up to findings and recommendations stemming from any internal or external audit report and evaluations as well as from OLAF investigations.[68] The executive director is responsible for preparing an action plan following up on the conclusions of internal or external audit reports and evaluations, as well as on investigations by OLAF.[69] There is responsibility to OLAF to carry out administrative investigations, including on-the-spot checks and inspections, in accordance with the provisions and

(2023) 0483), https://www.europarl.europa.eu/doceo/document/TA-9-2023-0483_EN.html, accessed 12 October 2024.

62 1999/352/EC, ECSC, Euratom: Commission Decision of 28 April 1999 establishing the European Anti-fraud Office (OLAF) [1999] OJ L 136/20.

63 Ibid art 2.

64 Ibid art 2(1)(b).

65 Ibid art 3.

66 2019 Frontex Regulation, art 117(1).

67 Ibid recital 113.

68 Ibid art 100(2)(u).

69 Ibid art 106(2)(r).

procedures of EU law,[70] and for establishing whether there has been fraud, corruption or any other illegal activity affecting the financial interests of the Union in connection with a grant agreement or grant decision or a contract funded by Frontex.[71] Working arrangements with third countries and with international organizations, grant agreements, grant decisions and contracts all must contain provisions empowering OLAF to conduct audits and investigations, in accordance with its competence.[72]

On 11 November 2020, the director-general of OLAF opened an investigation into:

1. potential misconduct and/or irregularities related to Frontex committed by named individuals (in the available version of the final report the names are redacted)[73] (the director-general of OLAF closed this part of the investigation on 3 May 2021 before completion);[74] and
2. potential misconduct and/or irregularities in the internal functioning and management of Frontex committed by named individuals (again redacted).

The decision was taken after OLAF had received by post on 8 October 2020 (and by email on 3 November 2020) from a named individual (redacted) information setting out six irregularities regarding the operation of the agency as follows:

1. possible witnessing by Frontex deployed assets, in particular aerial surveillance, of illegal pushbacks involving the Greek Coast Guard; the Frontex staff carrying out the surveillance were alleged to have received instructions not to politicize such events (understood to be not to report them through the serious incident reporting system);
2. intimidation and harassment of staff by senior personnel forcing them to circumvent the rules in interests of the actor; many staff members

70 Council Regulation (Euratom, EC) No 2185/96 of 11 November 1996 concerning on-the-spot checks and inspections carried out by the Commission in order to protect the European Communities' financial interests against fraud and other irregularities [1996] OJ L 292/2.

71 2019 Frontex Regulation, art 117(3).

72 Ibid art 117(5).

73 OLAF (n 2).

74 According to the report, the director-general of OLAF chose to split the case into two, close part (A) without waiting for the completion of the investigation on the allegations on the ground that this would cause significant delay in the finalization of the case. The director general widened part (B) to investigate additional persons suspected to be involved in the alleged pushbacks and/or their cover up (the new case number is OC/20221/0451/A1).

were reported to have been asked to be transferred internally or to leave Frontex altogether;
3. obsessive micro-management by a named individual (redacted) without respect for reporting lines and the failure to respect allocated responsibilities with the effect of paralysing Frontex's work and impairing its efficiency and effectiveness;
4. conflicts of interest in recruitment;
5. over-representation of (characteristic redacted) among senior positions after the appointment of the then executive director;
6. irregularities affecting contracts including arbitrary changes after projects had been finalized resulting in delays of payment to contractors.

This report has been referred to in Chapters 4 and 5 where the findings were related to the subject under consideration.[75] Here emphasis is placed on the way in which OLAF used its power to provide scrutiny in a manner more efficient than a number of other internal mechanisms had been able to do.

The report notes that the allegations referring to Frontex covering up or being involved in illegal pushbacks of migrants had already received wide coverage in 2020, specifically the EU Observer, Bellingcat, *Der Spiegel*, Respond and others.[76] The concerns of the LIBE Committee are also mentioned.[77] On 25 February 2021, it appears that OLAF received a letter from the head of a permanent representation (name redacted) expressing concern about the protection of migrants and asylum seekers at EU borders, possible pushbacks including severe human rights violations by Greek Coast Guard officers. The letter included a USB key (presumably) with digital data supporting the concerns expressed. A few days later, on 1 March 2021, OLAF received the management committee's Working Group on Fundamental Rights and Legal Operational Aspects of Operations report on its investigations into irregularities at Frontex which exonerated, almost completely, the agency of all allegations. The release of the management board's report appears to have unleashed a flurry of activity. Much of this activity is described under the headings relating to the relevant institution but they are repeated here as set out in the OLAF final report because they explain the chain of events which pushed OLAF to involve itself so decisively in the investigation of Frontex. Implicitly the description of the sequence of events as recounted in the report is a critique of lack of effectiveness of all the other internal and external mechanisms established to provide oversight of Frontex. The report details the Parliament budget committee's

[75] OLAF (n 2) 9.
[76] Ibid.
[77] Ibid.

refusal to discharge the Frontex budget on 23 March, stating that a named individual (name redacted but presumably the executive director) responded only after substantial delay to some of the FSWG's questions, the failure to reply to these questions was key to the refusal to discharge the budget. This was followed on 25 May by a letter to the FSWG from the responsible director general at the Commission providing detail about the timelines on development of the fundamental rights monitoring framework of Frontex among other things. The Court of Auditors released, on 7 June 2021, its report on Frontex, concluding that: 'Frontex has not fully implemented its 2016 mandate and … that there is a significant risk that Frontex will struggle to carry out the mandate assigned to it.'[78] A week later, on 15 June 2021, the European Ombudsman released her report on Frontex, concluding, 'it is regrettable that there has been delay by Frontex in implementing the important changes introduced by the 2019 Frontex Regulation. However, since the situation in the process is being resolved the Ombudsman does not find it justified to pursue the matter further'.[79] The OLAF report notes the release of the FSWG report on fact-finding into Frontex regarding allegations of fundamental rights violations on 14 July 2021.

OLAF divided the issues to be investigated into six:

1. possible irregularities concerning the handing of incidents;
2. possible irregularities in application of Frontex's Standard Operating Procedure on Serious Incident Reporting;
3. possible irregularities concerning the working relationship between the persons concerned and the FRO and the FRO's office;
4. possible unlawful restriction of, or exclusion to, access to information to the FRO;
5. possible irregularities or flaws in the communication by the persons concerned to stakeholders; and
6. external individuals, in particular concerning the fundamental rights related issues of Frontex.

Clearly, OLAF considered that its responsibility as an oversight mechanism of Frontex with direct authorization to work with the European Public Prosecutor's Office (EPPO) in respect of criminal activities was called for as all other oversight mechanisms were unable to get past the Frontex wall

[78] European Court of Auditors, 'Special Report 08/2021: "Frontex's Support to External Border Management: Not Sufficiently Effective to Date"' (7 June 2021).

[79] European Ombudsman, 'Decision in OI/5/2020/MHZ on the functioning of the European Border and Coast Guard Agency's (Frontex) Complaints Mechanism for alleged Breaches of Fundamental Rights and the Role of the Fundamental Rights Officer' (15 June 2021).

of denial regarding any fundamental rights irregularities. The report focuses on the capacity of the FRO and her staff to carry out their responsibilities to ensure the protection of fundamental rights by Frontex. The argument is that the internal fundamental rights mechanisms needed to be strengthened and supported so that they would be able to carry out their duties full and effectively. Overall, the OLAF report examined eight specific cases where the serious incident report system was compromised or circumvented by Frontex management at the highest levels. The next paragraphs summarize the findings.

With regard to the first, it found that the executive director had not ensured consistent compliance with Frontex's own Standard Operating Procedures regarding serious incident reporting. This resulted in the FRO being excluded from the assessment and handling of some incidents despite a clear fundamental rights component. Further the director had failed to initiate serious incident reports for some incidents with fundamental rights elements.[80] Secondly, the senior management [names redacted] decided to relocate a Frontex arial asset to a different operational area of activities with the apparent purpose (on the basis of evidence received) to avoid witnessing incidents at sea with a potential fundamental rights component.[81] Thirdly, the executive director did not ensure appropriate follow-up in relation to incidents witnessed by Frontex staff.[82] Fourthly, between 2016 and 2020, the executive director repeatedly acted directly or instructed others to act in a way which resulted in a severe limitation of access by the FRO and her staff to information within Frontex including the Eurosur system thus preventing the FRO's office from effectively performing its tasks.[83] Fifthly, he took the decision not to share with the FRO digital material received from the Turkish authorities in February 2021 and did not involve the FRO's office in the assessment of the material notwithstanding a fundamental rights component.[84] Sixthly, he did not request information and clarifications or otherwise take follow up action after having been informed by OLAF that Frontex co-financed assets appeared to have been involved in some incidents included in the digital material provided by the Turkish authorities.[85] Accordingly, OLAF concluded that the iterated actions affected the capacity of Frontex to fully comply with its tasks to contribute to the uniform application of EU fundamental rights law, including the Charter. The

80 OLAF (n 2).
81 Ibid.
82 Ibid.
83 Ibid.
84 Ibid.
85 Ibid.

misconduct uncovered by OLAF was also in breach of the Staff Regulation, the Frontex Code of Conduct and the 2019 Frontex Regulation.[86]

On the next ground covered by the investigation, a highly problematic recruitment process for the post of FRO and FRO deputy, OLAF found that the procedure had been flawed in order to delay the recruitment until a change of EU Commissioner for DG HOME because the incumbent was considered to be too favourable to the proper protection of fundamental rights.[87] This breached the Staff Regulation, the Code of Conduct, the Frontex Regulation and a management board decision.

The following ground related to a senior official's (name redacted) management of an administrative inquiry against the FRO and intentionally delaying any progress on it for 15 months, while leaking information about the inquiry to a member of the management board as well as providing misleading information to staff about the conclusions of the administrative inquiry. OLAF found misconduct in breach of the Charter, the Staff Regulation, the Code of Conduct and a management board decision.[88]

OLAF's next ground against the executive director was regarding failure to act when informed that Frontex deployed staff might have preferred not to report officially some incidents for fear of repercussions by the border guards of the host member state. No follow up or checks based on this information were reported. This affected the capacity of Frontex to fully comply with its tasks to monitor effective compliance with the respect for, the protection and promotion of fundamental rights in all of its activities at the external borders. This breached the Staff Regulation, the Code of Conduct and the Frontex Regulation. Further, OLAF found that the senior management [name redacted] had provided the Chair of the Parliament's LIBE Committee with incorrect information about the process of the revision of the Standard Operating Procedures on serious incident reports. OLAF made a further finding unlawful provision of partially untruthful or biased information to the LIBE Committee concerning the handling of fundamental rights matters within Frontex.[89]

The next misconduct related to senior management [name redacted] personally amending the text of two letters to be addressed to the authorities of a Member State to be 'politically softer', which meant less explicit on the gravity of the facts. He removed direct references to fundamental rights violations regarding incidents in the Member State's territorial waters. Further he showed lack of constructive cooperation in the implementation

86 Ibid.

87 Ibid.

88 Ibid.

89 Ibid.

of the (then new) legal framework as regards fundamental rights, thus causing severe delays in its implementation. OLAF noted that this appeared to be inspired by his personal opinions about the Commissioner of DG HOME and some officials whom he considered to lack competence and understanding of the operational challenges of Frontex. These negative opinions about the Commissioner and her staff were shared with external parties including representatives of Member States. He also apparently briefed a member of the management board to raise issues to put in difficulty the Commission's representative at a meeting. OLAF found that this misconduct was in breach of the Staff Regulation and the Code of Conduct. There were also incidents of the sharing of unpublished delicate or sensitive information about Frontex to persons unconnected with the agency contrary to the Staff Regulation.[90]

OLAF's reports includes additional findings regarding inappropriate handling of serious incident reports in order to prevent the FRO from being able to carry out an assessment, ordering the relocation of Frontex assets to avoid witnessing fundamental rights violations and otherwise hampering the FRO's access to information.[91] OLAF concluded that the senior management of Frontex within their differing roles and responsibilities committed serious misconduct and other irregularities. In doing so, they hindered the capacity of Frontex to fully comply with its responsibilities, namely the protection and promotion of fundamental rights as enshrined in the Charter. OLAF grouped the failing into three categories:

1. failure to follow procedures including the exclusion of the FRO from her duties to assess fundamental rights compliance and the relocation of assets to avoid witnessing fundamental rights violations;
2. failure in their duty of loyalty on the basis of their personal prejudices and the low esteem in which they held the Commission; and
3. failure in their managerial responsibilities.[92]

The OLAF report not only supported many criticisms levelled at the agency by NGOs and the Parliament but went further in revealing and condemning the agency's development as profoundly implicated in unlawful violence against persons in distress at sea and mafia-style cover-ups to prevent detection. It is a pity that the EPPO to date has not seen fit to commence criminal proceedings against those responsible.

[90] Ibid.

[91] Ibid.

[92] Ibid.

4 The Court of Justice of the European Union and halting operations under Article 46 of the 2019 Frontex Regulation

In this final section, the judgments of the CJEU regarding external border operations where the Court found serious violations of fundamental rights and which resulted in the executive director exercising his powers under Article 46 of the 2019 Frontex Regulation to end Frontex participating in a joint operation are analysed. There have only been two such cases. The first was brought by the Commission against Hungary regarding national legislation and practices which prevented asylum seekers travelling by land via Serbia and trying to enter Hungary to seek asylum from doing so.[93] The Commission claimed that the external border practices of Hungary were inconsistent with the Common European Asylum System (CEAS) and Article 6 (liberty of the person), Article 18 (the right to seek asylum) and Article 47 (the right to an effective remedy) of the EU Charter. In particular, the Commission challenged the Hungarian law which required all asylum applications to be lodged in person and exclusively in the transit zones of Röszke (Hungary) and Tompa (Hungary), access to which had been severely restricted by the Hungarian authorities. According to the Commission, the Hungarian authorities permit only a very limited number of daily entries into each of those transit zones: only one person per day could enter each of those transit zones, creating a waiting period of several months before one of them could be accessed for an application for international protection to be made there. This prevents people seeking international protection from making an application, a requirement of EU law. Furthermore, the Commission claimed that the Hungarian authorities had established a regime of systematic detention of asylum seekers contrary to EU law and further was expelling third-country nationals without the necessary protections and procedure required by EU law. The CJEU found against the Hungarian authorities on all grounds.

Frontex was engaged in a joint operation with the Hungarian border guards in the areas which were the subject of the judgment. There had been recommendations from the Consultative Forum and others to Frontex to cease participation in the joint operation on fundamental rights grounds under Article 46, but the executive director was reluctant to do so. Finally, in January 2021, in response to the judgment, Frontex suspended its operations in Hungary, as the country continued its practice of pushbacks across the

[93] Case C-808/18 *Commission v Hungary* [2020] EU:C:2020:1029.

border.[94] The cross-border crime prevention programme between Hungary and Frontex was however partially continued. When questioned about its continuation notwithstanding the CJEU judgment of violation of EU law, by the Parliament's FSWG, both the then acting executive director and the FRO argued that from a protection of fundamental rights perspective, it was better to continue joint operations as more Frontex presence was more effective in diminishing violations than less.[95]

In June 2022, the CJEU handed down a judgment in an expedited case regarding the treatment of an asylum seeker on the Lithuania–Belarus border.[96] In November 2021, Lithuania had declared a state of emergency on account of what it considered to be a mass influx of migrants, arriving mainly from Belarus. A week later a third-country national was arrested in Poland, along with a group of individuals who had arrived from Lithuania via Belarus for the reason that he was in possession of neither travel documents, nor the visa required in order to stay in that Member State or EU. The Polish authorities expelled him to Lithuania where he was detained on grounds that he might abscond. Further, on the basis of the Lithuanian state of emergency legislation, he was denied access to an asylum procedure and refused reception conditions as required by the CEAS. The CJEU found that the national legislation which excluded him from an asylum procedure and reception conditions was unlawful as it was not consistent with the Common European Asylum System.[97] The Court further found that in the event of a declaration of martial law or of a state of emergency or in the event of a declaration of an emergency due to a mass influx of aliens, an asylum seeker may not be placed in detention for the sole reason that he or she is staying illegally on the territory of that Member State.[98]

In July 2022, media reported that Frontex was withdrawing from its joint operation with Lithuania.[99] At the FSWG meeting of 12 July 2022, Frontex officials also confirmed that as a result of the CJEU judgment on Lithuanian border procedures, it had reduced its presence significantly in Lithuania and

---

94 Frontex, 'FRO Annual Report 2021' (2022), https://www.frontex.europa.eu/assets/FRO_Reports/The_Fundamental_Rights_Officer_Annual_Report_2021.pdf#page=13, accessed 12 October 2024.

95 Parliament, 'Video of meeting 12 July 2022', https://multimedia.europarl.europa.eu/en/webstreaming/libe-working-group-on-frontex-scrutiny_20220712-1630-COMMITTEE-LIBE, accessed 12 October 2024.

96 Case C-72/22 PPU *M.A. v Valstybės sienos apsaugos tarnyba* [2022] EU:C:2022:505.

97 Ibid para 75.

98 Ibid para 93.

99 Nikolaj Nielsen, 'Frontex Ends Lithuania Border Surveillance Operation' (*euobserver*, 14 July 2024), https://euobserver.com/migration/155523, accessed 12 October 2024.

ceased to assist that country on the disputed border with Belarus. The FRO in his annual report of 2022 confirmed that Frontex had stopped its Lithuanian border surveillance activities as of July 2022, but that the consequence of this was that the FRO had access to less information about fundamental rights violations at the Lithuania–Belarus border.[100] These are the two cases where the executive director has exercised powers to withdraw Frontex support for joint border operations on fundamental rights grounds.[101]

5 Conclusion

This chapter examined the three key external monitoring bodies which have engaged with Frontex on the question of fundamental rights protection and promotion. The OLAF investigation was by far the most impressive of all those carried out on Frontex operations, not least because of the very extensive investigatory powers which OLAF may use. These included access to the WhatsApp messages of Frontex officials which revealed much rich evidence of misconduct by them. It is clear from exchanges on WhatsApp that the officials incorrectly considered that these messages would not be available to any outside investigator. They were aware that their emails could be traced and so encouraged one another not to use emails to exchange vital information but to do so only by WhatsApp. Notwithstanding the seriousness of the violations revealed in the OLAF report, neither the EPPO now any other law enforcement body has chosen to prefer criminal charges against those responsible. This is unfortunate as prosecutions for complicity in fundamental rights violations would have sent a much clearer signal to all EU border guards that this behaviour is not tolerated (and that it is criminal). Instead, the executive director left his post precipitously, but he is currently a member of the European Parliament having been elected as a candidate for a French extreme right party. It is likely that he will seek to participate in the FSWG. OLAF is not the watchdog of Frontex. Its investigation was in the course of its more general duties to protect the EU from fraud and misconduct. Most of the investigations carried out by OLAF related to more general issues in the institutions. It cannot be expected that OLAF will be a regular investigator of allegations of fundamental rights violations in Frontex. From the framing of its investigation, to protect and enhance the position of the main internal Frontex fundamental rights institution, the FRO, it is clear that it may have been intended to strengthen internal

[100] Frontex, 'The Fundamental Rights Officer: Annual Report 2022' (2022).

[101] 'Frontex Suspends Operations in Spain' (*Informigrants*, 29 January 2024), https://www.infomigrants.net/en/post/54833/frontex-suspends-operations-in-spain, accessed 12 October 2024.

monitoring within the agency so that OLAF can leave the day-to-day work to the FRO rather than intervening again itself.

The CJEU judgments have been the most effective redress mechanism resulting in the actual cessation of cooperation on the grounds of fundamental rights violations. However, the judgments of the General Court on damages for individuals who claimed that they were victims of these violations have been particularly unsympathetic. Whether there will be any change to this trend when the CJEU examines the cases currently on appeal is unclear. The CJEU cases which have resulted in substantial change have come from two different sources: one was an infringement action by the Commission, and the other a reference from a national court. Notwithstanding substantial efforts by NGOs, the Commission has been reluctant to commence many infringement proceedings against Member States as regards migration and fundamental rights. The willingness of national courts to make references to the CJEU regarding these often sensitive, national issues varies substantially.[102]

The most durable of the monitoring mechanisms has been the European Parliament's LIBE Committee. Here, there has been sustained investigation, the collection of much evidence and the effective use of all powers available. In its primary role as part of the EU legislature, the Parliament has successfully introduced ever increasing fundamental requirements into the regulation to which Frontex is required to comply. It has monitored consistently the application of the legislation and called to account Frontex officials to explain where and why problems are occurring. It has also encouraged other monitoring mechanisms such as the EU Ombudsman to investigate allegations of violations of fundamental rights. The Parliament's use of its powers of budgetary discharge has been effective in obtaining some explanations for problems. However, the Parliament needs to have more purchase as regards transparency and powers to require action if it is to be able to turn around the internal culture with an agency where secrecy, the cover up of fundamental violations and violence appear to have become engrained.

[102] Minos Mouzourakis and Cathryn Costello, 'Effective Judicial Protection of Migrants and Refugees? The Role of Europe's Supranational Courts in Protecting and Generating Rights' in Evangelia (Lilian) Tsourdi and Philippe de Bruycker (eds), *Research Handbook on EU Migration and Asylum Law* (Edward Elgar 2022); Mariana Gkliati, 'Frontex Before the Judge: The Road to the Judicial Accountability before the CJEU, the ECtHR and National Courts' in Vasileios Pergantis (ed), *EU Responsibility in the International Legal Order: Human Rights – Comparative Approaches – Special Issues* (Sakkoulas Publishers 2023).

PART III

The Erosion of the Rule of Law through the Development of Europe's Techno-Borders

7

Technology-led Border Surveillance and the Rule of Law: Eurosur as a 'Foggy' Network of Information Exchange

1 Introduction

Chapters 5 and 6 examined Frontex from the perspectives of accountability and oversight, highlighting the agency's sub-standard internal and external monitoring mechanisms as significant rule of law deficits. What has not been covered so far though is the gradual evolution of the agency as a European Union (EU) migration information hub, underpinned by the proliferation of information-related tasks and the growing processing of personal data. At the heart of Frontex's data-related tasks is supporting the development and operation of the European Surveillance System (Eurosur), as mandated in Article 10(1)(f) of Regulation (EU) 2019/1896, the current legal basis of Frontex.[1] The latter, originally established by Regulation 10521/2013, is an information exchange platform linking national border control authorities and Frontex to facilitate exchange of information. Eurosur constitutes an information processing hub, designed to improve the management of the EU's external borders and become the backbone of Frontex's surveillance and intervention capabilities. Eurosur follows a risk-based approach and exemplifies the role of modern technological equipment in surveillance of movement in a bold manner; rather than creating data profiles through

[1] Regulation (EU) 2019/1896 of the European Parliament and of the Council of 13 November 2019 on the European Border and Coast Guard and repealing Regulations (EU) No 1052/2013 and (EU) 2016/1624 [2019] OJ L 295/1 (2019 Frontex Regulation).

extensive information collection, Eurosur is premised on the principle of interconnectivity of already existing monitoring sources in the various Member States with the ultimate goal of establishing a 'system of systems'[2] grounded on permanent surveillance. Eurosur has been within the academic radar, particularly from political scientists,[3] and recently, legal scholarship has emerged shedding light on the rise of Frontex as a data processing hub, which also discusses Eurosur.[4] However, an analysis on the rule of law challenges stemming from the development and operation of Eurosur is so far missing. To this end, the next section provides a bird's eye view on the evolution of Frontex's information-related tasks from the limited provisions in its founding Council Regulation (EC) No 2007/2004[5] to the current legal framework. It serves to not only lay the groundwork for the subsequent analysis on Eurosur, but also to demonstrate that the information-related tasks of the agency have over time raised rule of law challenges. Section 3 zooms into the operation of Eurosur to explain its purpose and operation, followed by an analysis of the rule of law challenges. These are centred on two axes: first, how the operation of Eurosur exacerbates and complicates the rule of law deficit of Frontex, and, second, the opacity and lack of foreseeability regarding the processing of personal data within the Eurosur ecosystem. The conclusion summarizes the main findings of the chapter.

---

2 Commission, 'Examining the Creation of a European Border Surveillance System (Eurosur)' (Communication) COM(2008) 68 final, 9.

3 See Sabrina Ellebrecht, *Mediated Bordering – Eurosur, the Refugee Boat and the Construction of an External EU Border* ([transcript] 2020); Julien Jeandesboz, 'Beyond the Tartar Steppe: EUROSUR and the Ethics of European Border Control Practices' in J. Peter Burgess and Serge Gutwirth (eds), *A Threat Against Europe? Security, Migration and Integration* (VB Press 2011) 114; Rocco Bellanova and Denis Duez, 'The Making (Sense) of EUROSUR: How to Control the Sea Borders?' in Raphael Bossong and Helena Carrapico (eds), *EU Borders and Shifting Internal Security* (Springer 2016); Martina Tazzioli, 'Spy, Track and Archive: The Temporality of Visibility in Eurosur and Jora' (2018) 49(4) *Security Dialogue* 272.

4 Mona Aviat, 'Externalising Refoulement through New Technologies: The Case of Frontex's Specific Situational Pictures under the Lens of EU Non-Contractual Liability' (2024) *Netherlands International Law Review*; Shrutika Gandhi, 'Frontex as a Hub for Surveillance and Data Sharing: Challenges for Data Protection and Privacy Rights' (2024) 53 *Computer Law & Security Review*. Analysis on Eurosur may also be found in Teresa Quintel, *Data Protection, Migration and Border Control: The GDPR, the Law Enforcement Directive and Beyond* (Hart 2022).

5 Council Regulation (EC) No 2007/2004 of 26 October 2004 establishing a European Agency for the Management of Operational Cooperation at the External Borders of the Member States of the European Union [2004] OJ L 349/1.

2 The emergence of Frontex as a 'migration information hub'

2.1 The early days

Frontex was established 'to facilitate the application of effective mechanisms for controlling the external borders of the EU'[6] and at first its mandate was rather restricted, being entrusted with the task of enhancing 'operational cooperation among Member States in external border management'.[7] The responsibility for surveillance and control of the borders remained with the Member States; Frontex was merely responsible for 'facilitating and rendering the effective application of existing and future mechanisms for controlling the external borders'.[8] At the time, the main aim of the agency was to coordinate Member States' actions to contribute to an efficient, high and uniform level of control on persons and surveillance at the external borders by conducting risk analyses, providing technical support to the European Commission and the Member States and assisting the latter in Joint Return Operations. Council Regulation (EU) No 2007/2004 contained only two provisions regarding processing personal data: Article 11 on information exchange systems, according to which the agency could take all necessary measures to facilitate the exchange of information relevant for its tasks with the Commission and the Member States, and Article 13 on cooperation with third countries, international organizations and Europol, notably through working arrangements. However, the former article did not specify what information could be shared,[9] whereas the latter article did not expressly allow exchanges of personal data to specify what such cooperation entailed.

2.2 Formalization and expansion of Frontex's information-related tasks

The competence to process personal data was formally introduced in the reform of the Frontex regime in 2011.[10] This is notwithstanding the fact that, in practice, Frontex was already processing and exchanging personal data particularly in relation to joint return operations for years before this reform, without undertaking any steps to implement the then applicable Regulation (EU) 45/2001 concerning the processing of personal data by

6 Ibid art 1.
7 Ibid.
8 Ibid art 1(2).
9 Gandhi (n 4) 2.
10 Regulation (EU) 1168/2011 of the European Parliament and of the Council of 25 October 2011 amending Council Regulation (EC) No 2007/2004 establishing a European Agency for the Management of Operational Cooperation at the External Borders of the Member States of the European Union [2011] OJ L 304/1 (2011 Frontex Regulation).

EU institutions, bodies, offices and agencies.[11] The practice of processing personal data without a clear basis – a clear violation of the rule of law, which obscures foreseeability in the tasks of the agency – was confirmed by the European Data Protection Supervisor (EDPS) in its opinion in 2010 on the Commission's Proposal for amending the 2007 Frontex Regulation.[12]

The adoption of Regulation (EU) No 1168/2011 was marked by a significant increase in the agency's powers and tasks to initiate and carry out joint operations and pilot projects in cooperation with Member States.[13] The Regulation expanded Frontex's role in conducting risk analyses and research,[14] with the agency being tasked to develop and operate information systems that enable swift and reliable exchanges of information regarding emerging risks at the external borders of the EU. It envisaged that Frontex would act as a hub for developing and operating a border surveillance system – Eurosur – and enabling the creation of an environment for common information sharing across EU agencies, such as Europol, to tackle the challenges posed by irregular immigration.[15] It also introduced an internal Frontex Data Protection Officer (DPO) for monitoring the agency's compliance with Regulation (EC) 45/2001, as well as the competence of the EDPS to monitor its activities.[16] However, the DPO was also charged with the task of reporting to and making recommendations to the executive director of Frontex on data protection matters, yet the latter was under no obligation to take the advice of the DPO and the recommendations were not binding.[17]

Eurosur was established in a separate legal instrument in 2013,[18] providing a common framework for the exchange of surveillance information and

---

[11] Regulation (EC) No 45/2001 Regulation (EC) No 45/2001 of the European Parliament and of the Council of 18 December 2000 on the protection of individuals with regard to the processing of personal data by the Community institutions and bodies and on the free movement of such data [2001] OJ L 8/1. It has been replaced by Regulation (EU) 2018/1725 of the European Parliament and of the Council of 25 November 2018 on the protection of natural persons with regard to the processing of personal data by the Union institutions, bodies, offices and agencies and on the free movement of such data [2018] OJ L 295/39.

[12] EDPS, 'Opinion on the proposal for a Regulation of the European Parliament and of the Council amending Council Regulation (EC) No 2007/2004 establishing a European Agency for the Management of Operational Cooperation at the External Borders of the Member States of the European Union (FRONTEX)' (17 May 2010) para 44.

[13] 2011 Frontex Regulation, art 3(a)(3).

[14] Ibid arts 2(c), 2(d), 2(h) and 2(i).

[15] Ibid art 2(i).

[16] Ibid art 11a.

[17] Gandhi (n 4) 5.

[18] Regulation (EU) No 1052/2013 of the European Parliament and of the Council of 22 October 2013 establishing the European Border Surveillance System (Eurosur) [2013] OJ L 295/11 (Eurosur Regulation).

cooperation between Member States' border surveillance authorities and the agency, thereby strengthening intelligence and risk assessment. For that purpose, the so-called National Coordination Centres (NCCs) and Frontex exchange information, data and intelligence in situational awareness pictures, to detect and monitor unauthorized crossings of the external Schengen borders.[19] In this respect, drones were considered an essential technology for acquiring information on happenings outside EU borders.[20] Eurosur significantly contributed to the transformation of Frontex into EU's migration information hub – Article 12 of the Eurosur Regulation allows Frontex to 'coordinate the common application of surveillance tools in order to supply the national coordination centres of Member States and itself with surveillance information on the external borders on a regular, reliable and cost-efficient basis'.

The next revision significantly increased Frontex's budget and powers, which now encompass the additional purposes of contributing to addressing serious crime with a cross-border dimension and ensuring 'a high level of internal security within the Union'.[21] Thus Frontex sits on two stools in-between border control and law enforcement and thus operates as a quasi-law enforcement agency. The agency was rebranded as the European Union Border and Coast Guard Agency, consisting of the national authorities responsible for border management and return as well as Frontex. Regulation (EU) 2016/1624 afforded the agency a more comprehensive monitoring role, improved its access to resources for joint operations, and considerably expanded Frontex's role in relation to the return of persons with no right to stay.[22] Frontex could collect and further process an increased amount of personal data in the context of its activities, including joint operations, pilot projects, rapid border interventions, return interventions and risk analyses. The Regulation aligned Frontex's formal mandate with its information-related role in practice, by including a separate section on 'information exchange and

[19] Commission, 'Commission Staff Working Document: Evaluation of the Regulation (EU) No 1052/2013 of the European Parliament and of the Council of 22 October 2013 establishing the European Border Surveillance System (Eurosur)', SWD (2018) 410 final, 7.

[20] Luisa Marin and Kamila Krajcíková, 'Deploying Drones in Policing Southern European Borders: Constraints and Challenges for Data Protection and Human Rights' in Ales Završnik (ed), *Drones and Unmanned Aerial Systems: Legal and Social Implications for Security and Surveillance* (Springer 2015).

[21] Regulation (EU) 2016/1624 of the European Parliament and of the Council of 14 September 2016 on the European Border and Coast Guard [2016] OJ L251/1 (2016 Frontex Regulation), art 1.

[22] Melanie Fink, 'European Border and Coast Guard Agency' in Violeta Moreno-Lax and Niovi Vavoula (eds), *Oxford Encyclopedia of European Union Law – Section on AFSJ* (Oxford University Press 2025).

data protection'.[23] The agency could process personal data for performing its tasks of organizing and coordinating joint operations, pilot projects, rapid border interventions and in the framework of the migration management support teams, organizing and coordinating return operations and return interventions, facilitating the exchange of information with Member States, the (former) European Asylum Support Office (now European Union Agency for Asylum), Europol or Eurojust, for performing risk analysis, identifying and tracking vessels in the framework of Eurosur and for its administrative tasks.[24] In addition, Frontex's mandate involved its participation 'in the development and management of research and innovation activities relevant for the control and surveillance of the external borders, including the use of advanced surveillance technology, and develop pilot projects'.[25]

2.3 The expansion of informational tasks under the 2019 Frontex Regulation

The 2019 revision of Frontex's legal basis via Regulation (EU) 2019/1896, motivated by the need to step up efforts to return irregular migrants,[26] increased the agency's autonomy and created the standing corps of the EU Border and Coast Guard Agency. In particular, its tasks were increased, ranging from monitoring migratory flows and the external borders,[27] to providing operational assistance to Member States and third countries,[28] assisting at all stages of the return process,[29] cooperating with Europol and Eurojust and other agencies,[30] as well as third countries through working arrangements.[31]

---

23 2016 Frontex Regulation, Chapter III, Section 2.

24 Ibid art 46(1). According to Article 46(3), the processing of personal data for other purposes was also permitted as long as it fell within the objective in Article 46(1) and it was authorised by the data provider of the information in question. Specific rules regarding the processing of personal data collected during joint operations, pilot projects and rapid interventions and by migration management support teams (Article 47) and in the context of return operations and return interventions (Article 48) are also foreseen.

25 Ibid arts 8(1)(q) and 37(1).

26 European Council, 'European Council Conclusions' (EUCO 9/18, 28 June 2018), https://www.consilium.europa.eu/en/press/press-releases/2018/06/29/20180628-euco-conclusions-final, accessed 12 October 2024.

27 2019 Frontex Regulation, art 10(1)(a) and (d).

28 Ibid art 10(1)(i).

29 Ibid art 10(1)(n).

30 Ibid art 10(1)(q)–(s). See David Fernández-Rojo, *EU Migration Agencies: The Operation and Cooperation of FRONTEX, EASO and EUROPOL* (Edward Elgar 2021).

31 Ibid art 10(1)(u). For the working arrangements see https://www.frontex.europa.eu/what-we-do/beyond-eu-borders/working-arrangements/, accessed 12 October 2024.

The key novelty of the 2019 Frontex Regulation is the creation of the standing corps consisting of members from different EU Member States and staff members employed by Frontex. Deployed in different Member States, the standing corps is meant to assist with border checks, to provide support to migration management, and assist with nationality screening, registration and fingerprinting.[32] The information-related tasks of the agency have been significantly emphasized. Personal data may be processed for a series of purposes:

- performing its tasks of organizing and coordinating joint operations, pilot projects, rapid border interventions and in the framework of the migration management support teams;
- performing its tasks of supporting Member States and third countries in pre-return and return activities, operating return management systems, as well as coordinating or organizing return operations and providing technical and operational assistance to Member States and third countries;
- facilitating the exchange of information with Member States, the Commission, the European External Action Service (EEAS) and various other EU agencies and bodies;
- facilitating the exchange of information with the law enforcement authorities of the Member States, Europol or Eurojust;
- risk analysis;[33]
- performing its tasks in the framework of Eurosur;
- operating the False and Authentic Documents Online (FADO) system; and
- administrative tasks.

In particular, while Eurosur and Frontex were previously established by two different legal instruments, Eurosur is now integrated within the Frontex architecture, although, as will be shown later in this chapter, the exact architecture and content are not explicitly regulated.[34] Furthermore, the agency may deploy operational staff and technical equipment to provide assistance in screening, debriefing, identification and recording biometric data.[35] Indeed, Frontex border guard officers can perform screening interviews with third-country nationals who do not possess valid identification documents and interview applicants for international protection.[36] In addition, Frontex was given more powers to access data held in both EU information systems and

[32] For further information see Fink (n 22).

[33] PeDRA, or 'Processing of Personal Data for Risk Analysis'.

[34] 2019 Frontex Regulation, arts 10(1)(f) and 18–28.

[35] Ibid art 10(1)(m).

[36] Frontex, 'Frontex Management Board Decision 1/2020 of 4 January 2020 on adopting the profiles to be made available to the European Border and Coast Guard Standing

in third-country databases.[37] Moreover, it can provide assistance at all stages of the return process, which involves information exchanges.[38] In addition, it can cooperate with Europol and Eurojust and provide support to Member States in circumstances requiring increased technical and operational assistance at the external borders in the fight against cross-border crime and terrorism.[39] It can process so-called operational personal data, collected while monitoring migratory flows, carrying out risk analyses or in the course of operations for the purpose of identifying suspects of cross-border crime[40] Finally, it can develop technical standards for information exchange, provide the necessary assistance for the development of a common information-sharing environment, including interoperability of systems, as appropriate[41] and even manage the FADO.[42] Overall, the 2019 Frontex Regulation establishes a duty to cooperate in good faith and an obligation to share information in a timely and accurate manner between the agency and the national authorities responsible for border management and return.[43]

Notwithstanding the elaborate provisions on the informational tasks of the agency, there is significant lack of foreseeability as to which data protection rules apply. In particular, as Quintel has pointed out, the agency's border guard officers may not only engage with interviewing applicants for international protection and registering biometric data, but also contribute to the detection of cross-border crime and the identification of persons suspected of being involved in cross-border crime activities, including migrant smuggling, terrorism, trafficking in human beings, supporting the collection of information concerning the apprehension of third-country nationals, and supporting the preservation of evidence when detecting illicit or smuggled goods or during the apprehension of individuals.[44] The boundaries between immigration control and law enforcement are significantly blurred in this context, whereby it becomes utterly unclear whether the processing of personal data by the agency constitutes processing of operational personal

Corps', https://www.frontex.europa.eu/assets/Key_Documents/MB_Decision/2020/MB_Decision_1_2020_adopting_the_profiles_to_be_made_available_to_the_EBC....pdf, accessed 12 October 2024.

37 For example, see 2019 Frontex Regulation, art 50(2).

38 Ibid art 49.

39 Ibid art 10(1)(q).

40 Ibid art 90. For criticism, see Ludek Stavinoha, Apostolis Fotiadis and Giacomo Zandonini, 'EU's Frontex Tripped in Its Plan for "Intrusive" Surveillance of Migrants' (*Balkan Insight*, 7 July 2022), https://balkaninsight.com/2022/07/07/eus-frontex-tripped-in-plan-for-intrusive-surveillance-of-migrants/, accessed 12 October 2024.

41 2019 Frontex Regulation, art 10(1)(y).

42 Ibid art 79.

43 Ibid art 11.

44 Quintel (n 4) 204–205.

data or not. The distinction is particularly important because it entails the application of different data protection rules. In particular, for the general rules on processing of personal data reference must be made to Article 86 of the 2019 Frontex Regulation, which refers to the European Union Data Protection Regulation, except its Chapter IX. However, for operational personal data, Chapter IX applies, the scope of which is unclear; it is defined solely by making reference to the processing of operational personal data.[45] This means that Frontex could process personal data under Chapter IX even though the relevant tasks may be primarily migration-related in nature and the law enforcement dimension may be secondary. Relying on Chapter IX is problematic, because it is incomplete and underdeveloped, in particular as regards international transfers and supervision. In particular, Article 94 of the EUDPR does not contain detailed provisions and safeguards for the transfer of personal data by an EU agency outside the EU, without any obligation to carry out a proportionality assessment or to require a justification of carrying out a particular transfer.[46] Thus, the lack of clarity as to when officers process operational personal data, relying on Chapter IX of the EUDPR, hinders foreseeability as to the applicable legal framework. It may also be heavily relied on by officers, with significant implications such as allowing in a streamlined and simplified manner the transfer of personal data outside the EU.[47]

Another significant task that was added to the mandate of Frontex was the setting up and operation of the European Travel Information and Authorisation System (ETIAS) Central Unit. ETIAS is the Schengen-wide large-scale IT system designed to process personal data from visa-free nationals who wish to travel to the Schengen area by carrying out pre-travel screening of these travellers to determine whether they pose a threat in terms of security, irregular migration or public health. For the performance of the risk assessment, the role of Frontex is crucial. The ETIAS watchlist against which the personal data of travel authorization applicants will be cross-checked is developed and will be managed by Frontex.[48] Furthermore, for the conduct of the automated risk assessment, Frontex is entrusted with the task of drafting special risk indicators, incorporated into an algorithm that will evaluate the personal data of applicants against the special risk indicators.

45 Ibid 206.

46 Ibid 199.

47 Ibid 206.

48 Regulation (EU) 2018/1240 of the European Parliament and of the Council of 12 September 2018 establishing a European Travel Information and Authorisation System (ETIAS) and amending Regulations (EU) No 1077/2011, (EU) No 515/2014, (EU) 2016/399, (EU) 2016/1624 and (EU) 2017/2226 [2018] OJ L 236/1 (ETIAS Regulation), art 20(4).

In addition, for the Visa Information System (VIS) risk assessments, Frontex has a similar task.[49]

Overall, Frontex can share vast amounts of information, including personal data, with Member States' authorities, including law enforcement agencies, EU agencies, such as Europol, and importantly with third countries. This is notwithstanding the fact that the agency has been heavily criticized for complicity in fundamental rights violations, as demonstrated in Part II of this book, and research shows that the data protection culture is also underdeveloped, with examples of sidelining the Frontex DPO being paradigmatic in this respect.[50]

3 Zooming in on Eurosur

3.1 Making sense of Eurosur: purpose and functions

Since before the official establishment of Frontex in 2005, a series of feasibility studies indicated the convergence and combination of all available information,[51] until the Commission announced the establishment of Eurosur in 2006 as a means of reinforcing the management of external borders.[52] Eurosur would be gradually established in three phases; under the first phase, Member States' surveillance systems would be linked and streamlined; the second phase focused on the improvement and development of surveillance tools and sensors, such as earth observation satellites and unmanned aerial vehicles; and under the third phase, 'a common information sharing environment' would integrate all existing maritime reporting and monitoring systems in the field of internal security.[53] To that end, in a rather questionable manner in terms of democratic legitimacy,[54] prior to the adoption of corresponding legislation, Frontex had commenced the organizational structure of the endeavour through the establishment of NCCs

49 Ibid art 7.

50 Sarah Tas, 'Frontex and Data Protection' (*Verfassungsblog*, 9 September 2022), https://verfassungsblog.de/frontex-and-data-protection/, accessed 12 October 2024; Stavinoha et al (n 40).

51 Council, 'Frontex Feasibility Study on Mediterranean Coastal Patrols Network—MEDSEA' (Doc. 12049/ 06, partly accessible, 20 November 2006); 'Frontex Study on Technical Feasibility of establishing a Surveillance System (European Surveillance System)—BORTEC (2007)', not publicly available.

52 Commission, 'Reinforcing the Management of the European Union's Southern Maritime Borders' COM(2006) 733 final, 8.

53 Ibid 5.

54 Jorrit Rijpma, 'Brave New Borders: The EU's Use of New Technologies for the Management of Migration and Asylum' in Marise Cremona (ed), *New Technologies and EU Law* (Oxford University Press 2017) 234.

and the Frontex Situation Centre,[55] which would eventually be integrated in Eurosur. Furthermore, the prevalence of the technical over the legal is evident from the conduct of feasibility studies – as opposed to impact assessments, which evaluate the impact of a proposed legislation on the protection of fundamental rights. As it has been pointed out, a key problem arising from the establishment of Eurosur is that it has been conceived as a technical fix to bypass parliamentary scrutiny and judicial review, thus minimizing the emergence of political issues in its adoption and implementation.[56] With the creation of the technical and organization infrastructure prior to the adoption of legislation, a series of modalities were pre-empted. Following years of operational and structural preparation, the Eurosur Regulation was adopted in 2013 requiring all Member States – not only those at the southern maritime borders – to 'make substantial investments in the alignment of their own border control systems with Eurosur's standards and requirements'.[57] It also considerably elevated Frontex to the status of a key actor in the overall functioning of the system. Article 8(1)(s) of the 2016 Frontex Regulation envisaged the role of Eurosur as providing the necessary assistance for its development and operation and, as appropriate, for the development of a common information-sharing environment, including interoperability of systems, in particular by developing, maintaining and coordinating the Eurosur framework. Eurosur was seen as a central way in which the agency could ensure proper and effective monitoring of the management of external borders. As mentioned earlier, the Eurosur rules – with some changes – were absorbed by the 2019 Frontex Regulation.

Eurosur provides an integrated framework for the exchange of real-time information and for operational cooperation between Member States' border surveillance authorities and the agency. According to Article 19(1) of the 2019 Frontex Regulation, Eurosur enables the performance of border checks at authorized border crossing points and for external land, sea and air border surveillance, understood as activities involving the monitoring, detection, identification, tracking, prevention and interception of unauthorized border crossings.[58] The stated purpose is threefold: to improve situational awareness

55 The Frontex Situation Centre was created in 2008 and is a central hub channelling all exchanges of information between the agency and the competent authorities of the Member States, whose task is also the administration of the Eurosur components.

56 Bellanova and Duez (n 3) 30.

57 Ben Hayes and Mathias Vermeulen, 'Borderline: The EU's New Border Surveillance Initiatives' (Heinrich Boll Foundation, 2012) 19.

58 Notably, under Article 2(2) of the Eurosur Regulation the use of Eurosur for the performance of border checks and air surveillance took place only on a voluntary basis if Member States provided such information. Furthermore, Eurosur information must not be used for any legal or administrative measure taken once the responsible authorities of a

and to increase reaction capability for the purposes of border management, including the detection, prevention and combating of illegal immigration and cross-border crime and contributing to ensuring the protection and saving the lives of migrants for the purpose of detecting, preventing and combating illegal immigration and cross-border crime and contributing to ensuring the protection and saving the lives of migrants.[59] Nevertheless, this humanitarian aim is more frequently invoked by the Commission rather than by the Member States,[60] which is why commentators have rightly argued that this appeared to be a secondary aim.[61] Similarly, the UN Special Rapporteur on the human rights of migrants has stated that the system 'is destined to become just another tool that will be at the disposal of Member States in order to secure borders and prevent arrivals, rather than a genuine life-saving tool'.[62]

In essence, Eurosur entails the setting up of an information processing factory, whereby maritime monitoring and different surveillance tools are deployed. The Eurosur Regulation mandated the creation of so-called situational pictures at different levels with the aim of improving the 'situational awareness' and increasing the 'reaction capability' at the external borders.[63] Ultimately, they allow to identify and trace events, operations and corresponding analysis relating to situations where human lives are at risk.[64] They are produced through the collection, evaluation, collation, analysis, interpretation, generation, visualization and dissemination of information. These pictures are continuously updated interfaces containing maps and reports that provide real-time information on the situations at the borders.[65] They are a 'virtual space' where information on the management of the EU's external borders is centrally compiled, sorted, selected and made accessible.[66] They consist of an events layer – reporting incidents of unauthorized border crossing and cross-border crime, an operational layer, with information on

Member State have intercepted cross-border criminal activities or unauthorised crossings by persons of the external borders.

59 Ibid art 19.

60 Bellanova and Duez (n 3) 29.

61 Jorrit Rijpma and Mathias Vermeulen, 'EUROSUR: Saving Lives or Building Borders?' (2015) 24(3) *European Security* 467. See Nicolas Nielsen, 'EU Border Surveillance System not Helping to Save Lives' (*EUobserver*, 2014), http://euobserver.com/justice/124136, accessed 12 October 2024.

62 UN General Assembly, 'Report of the Special Rapporteur on the Human Rights of Migrants, François Crépeau – Regional Study: Management of the External Borders of the European Union and Its Impact on the Human Rights of Migrants' (24 April 2013) 10, 11.

63 Eurosur Regulation, arts 8–11.

64 2019 Frontex Regulation, art 24(2).

65 Aviat (n 4).

66 Ibid.

different operations (plan, area, time and participating assets) and an analysis layer, whereby the information is analysed to attribute impact levels ('low' and 'medium' to 'high' and 'very high') to the incidents in the events layer (imagery and geo-data, key developments and indicators, analytical reports).[67]

There are three different situational pictures, in what Dijstelbloem has termed an example of infrastructural imagination:[68] the 'national situational picture' (NSP), the 'European situational picture' (ESP) and the 'specific situational picture' (SSP).[69] At the heart of these efforts are national coordination centres, which are entrusted with tasks related to the coordination, and exchange in a timely manner of information among, all authorities having responsibility for external border control at national level, as well as with the other national coordination centres and the agency.[70]

NCCs are inter alia entrusted with the key task of drawing up the NSP containing 'effective, accurate and timely information' on the state of their respective external borders. They shall establish and maintain a NSP in order to provide all authorities having responsibility for external border control at national level with effective, accurate and timely information. The authorities with which information is exchanged are search and rescue, law enforcement, asylum and immigration authorities, immigration liaison officers, and may even include in cases predefined at the national level competent authorities of a third country.[71] The majority of these centres are hosted either by the national police, the border guard or the border police of the Member States.[72] In practice, they cooperate with various authorities not listed here, such as the police, customs, coast guard, navy, tax authorities, fishery control and transport authorities, maritime authorities, army or intelligence services.[73]

The NSP is based on border section, a geographical unit,[74] and is composed of information collected from different sources:

- the national border surveillance system;
- stationary and mobile sensors operated by national authorities having responsibility for external border surveillance;

---

67 2019 Frontex Regulation, arts 24(1) and 25(3).

68 Huub Dijstelbloem, *Borders as Infrastructure: The Technopolitics of Border Control* (MIT Press 2021) 105.

69 2019 Frontex Regulation, art 20(1).

70 Ibid art 21(1).

71 Ibid arts 21(2)(b) and (i) and 21(6).

72 Commission, 'Commission Staff Working Document – Evaluation of the Regulation (EU) No 1052/2013 of the European Parliament and of the Council of 22 October 2013 establishing the European Border Surveillance System (Eurosur)' SWD (2018) 410 final, 13.

73 Ibid 15.

74 Aviat (n 4).

- patrols on border surveillance and other monitoring missions;
- local, regional and other coordination centres;
- other relevant national authorities and systems, including immigration liaison officers, operational centres and contact points;
- border checks;
- the agency;
- national coordination centres in other Member States;
- authorities of third countries based on bilateral or multilateral agreement and regional networks;
- ship reporting systems;
- other relevant European and international organizations as well as 'other sources'.[75]

This list raises concerns on the quality of information provided by third countries that could be included in the NSP and the lack of clarity raised by the term 'other sources'.

The national pictures combined with Frontex's own data form the foundation for the creation of an ESP covering the EU external borders. The ESP is also composed of information provided by immigration liaison officers, the agency, EU delegation and missions and operation in the content of the Common Security and Defence Policy, other relevant EU bodies, offices and agencies, such as Europol, authorities of third countries based on agreements of the Member States or the working arrangements of Frontex as such and other sources.[76] On the basis of the latter pictures, Frontex assigns impact levels to sections of the external land and sea borders[77] and provides 'effective, accurate and timely information and analysis, covering the external borders, the pre-frontier area and unauthorised secondary movements'.[78] Depending on the impact level, Member States have to improve their 'reaction capability' by strengthening their surveillance activities. However, the definition of this term does not include the ability to perform actions aimed at protecting the lives of migrants at the external borders.[79]

Compared to the Eurosur Regulation, which envisaged a 'common pre-frontier intelligence picture',[80] reporting on the areas beyond the external borders, the 2019 Frontex Regulation foresees the creation of SSP and

75 2019 Frontex Regulation, art 25(2).
76 Ibid art 26(2).
77 Ibid art 26(3).
78 Ibid art 26(1).
79 Council, Document 11437/12 (13 July 2012).
80 Eurosur Regulation, art 4(1)(e).

fusion services. The SSP 'transcribes an operation unit: the information displayed does not refer to the geographical unit border section, but to the unit operation x'.[81] As stressed by Aviat, in a joint operation between Montenegro, Italy and Frontex, the SSP will not cover the geographic area (Adriatic Sea), but rather the joint operation as such and the information may comprise of partly the NSP, the ESP and data relevant to the operation stemming from outside the EU.[82] According to Article 27 of the 2019 Frontex Regulation, the SSP is shared with international organizations[83] and third countries,[84] according to rules set out in the operational plan of the operation and a dedicated agreement, as well as subject to the principle of the originator's consent,[85] and possibly in an automated manner, without human intervention.[86]

Finally, the agency coordinates the so-called Fusion Services supplying the NCCs, the Commission and itself with information on the external borders and on the pre-frontier area on a regular, reliable and cost-efficient basis.[87] This information may stem from various sources, namely:

- the selective monitoring of designated third-country ports and coasts or pre-frontier areas;
- the tracking of vessels or other craft over high seas and the tracking of aircraft used for irregular immigration or cross-border crime, including in the case of persons in distress at sea;
- monitoring of designated areas in the maritime or air domain to detect, identify and track vessels, aircraft or other forms of equipment;
- environmental assessment of designated areas in the maritime domain and at the external land and air borders in order to optimize monitoring and patrolling activities;
- monitoring migratory flows in terms of trends, volume and routes;
- media monitoring, open source intelligence and analysis of internet activities; and
- analysis of information derived from large-scale information systems for the purpose of detecting changing routes and methods used for irregular immigration and cross-border crime.[88]

81 Aviat (n 4).
82 Ibid. See also 2019 Frontex Regulation, art 27(2).
83 Those listed in the 2019 Frontex Regulation, art 68(1).
84 Ibid art 27(1).
85 Ibid art 27(1) and (3).
86 Aviat (n 4).
87 2019 Frontex Regulation, art 28(1).
88 Ibid art 28(2).

The Fusion Services use optical and radar satellite technology to locate vessels suspected to be engaged in human smuggling and endangering individuals' lives at sea. Many of the services are delivered in cooperation with the European Maritime Safety Agency and the EU Satellite Centre.[89]

3.2 Eurosur: an accountability diffuser fuelling Frontex's rule of law deficit

The previous paragraphs show that areas beyond the external borders are also placed under surveillance, highlighting the agency's strong extraterritorial dimension and its close cooperation with third countries.[90] As such, Eurosur is symptomatic of the growing trend to focus on the external dimension of this policy area by co-opting third countries as gatekeepers with the EU, thus effectively expanding its border controls far beyond the physical borderline. It is also a paradigmatic example of a surveillance system underpinned by a preventive security approach based on pre-emptive risk assessment.[91] Eurosur's objective is to anticipate both geographically and temporally border crossing, by categorizing circulations based on their degree of riskiness, with person seeking into the EU being also grouped according to the degree of risk that can be inferred from their practices of circulation.[92] This pre-emptive border security approach generates important rule of law challenges adding to existing rule of law deficit in ensuring the accountability of Frontex operations, as discussed in Chapters 5 and 6. As highlighted by Aviat, the information built in the pictures helps strengthen the intelligence capabilities of third countries on the migratory routes of people, and the information gathered feeds the European situational awareness[93] and can lead to preventing individuals from reaching the EU territory through pushbacks and pullbacks in violation of the principle of *non-refoulement*. Eurosur adds a degree of remoteness in cases where the system produces intelligence resulting in the deflection of immigration flows already in the territory of third states[94] and thus diffuses the responsibility of the agency for violations for fundamental rights. As such, the technological intervention through Eurosur creates an additional layer of complexity in promoting Frontex's accountability. The

---

89 Quintel (n 4) 177.

90 A cross-border crime as 'any serious crime with a cross-border dimension committed at, along or *in the proximity of the external borders*', that is beyond the external border (emphasis added). See Article 3(c) of the Eurosur Regulation and Article 2(12) of the 2019 Frontex Regulation.

91 Valsamis Mitsilegas, 'Reconceptualising Security in the Law of the European Union' (European Papers, forthcoming).

92 Jeandesboz (n 3); Tazzioli (n 3).

93 Aviat (n 4).

94 Mitsilegas (n 92).

rule of law challenges are exacerbated by the lack of clarity in the working agreements on the basis of which information is shared with third countries as regards the types and the ways in which data are exchanged. This lack of clarity is particularly present in Frontex's delegated agreements, which provide specific information on the technical requirements and practical aspects of information exchange.[95] Regrettably, these agreements are not published as they contain sensitive information. The lack of transparency into Frontex's cooperation with third countries has thus a knock-on effect on Eurosur as well; the latter carries and exacerbates the agency's rule of law deficit.

3.3 The murky landscape regarding the processing of personal data by Eurosur

The drawing up of the pictures discussed earlier rests upon the collection and processing of a wide-ranging, heterogeneous and non-exhaustive ensemble of human and technological components: satellites, drones (unmanned aerial vehicles), stationary and mobile sensors, vessels and boats reporting systems, private companies, national and European experts' groups, patrols, information from Frontex, other Member States or third countries.[96] The information varies from raw data, such as images from drones and radars, to more subjective analytical elements, such as key developments and indicators relevant for the analysis of irregular migration and cross-border crime, risk rating trends, migrant profiles and routes. It has been reported that mobile radars and thermal cameras mounted on vehicles, as well as heartbeat detectors and CO_2 monitors used to detect signs of people concealed inside vehicles can also be used.[97] Research and innovation are part of Frontex's mandate and significant emphasis has been placed on tools predicting migration flows (such as ITFlows) and improving maritime surveillance capabilities (I-Seamore).[98]

The technical advantage is that the wide variety of information is centralized, updated and displayed on a single interface. Furthermore,

[95] Luisa Marin, 'The Cooperation Between Frontex and Third Countries in Information Sharing: Practices, Law and Challenges in Externalizing Border Control Functions' (2020) 26(1) *European Public Law* 157. See Aviat (n 4).

[96] Eurosur Regulation, art 9(2).

[97] Kaamil Ahmed and Lorenzo Tondo, 'Fortress Europe: The Millions Spent on Military-grade Tech to Deter Refugees' (*The Guardian*, 6 December 2021), https://www.theguardian.com/global-development/2021/dec/06/fortress-europe-the-millions-spent-on-military-grade-tech-to-deter-refugees, accessed 12 October 2024.

[98] See https://www.frontex.europa.eu/innovation/eu-research/horizon-projects/, accessed 12 October 2024.

Eurosur is perceived as contributing to the international framework on search and rescue through raising situational awareness.[99] However, its operative status is somewhat surrounded by secrecy, and it is hard to pinpoint its everyday role in the fabrication and management of the EU external border. This is particularly exemplified by the shortage of documentation on its operation, which beyond the Practical Handbook for implementing and managing Eurosur and Implementing Regulation (EU) 2021/581 of 9 April 2021 on the situational pictures does not exist.[100]

A key question that emerges in this context concerns the processing of personal data within Eurosur. As Marin and Krajcíková have stressed, at its core Eurosur constitutes a mass surveillance tool enabling exchange of data, including personal data on a massive scale.[101] This is true, but to demonstrate so, it is important to understand where personal data may be processed within Eurosur.

Article 46(1)(e) of the 2016 Frontex Regulation stated that processing of personal data was possible in the identifying and tracking vessels. Indeed, Article 13 of the Eurosur Regulation provided for the applicability of EU data protection law where NSPs are used for the processing of personal data, but the ESP and the common pre-frontier intelligence picture may be used only for the processing of personal data concerning ship identification numbers. This signified that the NSP could be used for the processing of personal data also in other cases, beyond the identification and tracking of vessels. Those data must be processed in accordance with the then applicable Frontex rules – the founding Council Regulation (EC) No 2007/2004. They must automatically be deleted within seven days of receipt by the agency or, where additional time is needed in order to track a vessel, within two months of receipt by the agency.

The 2019 Frontex Regulation leaves this matter more open for debate. Personal data could be processed within the framework of Eurosur Fusion Services and national situational pictures. With regard to the execution of Eurosur Fusion Services, Article 28(2)(h) foresees the application of Regulation (EU) 2016/679 (EU Data Protection Regulation – GDPR) and Directive 2016/680[102] (Law Enforcement

---

99 Rijpma (n 54) 238.

100 Annex to the Commission Recommendation adopting the Practical Handbook for implementing and managing the European Border Surveillance System (EUROSUR Handbook) C (2015) 9206 final.

101 Marin and Krajcíková (n 20).

102 Regulation (EU) 2016/679 of the European Parliament and of the Council of 27 April 2016 on the protection of natural persons with regard to the processing of personal data and on the free movement of such data, and repealing Directive 95/46/EC (General Data Protection Regulation – GDPR) [2016] OJ L119/1.

Directive)[103] as regards the processing of media monitoring, open source intelligence and analysis of internet activities, which means that at least in that regard it is possible for personal data to be processed. Furthermore, the analysis of information derived from large-scale information systems entails the processing of personal data. Importantly, Article 89 of the 2019 Frontex Regulation clearly leaves the possibility open for personal data to be processed within the framework of the NSPs.[104] It is foreseen that ship and aircraft identification numbers must be the only personal data that are permitted to be accessed in the ESP and SSP and the Eurosur Fusion Services.[105] However, the processing of personal data on an exceptional basis beyond this is also possible but 'any such processing shall be strictly limited to what is necessary for the purposes of Eurosur'.[106]

Similarly, it is foreseen that any exchange of personal data with third countries must be strictly limited to what is absolutely necessary,[107] but it is prohibited to exchange information that could be used to 'identify persons or groups of persons whose request for access to international protection is under examination or who are under a serious risk of being subjected to torture, inhuman and degrading treatment or punishment, or any other violation of fundamental rights'.[108] Whereas this is a necessary safeguard, it is difficult to be reconciled with practices of preventing people from reaching the EU external border via pushback or pull back operations, whereby the individual cases are not *a priori* known to the domestic authorities of the Member States which share such information. Furthermore, since the transmission may involve data from Frontex, thus transmission necessarily carries an EU law dimension, there must be a mechanism for verifying all information that is shared with third countries by an independent actor, who will regularly assess the type of information transmitted.[109] Coupled with the lack of clarity regarding the working arrangements of Frontex, as discussed earlier, the regulation of transfers of Eurosur data remains particularly opaque.

---

103 Directive (EU) 2016/680 of the European Parliament and of the Council of 27 April 2016 on the protection of natural persons with regard to the processing of personal data by competent authorities for the purposes of the prevention, investigation, detection or prosecution of criminal offences or the execution of criminal penalties, and on the free movement of such data, and repealing Council Framework Decision 2008/977/JHA [2016] OJ L119/89.

104 Also see 2019 Frontex Regulation, art 87(1)(f).

105 Ibid art 89(2).

106 Ibid art 89(3).

107 Ibid art 89(4).

108 Ibid art 89(5).

109 EU Fundamental Rights Agency, 'Fundamental Rights at Europe's Southern Sea Borders' (2012) p 61.

These provisions require further attention; in essence Eurosur does not provide any clarity as to what other personal data may be processed within NSPs, except the ship and aircraft identification numbers.[110] Indeed, with data received from ship reporting systems, drones and satellite images constituting a key element of Eurosur, it is likely that the images that the system takes when monitoring vessels, coasts or ports will also depict individuals, who may be identifiable, especially if these images are then compared to the facial images stored in EU or national large-scale IT systems. Drones in particular have the capacity to spot small boats from great distance and are fitted with thermal cameras that allow the detection of human movements. Their ability of being concealed and controlled remotely may generate the feeling of constant, secret surveillance. They can also autonomously collect images that they capture while flying and automatically transfer them to situational pictures without the intervention of a human agent.[111] Besides, how the information acquired by drones is processed as well as the purposes for which that information is used and by whom is utterly non-transparent.[112] Images that allow for identification of persons or groups of persons constitute personal data within the definition of personal data under the GDPR and it is also possible that the more advanced and sophisticated technologies are deployed within Eurosur, for instance through facial recognition technology, the more likely it is that such images allow for identification of individuals, for example, in vessels in distress. This is one example of personal data processing, but the lack of clarity in the 2019 Frontex Regulation creates significant opacity as the personal data processed and more categories of personal data may be processed through different tools deployed at national level. Interestingly, that amorphous personal data can be transferred to third countries,[113] even if those individuals could be then identified, provided that their request for access to international protection is not under examination or they are not under a serious risk of being subjected to torture, inhuman and degrading treatment or punishment, or any other violation of fundamental rights. The keeping of records of processing activities, as required by Article 89(6) of the 2019 Frontex Regulation, is particularly important so that national data protection authorities and the EDPS could supervise this aspect of Eurosur and provide clarity in this murky landscape. This is all the more important

[110] Daniel Deibler, 'EUROSUR – A Sci-fi Border Zone Patrolled by Drones?' in Jan Camenisch, Simone Fischer-Hübner and Marit Hansen (eds), *Privacy and Identity Management for the Future Internet in the Age of Globalisation: Privacy and Identity* (Springer 2015) 102.

[111] Aviat (n 4).

[112] Gandhi (n 4) 5.

[113] Also see 2019 Frontex Regulation, art 75.

considering that there is no specific retention period of the personal data in the 2019 Frontex Regulation – as opposed to the 2013 Eurosur Regulation, as discussed earlier. Article 40(2) of Implementing Regulation (EU) 2021/581 on the situational pictures states that personal data shall be deleted as soon as the purpose for which they have been collected has been achieved. This provision should not have been embedded in an Implementing Regulation as this is not a technical matter. Importantly, the provision in question is not clear at all regarding how long personal data can be retained.

Furthermore, there are no provisions substantially regulating the collection and processing of personal data, issues that remain at the discretion of Member States as long as these are compatible with the GDPR and the Law Enforcement Directive. The 2013 Eurosur Regulation stated in its Recital 13 that such processing must be an exception. That pronouncement did not seem realistic as even before the operation of Eurosur, nine NCCs confirmed the processing of personal data, whereas only two Member States stated that they were not planning on handling personal data for border surveillance purposes.[114] At the same time, Frontex claimed that during joint operations personal data was not exchanged through the Eurosur communication network, thus national structures were preferred for that purpose.[115] However, there was no information as regards other aspects of Frontex mandate, such as risk analysis. The 2019 Frontex Regulation does not state that the processing of personal data constitutes an exception, but equally does not regulate the processing within NSPs, ESPs and Fusion Services. The lack of any sector-specific data protection rules governing the operation of Eurosur is particularly problematic. Unlawful data collected at the national level may be exchanged with other Member States, institutions and agencies without any previous delimitation of the scope, categories of data, retention and use. How can surveillance at the national level and the unquestionable exchange of the proceeds of such surveillance be conducted without accompanying the rules on exchange with safeguards on the initial stage of collection and processing at the national level?[116] Moreover, the Regulation does not prescribe any rules regarding the centralized storage of information or events taking place at the border within EU-wide and Frontex-managed databases.

[114] Commission, 'Commission Staff Working Paper – Impact Assessment Accompanying the Proposal for a Regulation of the European Parliament and of the Council Establishing the European Border Surveillance System (EUROSUR)' SEC (2011) 1538 final, 31–32.

[115] Frontex, 'Report to the European Parliament and the Council on Art 22(2) of Regulation (EU) No 1052/2013 – The Functioning of Eurosur' (1 December 2015) 8.

[116] See Article 29 Data Protection Working Party, 'Letter to the Commissioner for Home Affairs Ms. Cecilia Malmström Regarding the Proposal for a Regulation Establishing the European Border Surveillance System' (12 June 2012) 1, 2.

The vagueness of the provisions has been coupled with the introduction of novel principles in the Eurosur Regulation, such as the principle of flexibility and the principle of information sharing, which demonstrate the 'foggy' legal framework.[117] Another point of concern involves the re-enactment of elements that were initially developed for a specific purpose within a different discourse; in other words, Eurosur enables the repackaging of information collected for significant purposes and its use for other aims.[118] This is particularly important if one considers that the mandate of Eurosur encompasses both migration and criminal justice objectives. In this context, another worrisome element involves the lack of a definition as to which crimes fall within the remits of Eurosur. According to Article 3(e) of the Eurosur Regulation, cross-border crime constituted 'any serious crime with a cross-border dimension committed at along or in the proximity of the external borders'. The same definition is included in Article 2(12) of the 2019 Frontex Regulation. In *Kennedy v UK*, where the applicant claimed that the term 'serious crime' as set out in the British act in question was not sufficiently clear, the European Court of Human Rights opined that as long as the term is further clarified in the interpretative provisions of the contested act and the act itself, the foreseeability requirement would be met, which is not the case of Eurosur.[119]

4 Conclusion

This chapter highlighted how the operation of Eurosur encompasses a 'foggy' information-exchange architecture, which raises significant rule of law challenges in terms of diffusing responsibility and accountability and in terms of concealing through broad flexibility the processing of personal data of individuals. The chapter stressed that Eurosur essentially constitutes a tool of mass surveillance, which extends extraterritorially beyond the EU/Schengen borders; this extensive geographical scope of Eurosur coupled with the broad and marked by secrecy leeway for transfer of data, including personal data, to third countries creates a layer of complexity in ensuring Frontex's accountability, especially in cases where the information provided results in deflecting immigration flows already in the territory of third states. The analysis further demonstrated that the 2019 Frontex Regulation, much like the Eurosur Regulation, does not provide sufficient clarity regarding the

[117] See Annex to Eurosur Regulation. According to the principle of flexibility, 'organisation, information and technology shall be designed to enable the EUROSUR stakeholders to react to changing situations in a flexible and structured manner'.

[118] Bellanova and Duez (n 3) 33.

[119] *Kennedy v UK* (2011) 52 EHRR 4, para 159.

processing of personal data in terms of whether personal data are processed, how they are collected as well as how they are stored and further processed at the national and EU level, thus in clear violation of the legality principle. Overall, the chapter demonstrates through the example of Eurosur how technological advancements exacerbate rule of law challenges in favour of promoting a securitized, preventive risk-based approach, whereby deflecting migration flows takes precedence over saving them.

8

EU Large-scale IT Systems for Third-country Nationals Beyond the Rule of Law

1 Introduction

Chapter 7 highlighted the rule of law challenges raised by the establishment and operation of Eurosur and the role of Frontex in this context as an emerging information hub for migration at the European Union (EU) level. In this chapter, the analysis on how the development and use of new technologies in the border controls erodes the rule of law is shifted to examine the primary manifestation of digitalization of EU immigration and asylum policy; the setting up, operation and reconfiguration of EU/Schengen-wide large-scale IT systems. This 'millefeuille' of IT systems concerns the currently operational Schengen Information System (SIS), Visa Information System (VIS) and Eurodac, as well as the forthcoming Entry/Exit System (EES), the European Travel Information and Authorisation System (ETIAS) and the European Criminal Record Information System for Third-country Nationals (ECRIS-TCN). The IT systems store and further process different categories of personal data from various groups of third-country nationals, which are then accessed and consulted by a wide array of national authorities and some EU agencies, such as Frontex, Europol or the European Union Agency for Asylum (EUAA) for a series of purposes, from immigration-related to (more controversially) law enforcement. The IT systems are scheduled to become interoperable, in other words, the personal data stored will be interconnected in various ways, by 2027.

Whereas the IT systems have been on the academic radar for around two decades, legal scholarship has primarily been focused on the fundamental rights concerns raised by their operation.[1] In turn, the rule of law challenges have largely evaded scholarly attention. This chapter will provide an

[1] See among others Niovi Vavoula, *Immigration and Privacy in the Law of the European Union: The Case of Information Systems* (Brill Nijhoff 2022); Stephen Kabera Karanja,

anthology of the rule of law challenges focusing on three key manifestations of the rule of law deficit: first, the prevalence of the technical aspects over legality; second, the blurring of the boundaries between migration and law enforcement; and, third, the significant legal obstacles inherent in the operation of IT systems as multinational in accessing judicial protection.

2 The emergence of a complex architecture of interoperable large-scale IT systems for third-country nationals

At EU level, the use of digital technologies in the field of migration, asylum and border management is not a new phenomenon; it goes back to the late 1980s and has been inextricably linked with the abolition of internal border controls and the development of a borderless Schengen area. The establishment of the Schengen area as a space of free movement of persons has been accompanied by common policies on the management of the external (Schengen) borders, on visas and police cooperation.[2] Their aim has been to ensure a high level of internal security, prevent irregular immigration and filter out perceived 'risky' migrants and asylum seekers, considering that anyone who crossed the external borders would then be able to freely circulate within the area.[3] An indispensable component in this respect has been the development of EU/Schengen-wide large-scale IT systems (databases) to enable the storage and further processing of personal data collected from different groups of third-country nationals in various administrative and law enforcement settings.

Transparency and Proportionality in the Schengen Information System and Border Control Co-operation (Martinus Nijhoff 2008); Evelien Brouwer, *Digital Borders and Real Rights: Effective Remedies for Third-Country Nationals in the Schengen Information System* (Martinus Nijhoff 2008); Annaliese Baldaccini, 'Counter-Terrorism and the EU Strategy for Border Security: Framing Suspects with Biometric Documents and Databases' (2008) 10(1) *European Journal of Migration and Law* 31; Valsamis Mitsilegas, 'Border Security in the European Union: Towards Centralised Controls and Maximum Surveillance' in Elspeth Guild, Helen Toner and Annaliese Baldaccini (eds), *Whose Freedom, Security and Justice? EU Immigration and Asylum Law and Policy* (Hart 2007); 'The Border Paradox: The Surveillance of Movement in a Union without Internal Frontiers' in Hans Lindahl (ed), *A Right to Inclusion and Exclusion? Normative Fault Lines of the EU's Area of Freedom, Security and Justice* (Hart 2009).

2 Agreement between the Governments of the States of the Benelux Economic Union, the Federal Republic of Germany and the French Republic on the gradual abolition of checks at their common borders, Schengen Agreement [2000] OJ L 239/13.

3 Thomas Gammeltoft-Hansen, 'Filtering Out the Risky Migrant: Migration Control, Risk Theory and the EU' Akademiet for Migrationsstudier i Danmark, Aalborg Universitet (2006).

2.1 The first generation of IT systems

Perhaps the best-known database is SIS, the purpose of which is to maintain a high level of security within the Schengen area.[4] At the heart of the compensatory measures for the abolition of internal border controls, SIS registers 'alerts' on various categories of persons and objects, for example, people wanted for arrest for extradition, or persons or objects subject to discreet inquiry or specific checks.[5] In addition, it stores alerts on third-country nationals to be refused entry into or stay in the Schengen area,[6] or who are subject to return proceedings.[7] Hence, by its very hybrid nature, SIS serves as both immigration and criminal law instrument and essentially has two branches; immigration and law enforcement. In connection to each alert, the system stores basic alphanumeric information, as well as biometric data (dactyloscopic data, facial images and DNA files)[8] and alerts based on different legal bases can be interlinked. SIS is complemented by SIRENE, an auxiliary system that enables searches for supplementary information in cases of a 'hit' at the national level.

VIS was conceptualized in the aftermath of the 9/11 events[9] to modernize the administration, issuance and checks of short-stay visas by enabling the exchange of personal data on visa applicants.[10] Its overarching aim is

---

4 The legal bases of SIS are: Regulation (EU) 2018/1860 of the European Parliament and of the Council of 28 November 2018 on the use of the Schengen Information System for the return of illegally staying third-country nationals [2018] OJ L 312/1 (SIS Regulation for return); Regulation (EU) 2018/1862 of the European Parliament and of the Council of 28 November 2018 on the establishment, operation and use of the Schengen Information System (SIS) in the field of police cooperation and judicial cooperation in criminal matters, amending and repealing Council Decision 2007/533/JHA, and repealing Regulation (EC) No 1986/2006 of the European Parliament and of the Council and Commission Decision 2010/261/EU [2018] OJ L 312/56 (SIS Regulation regarding police and judicial cooperation in criminal matters); Regulation (EU) 2018/1861 of the European Parliament and of the Council of 28 November 2018 on the establishment, operation and use of the Schengen Information System (SIS) in the field of border checks, and amending the Convention implementing the Schengen Agreement, and amending and repealing Regulation (EC) No 1987/2006 [2018] OJ L 312/14 (SIS Regulation for border checks).

5 For these alerts see SIS Regulation regarding police cooperation and judicial cooperation in criminal matters, arts 26–41.

6 SIS Regulation for border checks, arts 20–31.

7 SIS Regulation for return, art 3.

8 SIS Regulation regarding police cooperation and judicial cooperation in criminal matters, arts 42–43.

9 Baldaccini (n 1).

10 Council Decision 2004/512/EC of 8 June 2004 establishing the Visa Information System (VIS) [2004] OJ L 213/5; Regulation (EC) 767/2008 of the European Parliament and of the Council of 9 July 2008 concerning the Visa Information System (VIS) and the exchange of data between Member States on short-stay visas (VIS Regulation) [2008] OJ L 218/60, as amended by Regulation (EC) No 810/2009 of the European Parliament

to assist in the development of the common visa policy, however, no less than seven wide-ranging sub-purposes are set out, among which is the prevention of threats to the internal security of the EU Member States. To that end, a separate instrument has been adopted, Decision 2008633/JHA (VIS Decision),[11] that lays down the modalities by which visa data may be consulted by law enforcement authorities and Europol. In 2021, the VIS legal framework was reformed, extending the personal scope of VIS to long-stay visa applicants and residence permits applicants.[12] Overall, the system stores a broad range of personal data, including fingerprints and photographs of all persons subject to VIS requirements for individuals as young as six years old, irrespective of the status of their application.[13] A novelty of the 2021 revision is that under the new rules personal data from the Schengen visa applications must be subject to automated processing, consisting of checks against European and international databases and algorithms.

Eurodac first became operational in 2003 as the 'path tracker' of the Common European Asylum System, aimed to assist in the implementation of the Dublin system on the allocation of the Member State responsible for examining an application for international protection.[14] To that end, the system has processed the fingerprints of applicants for international protection over the age of 14,[15] as well as those persons found irregularly crossing the

---

and of the Council of 13 July 2009 establishing a Community Code on Visas (Visa Code) [2009] OJ L 243/1 (VIS Regulation).

[11] Council Decision 2008/633/JHA of 23 June 2008 concerning access for consultation of the Visa Information System (VIS) by designated authorities of Member States and by Europol for the purposes of the prevention, detection and investigation of terrorist offences and of other serious criminal offences [2008] OJ L 218/129 (VIS Decision). The need for a separate EU instrument is attributed to the then pillar structure.

[12] Regulation (EU) 2021/1134 of the European Parliament and of the Council of 7 July 2021 amending Regulations (EC) No 767/2008, (EC) No 810/2009, (EU) 2016/399, (EU) 2017/2226, (EU) 2018/1240, (EU) 2018/1860, (EU) 2018/1861, (EU) 2019/817 and (EU) 2019/1896 of the European Parliament and of the Council and repealing Council Decisions 2004/512/EC and 2008/633/JHA, for the purpose of reforming the Visa Information System [2021] OJ L 248/11 (revised VIS Regulation).

[13] Ibid art 9.

[14] Regulation 603/2013 Regulation (EU) No 603/2013 of the European Parliament and of the Council of 26 June 2013 on the establishment of 'Eurodac' for the comparison of fingerprints for the effective application of Regulation (EU) No 604/2013 establishing the criteria and mechanisms for determining the Member State responsible for examining an application for international protection lodged in one of the Member States by a third-country national or a stateless person and on requests for the comparison with Eurodac data by Member States' law enforcement authorities and Europol for law enforcement purposes, and amending Regulation (EU) No 1077/2011 establishing a European Agency for the operational management of large-scale IT systems in the area of freedom, security and justice (recast) [2013] OJ L 180/1 (recast Eurodac Regulation).

[15] Ibid arts 9–13.

external borders or staying on national territory,[16] to check whether these have already been recorded by another Member State. If a Eurodac check reveals that the fingerprints have already been recorded, the individual may be sent to that Member State. With the revision of the Eurodac via Regulation 603/3013, the system has been opened up for consultation by national law enforcement authorities and Europol.[17] In 2024, the revised Eurodac rules were adopted; among the reforms, Regulation (EU) 2024/1358 prescribes that the system will be used for additional migration-related purposes, such as resettlement and returns, and will store additional categories of personal data apart from fingerprints – the threshold for which is lowered to six years, including biographical information, facial images and copies of travel documents.[18]

2.2 The second generation of IT systems

Since 2015, the so-called 'refugee crisis' coupled with the various terrorist events reinvigorated the techno-solutionist drive, and information gaps in the EU's technological architecture were equated with security gaps.[19] On top of reforms to the existing IT systems, three additional ones were designed and several interoperability components – that is technological tools aimed at interconnecting in various ways the systems – were conceived to fill in those gaps.

In particular, influenced by similar initiatives in the United States, the EES was adopted in November 2017 as a multi-purpose tool to enhance

[16] Ibid arts 14–17.

[17] Niovi Vavoula, 'The Recast Eurodac Regulation: Are Asylum Seekers Treated as Suspected Criminals?' in Céline Bauloz, Celine Bauloz, Sarah Singer and Vladislava Stoyanova (eds), *Seeking Asylum in the European Union: Selected Protection Issues Raised by the Second Phase of the Common European Asylum System* (Brill 2015).

[18] Regulation (EU) 2024/1358 of the European Parliament and of the Council of 14 May 2024 on the establishment of 'Eurodac' for the comparison of biometric data in order to effectively apply Regulations (EU) 2024/1351 and (EU) 2024/1350 of the European Parliament and of the Council and Council Directive 2001/55/EC and to identify illegally staying third-country nationals and stateless persons and on requests for the comparison with Eurodac data by Member States' law enforcement authorities and Europol for law enforcement purposes, amending Regulations (EU) 2018/1240 and (EU) 2019/818 of the European Parliament and of the Council and repealing Regulation (EU) No 603/2013 of the European Parliament and of the Council [2024] OJ L 2024/1358. For an analysis, see Niovi Vavoula, 'The Transformation of Eurodac from an Asylum Tool into an Immigration Database' (*EU Migration and Asylum Blog*, 16 October 2024), https://eumigrationlawblog.eu/the-transformation-of-eurodac-from-an-asylum-tool-into-an-immigration-database/, accessed 20 October 2024.

[19] Commission, 'Stronger and Smarter Information Systems for Borders and Security' (Communication) COM(2016) 205 final.

the efficiency and automation of border checks; assist in the identification of irregular migrants and overstayers; combat identity fraud and misuse of travel documents; and strengthen internal security by allowing law enforcement authorities access to travel history records.[20] It is designed to record the identities of short-stay travellers irrespective of whether they are subject to visa requirements, by storing alphanumeric data, four fingerprints and a facial image, along with details of their travel documents, which will be linked to electronic entry and exit records.

ETIAS will require all visa-free travellers to the Schengen area to undergo a pre-screening process to obtain authorization prior to their departure by applying online and disclosing a series of personal data in what could be described as a 'light' visa process.[21] The pre-screening and provision of authorization shall take place on the basis of cross-checking against:

- data held in existing immigration and law enforcement databases, thus enabling the use of data from other sources;
- screening rules enabling profiling on the basis of risk indicators;[22] and
- a special ETIAS watchlist of individuals suspected of having participated in terrorism or other serious crimes or in respect of whom there are factual indications or reasonable grounds to believe that they will commit such offences.[23]

The latest member in the IT systems family is ECRIS-TCN.[24] This emerged as a necessity in the law enforcement context, as in order to obtain complete information on previous convictions of third-country

[20] Regulation (EU) 2017/2226 of the European Parliament and of the Council of 30 November 2017 establishing an Entry/Exit System (EES) to register entry and exit data and refusal of entry data of third-country nationals crossing the external borders of the Member States and determining the conditions for access to the EES for law enforcement purposes, and amending the Convention implementing the Schengen Agreement and Regulations (EC) No 767/2008 and (EU) No 1077/2011 [2017] OJ L 327/20 (EES Regulation).

[21] Regulation (EU) 2018/1240 Regulation (EU) 2018/1240 of the European Parliament and of the Council of 12 September 2018 establishing a European Travel Information and Authorisation System (ETIAS) and amending Regulations (EU) No 1077/2011, (EU) No 515/2014, (EU) 2016/399, (EU) 2016/1624 and (EU) 2017/2226 [2018] OJ L 61/1 (ETIAS Regulation).

[22] Ibid art 33.

[23] Ibid art 34.

[24] Regulation (EU) 2019/816 of the European Parliament and of the Council of 17 April 2019 establishing a centralised system for the identification of Member States holding conviction information on third-country nationals and stateless persons (ECRIS-TCN) to supplement the European Criminal Records Information System and amending Regulation (EU) 2018/1726 [2019] OJ L135/1 (ECRIS-TCN Regulation).

nationals, states were obliged to send 'blanket requests' to all other Member States. The ECRIS-TCN will be a centralized system for the exchange of criminal records on convicted third-country nationals and stateless persons, including dual nationals, and is meant to complement the already existing, decentralized ECRIS system through which information on the criminal records of EU nationals is exchanged. A novelty of ECRIS-TCN is that an EU database primarily set up in the context of judicial cooperation may be used for immigration control purposes if allowed and in accordance with national laws.

2.3 Synthesis

In light of this, one could distinguish a series of characteristics common to all systems; first, they primarily process personal data of *different categories of third-country nationals*, be it asylum seekers, refugees, irregular migrants, short-stay tourists subject to visa requirements or visa-free travellers and convicted criminals. EU citizens are not entirely let off the hook, but their personal data are only processed in an incremental manner, for example, by the law enforcement branch of SIS. There can be some overlapping as to the categories of individuals affected,[25] but the full picture – or 'puzzle' – is only revealed if all systems are viewed collectively.[26] In relation to each third-country national every database stores and enables the further processing of *a wide range of personal data* (from standard biographical or travel documentation data to biometric data) in various fora and contexts; before their entry, at the borders, on national territory and after they leave. Databases are *adaptable, flexible and dynamic* in nature. This is particularly exemplified by the progressive beefing up of information systems with additional functionalities and new purposes, as a response to perceived threats to the EU, primarily linked to terrorism, and the evolving digital technologies. As a result, the systems are used for a multiplicity of –often diverging – purposes spanning from modernizing immigration control to law enforcement, thus heavily blurring the boundaries between immigration and criminal law.[27] Indeed, every system is at the disposal of national law enforcement authorities, at least to a certain extent, either because of its direct law enforcement (security) mandate, as in the cases of SIS and ECRIS-TCN, or because

[25] For example, both Eurodac and SIS store records on irregular migrants. EES will monitor the movement of third-country nationals covered by VIS and ETIAS. Convicted individuals' data will be stored in both SIS and ECRIS-TCN.

[26] Niovi Vavoula, 'The "Puzzle" of EU Large-Scale Information Systems for Third-Country Nationals: Surveillance of Movement and Its Challenges for Privacy and Data Protection' (2020) 45(3) *European Law Review* 348.

[27] Mitsilegas (n 1).

criminal law is listed as an ancillary objective, as in the cases of Eurodac, VIS, EES and ETIAS.

2.4 Interoperability: the missing glue

This already elaborate landscape is further complexified by the design of several interoperability components. For years, the evolution of IT systems followed a gradual, *compartmentalized*, salami approach, whereby each system was established under different institutional, legal and policy contexts, whereas the data pots remained air-gapped, separate from each other, without the possibility to establish direct communication among them. Regulations 2019/817 and 2018/818 (the Interoperability Regulations) aim to alter this structure by allowing the underlying systems to interconnect in a variety of ways.[28] They establish several tools designed to process all the data collected by each individual system and generate combined results.

In particular, the European Search Portal will enable competent authorities to simultaneously query the underlying systems to which they have access and the combined results will be displayed on one single screen.[29] Even though the screen will indicate in which databases the information is held, access rights will remain unaltered and will proceed following the rules of each database.[30] The shared Biometric Matching Service (sBMS) will generate and store biometric templates obtained from all biometric data registered in each underlying system and compare them to the biometric data of new applicants to detect possible matches (biometric identification).[31] It thus effectively becomes a new database compiling biometric templates from the SIS, VIS, Eurodac, EES and ECRIS-TCN, and will substitute separate searches. The Multiple Identity Detector (MID) will enable the

[28] Regulation (EU) 2019/817 of the European Parliament and of the Council of 20 May 2019 on establishing a framework for interoperability between EU information systems in the field of borders and visa and amending Regulations (EC) No 767/2008, (EU) 2016/399, (EU) 2017/2226, (EU) 2018/1240, (EU) 2018/1726 and (EU) 2018/1861 and Council Decisions 2004/512/EC and 2008/633/JHA [2019] OJ L 135/27; Regulation (EU) 2019/818 of the European Parliament and of the Council of 20 May 2019 on establishing a framework for interoperability between EU information systems in the field of police and judicial cooperation, asylum and migration and amending Regulations (EU) 2018/1726, (EU) 2018/1862 and (EU) 2019/816 [2019] OJ L 135/85 (collectively Interoperability Regulations).

[29] Interoperability Regulations, arts 6–11.

[30] Ibid recital 15.

[31] Ibid arts 12–16. Biometric templates are personal data. The template does not contain the full (biometric) information as contained in the collected sample, but only represents the particular features selected by the algorithm(s). See Els Kindt, *Privacy and Data Protection Issues of Biometric Identifiers* (Springer 2013) 98.

automated identification of third-country nationals based on alphanumeric data to detect those who have used multiple identities, constituting, thus, a complementary identification system to the sBMS based on non-biometric data.[32] It will create links between identical data to indicate whether the individual is lawfully registered in more than one system or whether identity fraud is suspected. Therefore, its dual purpose is to facilitate identity checks for *bona fide* travellers and combat identity fraud.[33] Four types of links are envisaged; white (in the case of clear identity);[34] yellow (in the case of unclear identity);[35] green (in the cases of confused identity, such as two different persons with similar data);[36] and red (in the case of identity fraud).[37] The Common Identity Repository (CIR) will store an individual file for each person registered in the systems (except SIS) containing both biometric and biographical data as well as a reference indicating the system from which the data were retrieved.[38] Its main objectives are to enable identification of third-country nationals without (proper) travel documents, assist in the detection of individuals with multiple identities and streamline the procedure for consulting databases for law enforcement purposes.[39] As regards the latter issue, a two-step process is foreseen. In the first step, a law enforcement officer shall be able to query all systems at once so as to identify whether any records on an individual exist in any of these without obtaining prior authorization or need to fulfil specific conditions. In the event of a 'hit', the officer will request full access to those information systems that generated hits. The officer would need to justify the need to access these systems through the procedure prescribed for each database and subject to prior authorization by a designated authority (hit-flag procedure).[40] Finally, the Common Repository for Reporting and Statistics (CRRS) will provide cross-system statistical data and analytical reports for policy, operational and data quality purposes.[41] One of these operational purposes is the provision of statistical data and customizable reports allowing the analysis and specification of risk profiles that will be subsequently used for the pre-vetting of visa applicants and visa-exempt travellers.[42]

32 Interoperability Regulations, arts 25–36.
33 Ibid recital 39 and art 25.
34 Ibid art 33.
35 Ibid art 30.
36 Ibid art 31.
37 Ibid art 32.
38 Ibid arts 17–24.
39 Ibid art 17(1).
40 Ibid art 22.
41 Ibid art 39.
42 Commission Delegated Decision of 23 November 2021 on further refining security, illegal immigration or high epidemic risks [2021 OJ C(2021)4981, art 3.

3 IT systems as a highly complex ecosystem

The previous sections aimed to highlight the highly complex architecture of large-scale IT systems and their interoperability. As argued elsewhere, the development of the EU/Schengen large-scale IT systems can be systematically categorized in three distinct eras: the initial steps to employ technological means for the purposes of immigration control and law enforcement; the systematization of databases and the gradual expansion of their capacities; and the current stage of generalized and normalized surveillance of movement of almost the entirety of third-country nationals.[43] It is true that in general the legal instruments follow a specific logic in terms of structure and to an extent the IT systems are developed consistently, in the sense that the provisions are similarly worded and the different modalities – who has access, to which personal data, for which purposes, for how long, and so on – are relatively regulated in a manner that allows for progressive convergence of the different systems and their fusion into a distinct policy field. This comes at the price of progressively assimilating different groups of third-country nationals under the banner of 'third-country nationals' and blurring the distinction between policy areas in the area of freedom, security, and justice, and notably: asylum, migration, police cooperation, internal security and criminal justice.

Aside from this assimilation for the purposes of technical efficiency and enabling connections between the data pots, the emergence of six separate large-scale IT systems, which are bound to become interoperable, has created an extremely complex ecosystem. A paradigmatic example of this complexity concerns the fact that the interoperability framework has created three additional databases containing personal data. In addition, the ETIAS watchlist will also function as a database storing personal data of (potentially) dangerous third-country nationals. This is just one example of how the wording and structure of the legal instruments governing the operation of the IT systems, viewed both separately and holistically, as part of the broader picture, is extremely complex and does not allow full foreseeability of the infrastructure and its implications. This complexity can be attributed to (and significantly exacerbated by) three main factors:

1. the technical understanding of the IT systems, inherent in their very nature, evidenced by entrusting the management of the IT systems to a technical agency, European Union Agency for the Operational

[43] See Niovi Vavoula, 'Digitalising the EU Migration and Asylum Policy: The Fundamental Rights Implications of Information Systems' in Evangelia (Lilian) Tsourdi and Philippe De Bruycker (eds), *Research Handbook in EU Immigration and Asylum Law* (Edward Elgar 2022).

Management of Large-Scale IT Systems in the Area of Freedom, Security and Justice (eu-LISA);
2. the not only constant, but also incremental, revisions of the legal instruments governing the IT systems; and
3. the proliferation of non-legislative and often non-public instruments (delegated and implementing acts) regulating significant (non-technical) aspects.

Let us see each of these issues in turn.

3.1 The promotion of the technical nature of interoperable IT systems

IT systems have an inherently technical nature. The use of technological jargon is inevitable in the legislation, which in itself hinders a proper understanding of how the systems operate in silos and altogether. The technical understanding of the systems has promoted a highly 'techno-solutionist' approach whereby the systems have been viewed as a panacea for addressing various security and migration-related concerns, such as the enhancement of returns of irregular migrants, or of EU internal security or the modernization of border controls. On several occasions, the prevalence of this approach has signified that various revisions have not followed from an Impact Assessment, examining the various ethical and fundamental rights implications of the IT systems developed from scratch or reformed. This has been the case with ETIAS, which was only subject to a Feasibility Study emphasizing the technical side of the system rather than a legal assessment.[44] In the case of Eurodac, there has never been conducted a self-standing evaluation of the database, testament to its status as a 'sidekick' of the Dublin system.

The prevalence of the technical over the legal is also evident in the understanding of interoperability as a technical issue, particularly in the discourse prior to the adoption of the Commission proposals on interoperability. Debates over interconnecting databases started in the aftermath of 9/11,[45] with a key issue being whether the VIS, which had been recently negotiated, could be linked or incorporated into the SIS.[46] The Hague Programme also mentioned interoperability both in the context of strengthening security, encouraging interoperability of

[44] Commission, 'Feasibility study for a European Travel Information and Authorisation System (ETIAS)' (2016).

[45] Council, Document 13176/01 (24 October 2001).

[46] Commission, 'Development of the Schengen Information System II' (Communication) COM(2001) 720 final, 8.

national databases or direct online access to existing central EU databases, including by Europol,[47] and in the context of migration management, where the European Council called on the Council to examine 'how to maximise the effectiveness and interoperability of EU information systems'.[48] In its Communication on improved effectiveness, enhanced interoperability and synergies among EU databases, the Commission defined interoperability as the 'ability of IT systems and of the business processes they support to exchange data and to enable the sharing of information and knowledge'.[49] However, details on the legal aspects for the interoperability of databases were omitted, as the concept was reduced to a technical rather than a legal or political matter.[50] This was a clear attempt 'to de-politicise the issues and to shield it from legal and democratic scrutiny'.[51] When the interoperability project gained fresh impetus in order to address perceived migration and security threats, stemming from the rise in irregular border crossings as a result of the so-called 'refugee crisis' and the series of terrorist attacks, the agenda was advanced by the High-Level Expert Group on Information Systems and Interoperability, comprised of experts from Member States and associated Schengen countries as well as eu-LISA, Europol, EUAA, Frontex and the EU Fundamental Rights Agency.[52] In its report from May 2017 the Group proposed certain interoperability components, which featured in the Commission proposal, along with MID, which emerged without prior deliberations. This technocratic framing of the issue is in striking contrast with the significant fundamental rights consequences, particularly in relation to privacy and data protection, that maximized information access and exchange backed up by interoperability entails.[53]

[47] Hague Programme: Strengthening Freedom, Security and Justice in the European Union [2004] OJ C53/1, 7–8.

[48] Ibid 7.

[49] Commission, 'Improved effectiveness, enhanced interoperability and synergies among European databases in the area of Justice and Home Affairs' (Communication) COM(2005) 597 final, 3.

[50] For a critique see Paul De Hert and Serge Gutwirth, 'Interoperability of Police Databases within the EU: An Accountable Political Choice?' (2006) 20(1–2) *International Review of Law, Computers & Technology* 21.

[51] On interoperability as de-politicization, see Mitsilegas (n 1).

[52] Commission, 'Decision of 17 June 2016 setting up the High Level Expert Group on Information Systems and Interoperability' [2016] OJ C 257/3.

[53] Niovi Vavoula, 'Interoperability of EU Information Systems: The Deathblow to the Rights to Privacy and Personal Data Protection of Third-Country Nationals?' (2020) 26(1) *European Public Law* 131.

Interoperability in particular raises significant rule of law concerns because it fundamentally alters the nature, structure and logic of IT systems, which should no longer be viewed as single structure, but rather holistically as an interconnected ecosystem. As mentioned earlier, breaking the silos and bringing the data pots together signifies that to the six large-scale IT systems processing personal data of different groups of third-country nationals one must add sBMS, MID and CIR, which also process specific groups of personal data from underlying systems. The Common Repository for Reporting and Statistics (CRRS) is also a database with non-personal data – though the processing of personal data cannot be excluded in cases of very specialized statistical data through which individuals can be re-identified. The Interoperability Regulations do not explicitly state that the revamped architecture entails the building of new databases, hiding behind the fancier term 'repository' and deliberately creating confusion as to the nature of the interoperability components. Aside from the structural ambiguity of the IT systems there exists inherent confusion in the various processing operations that take place attributed to the technical language prevailing in the law. For example, the MID will conduct searches to identify links among personal data stored in the IT systems on a constant basis, whenever the data are processed; in the life cycle of a single record in an IT system one could imagine that the MID check may take place an endless amount of times, even in cases where the individual has no interaction with administrative or law enforcement agencies of a Member State or an EU agency. The technical tools of interoperability, for example, the use of artificial intelligence, are equally unclear, but this is a matter to which the next chapter will return.

Entrusting the management of large-scale IT systems to eu-LISA, an agency with a purely technical mandate, is another testament to their technical perception.[54] It has been established to enable the continuous and uninterrupted exchange of personal data between the national authorities and EU agencies using them. It has been promoting the proliferation of IT systems and advancing their interoperability and participates in preparatory processes to design, develop and implement new systems, including execution of pilot projects. eu-LISA is, however, a technical agency,[55] primarily composed of engineers, with very limited legal staff and even less clarity

[54] Regulation (EU) 2018/1726 of the European Parliament and of the Council of 14 November 2018 on the European Union Agency for the Operational Management of Large-Scale IT Systems in the Area of Freedom, Security and Justice (eu-LISA), and amending Regulation (EC) No 1987/2006 and Council Decision 2007/533/JHA and repealing Regulation (EU) No 1077/2011 [2018] OJ L 295/99.

[55] Didier Bigo and Laurent Bonelli, 'Digital Data and the Transnational Intelligence Space' in Didier Bigo, Engin Isin and Evelyn Ruppoert (eds), *Data Politics: Worlds, Subjects, Rights* (Routledge 2019).

as to the processing of personal data by the agency itself. For example, the Interoperability Regulations envisage a central role for eu-LISA in developing and hosting the interoperability components and ensuring that their central infrastructures are operated in accordance with the Interoperability Regulations.[56] The establishment of a technical, single-agenda agency in this context poses further challenges to the rule of law requirements of transparency and accountability in the access and processing of personal data and may serve to mask the fundamental rights consequences of interoperable data sharing and processing from meaningful legal scrutiny.

3.2 Continuous and inconsistent reforms

The techno-solutionist approach has resulted in constant revisions of the legal instruments of the IT systems. However, these revisions have taken place in an incremental and inconsistent manner. To illustrate the issue, as mentioned earlier, the ETIAS Regulation requires the automated processing of personal data against (among others) the existing IT systems. This has resulted in various amendments to the legal instruments of the other IT systems through consequential amendments,[57] which were negotiated at the same time as the Commission proposals for interoperability, which also entailed cross-cutting reforms to the IT systems to regulate the interconnections foreseen among the IT systems.[58] At the same time, the Commission proposal for a revised Eurodac was also under negotiation and, in fact, a secret, partial interinstitutional agreement had been made between the Council and the European Parliament in 2018,[59] thus the amendments to Eurodac following

[56] Interoperability Regulations, art 54.

[57] Regulation (EU) 2021/1150 of the European Parliament and of the Council of 7 July 2021 amending Regulations (EU) 2018/1862 and (EU) 2019/818 as regards the establishment of the conditions for accessing other EU information systems for the purposes of the European Travel Information and Authorisation System [2021] OJ L 249/1; Regulation 2018/1861 of the European Parliament and of the Council of 28 November 2018 on the establishment, operation and use of the Schengen Information System (SIS) in the field of border checks, and amending the Convention implementing the Schengen Agreement, and amending and repealing Regulation (EC) No 1987/2006 [2018] OJ L312/14; Regulation 2018/1862 of the European Parliament and of the Council of 28 November 2018 on the establishment, operation and use of the Schengen Information System (SIS) in the field of police cooperation and judicial cooperation in criminal matters, amending and repealing Council Decision 2007/533/JHA, and repealing Regulation (EC) No 1986/2006 of the European Parliament and of the Council and Commission Decision 2010/261/EU [2018] OJ L312/56.

[58] Regulation 2019/817, arts 58–65; Regulation 2019/818, arts 59–62.

[59] The interinstitutional agreement may be found here: https://www.europarl.europa.eu/RegData/publications/divers/2016/0132/NEGO_CT(2016)0132(2018-06-21)_XL.pdf, accessed 12 October 2024.

the introduction of interoperability were not concretely regulated. Only few years later, the revised VIS was negotiated, also encompassing automated processing of visa applications and leading to additional reforms to the legal instruments of the IT systems.[60]

The constant revisions have had a series of consequences for safeguarding the rule of law; individuals, non-governmental organizations (NGOs) and legal practitioners representing third-country nationals cannot rely on the founding legal instruments but must have a broad overview of the database ecosystem to understand how they operate and to what extent they are interconnected. However, such a task is impossible not only because of the IT systems' inherent technical nature, but because, due to constant reforms, the full overview of how an IT system operates on its own requires to also consult the legal instruments of the IT systems and interoperability which contain provisions that have changed and the existence of consolidated legal instruments remains elusive. To this, there exists an additional serious challenge for foreseeability and clarity in the law: the fact that in various cases the legislation reforming the legal instruments of the IT systems solely contains the changes to the previous law. For example, in the case of VIS, the revised VIS Regulation is composed of provisions which have changed compared to the pre-existing VIS Regulation. As a result, an individual may have to consult at the same time: the founding legal instrument (the VIS Regulation), the revised VIS Regulation, as well as any consequential amendments scattered in the legal instruments of other IT systems.

3.3 Delegated and implementing acts

The complex landscape becomes even more untenable considering that various technical matters are not even laid down in the legislative instruments, but are rather laid down in many delegated and implementing acts. This involves matters that may have significant legal consequences on individuals, for example, on the additional questions an ETIAS applicant may have to answer in case there is a hit against any of the elements which are cross-checked during the automated assessment.[61] In fact, the more complex the

---

60 Regulation (EU) 2021/1133 of the European Parliament and of the Council of 7 July 2021 amending Regulations (EU) No 603/2013, (EU) 2016/794, (EU) 2018/1862, (EU) 2019/816 and (EU) 2019/818 as regards the establishment of the conditions for accessing other EU information systems for the purposes of the Visa Information System [2021] OJ L 248/1.

61 Commission Delegated Decision (EU) 2023/2424 of 28 July 2023 specifying the content and format of the questions and laying down the additional set of predetermined questions for the European Travel Information and Authorisation System (ETIAS) pursuant to Articles 17(5) and (6) of Regulation (EU) 2018/1240 of the European Parliament and of the Council [2023] OJ L 2023/2424.

data processing operations of an IT system, the greater the number of non-legislative instruments adopted and the more legal implications for third-country nationals they may entail. For example, in the case of ETIAS the list of delegated and implementing acts is extremely long.[62] In addition, many

[62] Ibid; Commission Delegated Regulation (EU) 2024/2510 of 2 May 2024 supplementing Regulation (EU) 2018/1240 of the European Parliament and of the Council as regards the payment methods and collection process for the travel authorisation fee provided for by that Regulation [2024] OJ L 2024/2510; Commission Delegated Regulation (EU) 2024/2511 of 2 May 2024 supplementing Regulation (EU) 2018/1240 of the European Parliament and of the Council as regards the identification of increases in the costs of operation and maintenance of the European Travel Information and Authorisation System (ETIAS) for the purpose of changing the amount of the travel authorisation fee [2024] OJ L 2024/2511; Commission Delegated Decision (EU) 2022/1612 of 16 February 2022 specifying the content and format of the predetermined list of options to be used to request additional information or documentation pursuant to Article 27(3) of Regulation (EU) 2018/1240 of the European Parliament and of the Council [2022] OJ L 241/7; Commission Delegated Regulation (EU) 2021/916 of 12 March 2021 supplementing Regulation (EU) 2018/1240 of the European Parliament and of the Council establishing a European Travel Information and Authorisation System (ETIAS) as regards the predetermined list of job groups used in the application form [2021] OJ L 201/1; Commission Delegated Decision (EU) 2019/969 of 22 February 2019 on the tool enabling applicants to give or withdraw their consent for an additional retention period of their application file pursuant to Article 54(2) of Regulation (EU) 2018/1240 of the European Parliament and of the Council [2019] OJ L 156/10; Commission Delegated Decision (EU) 2019/970 of 22 February 2019 on the tool for applicants to check the status of their applications and to check the period of validity and status of their travel authorisations pursuant to Article 31 of Regulation (EU) 2018/1240 of the European Parliament and of the Council [2019] OJ L 156/15; Commission Delegated Decision (EU) 2019/971 of 26 February 2019 on the definition of the requirements of the secure account service pursuant to Article 6(4) of Regulation (EU) 2018/1240 of the European Parliament and of the Council, enabling applicants to provide any additional information or documentation required [2019] OJ L 156/20; Commission Implementing Decision (EU) 2023/1802 of 20 September 2023 laying down the technical arrangements for data retention [2023] OJ L 233/85; Commission Implementing Decision (EU) 2022/1620 of 19 September 2022 laying down model contingency measures for cases of technical impossibility to access data at the external borders, including fall-back procedures to be followed by border authorities pursuant to Article 48(4) of Regulation (EU) 2018/1240 of the European Parliament and the Council [2022] OJ L 243/144; Commission Implementing Decision (EU) 2022/1462 of 2 September 2022 on the requirements for the means of audio and video communication for the interview pursuant to Article 27(5) of Regulation (EU) 2018/1240 of the European Parliament and of the Council [2022] OJ L 229/77; Commission Implementing Regulation (EU) 2022/1380 of 8 August 2022 laying down the rules and conditions for verification queries by carriers, provisions for data protection and security for the carriers' authentication scheme as well as fall back procedures in case of technical impossibility and repealing Implementing Regulation (EU) 2021/1217 [2022] OJ L 207/1; Commission Implementing Decision (EU) 2022/102 of 25 January 2022 laying down forms for refusal, annulment or revocation of a travel authorisation [2022] OJ L 17/59; Commission Implementing Regulation (EU)

of these non-legislative acts are not even publicly available for consultation in many cases, or they have become public following access to information requests, or they remain secret notwithstanding efforts to secure them through such requests. This involves in particular two highly important non-legislative instruments that concern the establishment of the screening rules for the automated risk assessment of ETIAS applicants.[63] Similarly, the revised VIS Regulation mandates the adoption of various delegated and implementing acts.[64] At the time of finalizing this book, none of these

---

2021/1217 of 26 July 2021 laying down the rules and conditions for verification queries by carriers, provisions for data protection and security for the carriers' authentication scheme as well as fall-back procedures in case of technical impossibility [2021] OJ L 267/1; Commission Implementing Decision (EU) 2021/1028 of 21 June 2021 adopting measures for the application of Regulation (EU) 2018/1240 of the European Parliament and of the Council as regards accessing, amending, erasing and advance erasing of data in the ETIAS Central System [2021] OJ L 224/31; Commission Implementing Decision (EU) 2021/627 of 15 April 2021 laying down rules on keeping and accessing of the logs in the European Travel Information and Authorisation System (ETIAS) pursuant to Regulation (EU) 2018/1240 of the European Parliament and of the Council [2021] OJ L 131/87; Commission Implementing Regulation (EU) 2021/331 of 24 February 2021 on the reporting of abuses committed by commercial intermediaries providing application services for travel authorisation under Regulation (EU) 2018/1240 of the European Parliament and of the Council [2021] OJ L 65/47; Commission Delegated Regulation (EU) 2024/2510 of 2 May 2024 supplementing Regulation (EU) 2018/1240 of the European Parliament and of the Council as regards the payment methods and collection process for the travel authorisation fee provided for by that Regulation [2024] OJ L 2024/2510; Commission Delegated Regulation (EU) 2024/2511 of 2 May 2024 supplementing Regulation (EU) 2018/1240 of the European Parliament and of the Council as regards the identification of increases in the costs of operation and maintenance of the European Travel Information and Authorisation System (ETIAS) for the purpose of changing the amount of the travel authorisation fee [2024] OJ L 2024/2511.

[63] For example, Commission Delegated Decision of 23 November 2021 on Further Defining Security, Illegal Immigration or High Epidemic Risks [2021] OJ C(2021)4981; Commission Implementing Decision of 23 November 2021 on specifying risks related to security, illegal immigration or high epidemic risk as defined in Regulation (EU) 2018/1240 of the European Parliament and of the Council C(2021) 4980 final.

[64] The Commission shall adopt delegated acts to lay down the predetermined list of occupations (job groups); to lay down in a manual the procedures and rules necessary for queries, verifications and assessments; to further define the risks related to security or illegal immigration or a high epidemic risk; to lay down detailed rules on managing the functionality for the centralised management of the list of recognised travel documents and of the notification of the recognition or non-recognition of the listed travel documents. The Commission shall adopt implementing acts to lay down the detailed rules on managing the functionality for the centralised management of the list of competent authorities; to lay down and develop the mechanism and the procedures for carrying out quality checks and appropriate requirements for data quality compliance; to specify the risks defined in the delegated act; to lay down the specification of the quality standards; to lay down the measures necessary for the development of the VIS Central System, the NUIs in each

acts has been made public and there is no public information about the adoption of Commission proposals in this regard. This is notwithstanding the fact that preparations for the upgrade of VIS have been underway since 2021. The Interoperability Regulations also foresee the adoption of various delegated and implementing acts.[65] As a result, the legal framework

---

Member State and the communication infrastructure between the VIS Central System and the NUIs concerning the following: (a) the design of the physical architecture of the VIS Central System including its communication network; (b) technical aspects which have a bearing on the protection of personal data; (c) technical aspects which have serious financial implications for the budgets of the Member States or which have serious technical implications for the national systems; (d) the development of security requirements, including biometric aspects. In addition, the Commission shall adopt implementing acts to lay down measures necessary for the technical implementation of the functionalities of the VIS Central System, in particular: (a) for entering the data and linking applications; (b) for accessing the data; (c) for rectification, erasure and advance erasure of data; (d) for keeping and accessing the logs; (e) for the consultation mechanism and the procedures; (f) for accessing the data for the purposes of reporting and statistics. The Commission shall also adopt implementing acts to lay down the technical specifications for the quality, resolution and use of fingerprints and of the facial image for biometric verification and identification in the system. Moreover, the Commission shall adopt implementing acts to lay down detailed rules concerning the conditions for the operation of the carrier gateway and the data protection and security rules applicable. implementing acts to lay down the authentication scheme for carriers. implementing act to lay down the details of the fall-back procedures in the case of technical impossibility to access data by carriers. Finally, the Commission shall adopt implementing acts for the adoption of specifications of the technical solution regarding the generation of statistics.

65 As regards Regulation (EU) 2019/817: Commission Delegated Regulation (EU) 2023/333 of 11 July 2022 supplementing Regulation (EU) 2019/817 of the European Parliament and of the Council as regards determining cases where identity data are considered as same or similar for the purpose of the multiple identity detection [2023] OJ L 47/17; Commission Delegated Regulation (EU) 2021/2223 of 30 September 2021 supplementing Regulation (EU) 2019/817 of the European Parliament and of the Council with detailed rules on the operation of the central repository for reporting and statistics [2021] OJ L 448/7; Commission Delegated Regulation (EU) 2021/2104 of 19 August 2021 laying down detailed rules on the operation of the web portal, pursuant to Article 49(6) of Regulation (EU) 2019/817 of the European Parliament and of the Council [2021] OJ L 429/72; Commission Implementing Regulation (EU) 2024/2106 of 31 July 2024 amending Implementing Decision C(2021) 5052 laying down technical details for European search portal user profiles, pursuant to Article 8(2) of Regulation (EU) 2019/817 of the European Parliament and of the Council [2024] OJ L 2024/2106; Commission Implementing Decision (EU) 2023/220 of 1 February 2023 laying down and developing the universal message format (UMF) standard pursuant to Regulation (EU) 2019/817 of the European Parliament and of the Council [2023] OJ L 30/18; Commission Implementing Regulation (EU) 2021/2225 of 16 November 2021 laying down the details of the automated data quality control mechanisms and procedures, the common data quality indicators and the minimum quality standards for storage of data, pursuant to Article 37(4) of Regulation (EU) 2019/817 of the European Parliament and of the Council [2021] OJ L 448/23. As regards Regulation (EU) 2019/818: Commission

of IT systems becomes a conundrum of an increasingly large number of legislative and non-legislative instruments, which viewed together makes the foreseeability and legal certainty impossible even for expert readership, let alone for individuals affected by the operation of the systems.

4 Large-scale IT systems as security systems

As already mentioned, large-scale IT systems can be accessed by multiple actors at the national level and certain EU agencies in an approach which promotes maximized exchanges of personal data. This approach reflects what Bigo has called the (in)security continuum, whereby the securitization of crime and terrorism is being transferred to migration and mobility.[66] Such (in) security continuum justifies allowing access by law enforcement authorities to immigration – thus administrative IT systems for 'security' purposes, in particular allowing under specific conditions national law enforcement authorities and Europol to consult data in the systems for the purposes of combatting terrorism and other serious crimes. This approach is not new: it was already highlighted in European Council responses after the Madrid attacks, including in the Hague Programme. The latter placed emphasis on the interoperability of databases, including in the context of migration management. It called on the Council to examine 'how to maximise the effectiveness and interoperability of EU information systems' and invited the

Delegated Regulation (EU) 2023/332 of 11 July 2022 supplementing Regulation (EU) 2019/818 of the European Parliament and of the Council as regards determining cases where identity data are considered as same or similar for the purpose of the multiple identity detection [2022] OJ L 47/6; Commission Delegated Regulation (EU) 2021/2222 of 30 September 2021 supplementing Regulation (EU) 2019/818 of the European Parliament and of the Council with detailed rules on the operation of the central repository for reporting and statistics [2021] OJ L 448/1; Commission Delegated Regulation (EU) 2021/2103 of 19 August 2021 laying down detailed rules on the operation of the web portal, pursuant to Article 49(6) of Regulation (EU) 2019/818 of the European Parliament and of the Council [2021] OJ L 429/65; Commission Implementing Regulation (EU) 2024/2107 of 31 July 2024 amending Implementing Decision C(2021) 5053 laying down technical details for European search portal user profiles, pursuant to Article 8(2) of Regulation (EU) 2019/818 of the European Parliament and of the Council [2024] OJ L 2024/2107; Commission Implementing Decision (EU) 2023/221 of 1 February 2023 laying down and developing the universal message format (UMF) standard pursuant to Regulation (EU) 2019/818 of the European Parliament and of the Council [2023] OJ L 30/26; Commission Implementing Regulation (EU) 2021/2224 of 16 November 2021 laying down the details of the automated data quality control mechanisms and procedures, the common data quality indicators and the minimum quality standards for storage of data, pursuant to Article 37(4) of Regulation (EU) 2019/818 of the European Parliament and of the Council [2021] OJ L 448/14.

66 Didier Bigo, *Polices en Réseax. L'Éxperience Européenne* (Presses de Sciences Po 1996).

Commission to present a Communication on the interoperability between the SIS, the VIS and Eurodac.[67] In the Commission Communication on improved effectiveness, enhanced interoperability and synergies among European databases of 2005, the Commission highlighted how, beyond their present purposes, databases 'can more effectively support the policies linked to the free movement of persons and serve the objective of combating terrorism and serious crime'.[68] The result of this fusion of immigration and security purposes is noteworthy: VIS, Eurodac, EES and ETIAS are designed to allow for the personal data stored to be accessed by national law enforcement authorities and Europol. Furthermore, the case of ETIAS solidifies the link between immigration control and security, as one of its main objectives is to contribute to a high level of security by thoroughly assessing whether travellers pose a 'security risk'.[69] That IT system is therefore a pre-emptive control mechanism that also serves many other purposes, including the prevention of irregular migration and the contribution to the prevention, detection and investigation of terrorist offences and other serious offences.[70] Access for law enforcement purposes was originally foreseen to take place under specific – albeit slightly different – conditions and modalities for each system.[71] In general, IT systems are conceived and designed as multi-purpose tools serving a series of (divergent) objectives, thereby heavily blurring the boundaries between immigration and criminal law. In fact, the more EU systems proliferated and the more banal law enforcement access became, the less the tensions and dissenting voices against the merging of immigration with security objectives. This is not surprising; once resistance in relation to heavily debated dossiers – such as Eurodac, which stored personal data on applicants of international protection and refugees, thus potentially vulnerable individuals – was curbed, the trend of law enforcement access has been since generalized and normalized.

Conversely, ECRIS-TCN, which appears to have a single purpose, to help identify a Member State that holds criminal conviction data on a third-country national, may also be used under national law in immigration control procedures.[72] In fact the purposes of consulting this system remain solely regulated under national law and the ECRIS-TCN rules do not provide an

---

67 European Council, 'The Hague Programme: Strengthening Freedom, Security and Justice in the European Union' [2004] OJ C 53/1, 7.

68 Commission, 'Improved effectiveness, enhanced interoperability and synergies among European databases in the area of Justice and Home Affairs' (Communication) COM(2005) 597 final.

69 ETIAS Regulations, art 4(a).

70 Ibid art 4(b)–(f).

71 For a detailed analysis see Niovi Vavoula, 'Consultation of EU Immigration Databases for Law Enforcement Purposes: A Privacy and Data Protection Assessment' (2020) 22 *European Journal of Migration and Law* 139.

72 ECRIS-TCN Regulation, art 7.

exhaustive list of its purposes. ECRIS-TCN is also testament to the blurring of boundaries between immigration and security taking place *in reverse* via the addition of an immigration component to criminal law measures, as seen by the extension of ECRIS to include data on third-country nationals in ECRIS-TCN.

As for the case of SIS, the system aims to ensure a high level of security in the area of freedom, security and justice, and facilitate the movement of persons. The vague wording of the overarching purpose of the database poses legality concerns regarding the gradual transformation from a reporting system into a powerful investigative tool, the full potential of which has yet to be reached.[73] The intertwining of immigration control with security disregards the specificity of the immigration branch of the SIS as a tool solely for the refusal of entry and stay in the territory of the Member States. In view of the growing convergence of alerts inserted, particularly through interlinking and the inclusion of biometric data, which allow for multiple uses of the data, the broad wording of the purpose of the database is problematic, as it leaves huge leeway to introduce further new functionalities which are unforeseeable to the individuals concerned. Access to SIS data by Europol, including all immigration alerts, is another indication of the evolution of the system towards intelligence gathering. An example of this leeway is the broadening of the functions of SIS in the context of law enforcement, shifting away from border checks; Article 34(1)(c) of the SIS Regulation for border checks enables the unconditional for the purposes of the prevention, detection, investigation or prosecution of terrorist or other serious criminal offences or the execution of criminal penalties.

Opening up the IT systems established primarily for administrative purposes to law enforcement has become a banality, even though the justification has been fragile and not convincing and the actual effectiveness of such access is still in embryonic stage with limited anecdotal information. Besides, prevention of terrorist offences and serious crimes is difficult to measure, which means that the justification of the pre-emptive use of databases in the law enforcement context will probably remain elusive. Behind the trend of granting access to immigration data by law enforcement authorities are two perceptions; firstly, that third-country nationals collectively are de facto risky individuals suspected of criminality, the movement of whom constitutes an inherently dangerous activity that must be controlled and monitored.[74] IT systems as risk technology tools are thus redeployed from the immigration control domain to the domain of the fight against impunity in an attempt to 'to feign control over the uncontrollable'.[75] In that regard, the stigmatizing

73 Vavoula (n 1) 133–134.

74 Gammeltoft-Hansen (n 3).

75 Ulrich Beck, 'The Terrorist Threat: World Risk Society Revisited' (2002) 19(4) *Theory, Culture & Society* 39, 41.

effect of law enforcement access, which has been stressed in *S and Marper v UK*,[76] particularly since the data are stored for a significant period of time, has been largely disregarded.[77] Secondly, it is evident that once data has been collected and is already stored, there is no deal-breaking reason why these should not be available even for objectives unrelated to their original context. The Eurodac example, whereby the data are used for law enforcement and in the future for wider migration purposes, illustrates the inherent danger of function creep when personal data is centrally stored: once information is stored for a specific purpose, there is a real possibility of the system being repurposed for objectives that were not initially contemplated.

Importantly, the expansion of the purposes for which data may be used and/or the development of multi-functional databases from the outset is difficult to reconcile with the principle of purpose limitation, envisaged in Article 5(1)(b) of Regulation (EU) 2016/679 (General Data Protection Regulation – GDPR).[78] Personal data may only be collected for specified, explicit and legitimate purposes and must not be further processed in a manner incompatible with those purposes. The multi-purpose character of information systems challenges the limits of the purpose limitation principle and raises doubts about the threshold for finding that the stated purposes are mutually incompatible. This function creep, that is the widening of the purposes for which the data is used, is inherent in the functioning of the IT systems, whereby the data are casually repurposed for additional purposes other than those for which they were initially collected, without explicit justification or transparent debate.

The Court of Justice of the European Union (CJEU) has clarified that the limited conditions laid down in the legal instruments are testament that law enforcement access is an ancillary purpose to the main functions of the system.[79] Admittedly, the modalities of law enforcement access are carefully drafted, yet loopholes remain raising not only proportionality concerns,[80] but also *legality* ones. In particular, the vague definitions of offences provided in EU legal instruments has a knock-on effect on law enforcement access. For instance, terrorist crimes correspond, or are equivalent, to those referred to

[76] *S and Marper v UK* (2009) 48 EHRR 50, para 122.

[77] Data may be stored between five and ten years and even longer depending on whether, for example, an individual is a regular visitor to the EU/Schengen area and re-applied for a visa once that has expired.

[78] Regulation (EU) 2016/679 of the European Parliament and of the Council of 27 April 2016 on the protection of natural persons with regard to the processing of personal data and on the free movement of such data, and repealing Directive 95/46/EC (General Data Protection Regulation) [2016] OJ L 119/1.

[79] CJEU, *UK v Council*, C-482/08, ECLI:EU:C:2010:631.

[80] Vavoula (n 71).

in Articles 3 to 12 of Directive (EU) 2017/541 on combatting terrorism.[81] Serious crimes are specified in Article 2(2) of Framework Decision 2002/584/JHA on the European Arrest Warrant.[82] The fact that the offences in question are specified by reference to other EU instruments does not present a legality issue. In *Kennedy v UK*, the applicant claimed that the term 'serious crime' as set out in the British act in question was not sufficiently clear, but the European Court of Human Rights opined that as long as the term is further clarified in the interpretative provisions of the contested act and the act itself, the foreseeability requirement would be met.[83] In Opinion 1/15, concerning the transfer of Passenger Name Record (PNR) data from the EU to Canada for law enforcement purposes, the Grand Chamber was satisfied that the definitions of 'terrorist offences' and 'serious transnational crime' were provided with clarity and precision by requiring that they must be punishable by a maximum deprivation of liberty of at least four years or a more serious penalty and must be defined by Canadian law.[84] In that respect, it must be stressed that the delineation of terrorist acts has been subject to consecutive reforms as a response to the phenomenon of 'foreign terrorist fighters' and new trends in terrorism. However, the inclusion of additional offences, such terrorist travel, has been criticized as raising legality concerns, due to its vagueness, and leading to legal uncertainty.[85] Therefore, immigration data may be consulted in relation to criminal offences that do not stand the legality test due to lack of clarity in their definition. Blurring boundaries in this manner results in an all-encompassing, yet at the same time amorphous concept of security, which is repeatedly prioritized and stressed, but may serve to undermine key distinctions and limits to the reach of the state in the lives of individuals.

Interoperability serves to take this this catch-all concept of security to the next level, and further strains the purpose limitation principle by enabling the data present in information systems to be used in a far more rigorous manner. The threshold for incompatibility is impossible to reach and the

81 Directive (EU) 2017/541 of the European Parliament and of the Council of 15 March 2017 on combating terrorism and replacing Council Framework Decision 2002/475/JHA and amending Council Decision 2005/671/JHA [2017] OJ L 88/6.

82 Council Framework Decision 2002/584/JHA of 13 June 2002 on the European arrest warrant and the surrender procedures between Member States – Statements made by certain Member States on the adoption of the Framework Decision [2002] OJ L 190/1.

83 *Kennedy v UK* (2011) 52 EHRR 4.

84 Opinion 1/15 ECLI:EU:C:2017:592, paras 176–177.

85 Niovi Vavoula, 'The EU Response to the Phenomenon of Foreign Fighters: Challenges for Fundamental Rights and the Rule of Law' in Ulrich Sieber, Valsamis Mitsilegas, Christos Mylonopoulos, Emmanouil Billis and Nandor Knust (eds), *Alternative, Informal, and Transitional Types of Criminal Justice and the Legitimacy of New Sanction Models in the Global Risk Society* (Duncker & Humblot 2018).

limits of these systems are far from being exceeded.[86] Through the two-step approach described earlier, the Interoperability Regulations water down the conditions for law enforcement access. As noted by the European Data Protection Supervisor (EDPS), the existence of a 'hit' – that the database holds a file on the individual in question – is significant, since it reveals elements of an individual's personal life, for instance that they are visa-free travellers, and therefore the first step of checking whether there is personal data should be covered by the conditions of access. Conversely, if there is no 'hit', the authorities may have still acquired some information as regards the individual in question, for example, that most probably they belong to a specific group of third-country nationals. Importantly, it is hard to believe that upon finding that a database holds information on a person, the verifying authority ensuring the conditions for access have been met will not allow such access. This will be particularly the case when this function will be used in cases of *unknown* perpetrators or victims of offences, where the existence of information on the individual in a system will pre-empt the verification of the conditions of access. In other words, not only the independence and objectivity, but also the very existence of the verification process may be biased by the two-step approach. Arguably, this new function may enable national authorities to engage in fishing expeditions. Therefore, more prosecutions and/or convictions of third-country nationals may take place, merely because a pool of information exists, since no equivalent EU-wide catalogue of records on EU citizens exists. The end result will be that the mere existence of data stored in a system can legitimize access by law enforcement authorities. In such a scenario, the conditions of access may *de facto* be replaced by merely one condition: the presence of data relating to an individual within a system.[87] Since every third-country national will be listed in at least one system, access will become a routine practice of law enforcement authorities and the limitations on access will remain on paper only. In turn, since the character of law enforcement access will no longer be exceptional, this purpose will cease to be an ancillary objective by default.

In addition, Article 20(4) of the Interoperability Regulations enables a police authority empowered under national law in the event of a natural disaster, an accident or a terrorist attack and solely for the purpose of identifying unknown persons who are unable to identify themselves or unidentified human remains, to query CIR with the biometric data of those persons. Arguably in cases concerning terrorist offences and potentially other serious crimes that may have been committed in the context of an accident, for example, murder, or even in cases where the victims of an offence, such

[86] See Vavoula (n 53).

[87] Vavoula (n 26) 370.

as smuggling or human trafficking, are in shock, police authorities could entirely circumvent the two-step process and resort to Article 20(4) of the Interoperability Regulations to access information systems for third-country nationals. In such cases, the regularized access to the IT systems completely breaks down the walls between the immigration and the law enforcement functions of the systems.

Finally, it must be emphasized that though interoperability has commenced by interconnecting the large-scale IT systems, it has since then been further expanded to integrate in various ways other decentralized information exchange systems in the field of migration and law enforcement. These involve the integration of Prüm,[88] the Advanced Passenger Information data and PNR[89] within this ecosystem. As a result, the security continuum becomes even more apparent by fusing not only personal data of different groups of third-country nationals, but of suspects and criminals or merely of mobile individuals. As highlighted by Mitsilegas, these developments transform Bigo's (in)security continuum into 'a continuum transferring securitisation also to generalised citizen mobility'[90] and a 'generalised security control system'.[91]

5 Interoperable large-scale IT systems and effective judicial protection: 'mission impossible'?

In a complex area of multi-layered actorness, such as that of interoperable large-scale IT systems, the availability of effective judicial remedies is crucial to ensure the protection of individual rights, accountability in the exercise of public powers and to safeguard the rule of law.[92] These remedies are essential as the existence of a record/file/alert on a third-country national has a significant impact on individuals; not only in that it enables their visibility as data subjects, benefiting from the protection of the EU Charter, but it can have significant negative implications: on their prospects for receiving

88 Regulation (EU) 2024/982 of the European Parliament and of the Council of 13 March 2024 on the automated search and exchange of data for police cooperation, and amending Council Decisions 2008/615/JHA and 2008/616/JHA and Regulations (EU) 2018/1726, (EU) No 2019/817 and (EU) 2019/818 of the European Parliament and of the Council (the Prüm II Regulation) [2024] OJ L 2024/982.

89 Council Directive 2004/82/EC of 29 April 2004 on the obligation of carriers to communicate passenger data [2004] OJ L 261/24, to be replaced. The revised rules have been agreed upon, but at the time of writing they have not yet been published.

90 Valsamis Mitsilegas, 'Interoperability as a Rule of Law Challenge' (*EUI*, 13 February 2020) (not publicly available anymore).

91 Ibid.

92 Herwig C.H. Hofmann and Morgane Tidghi, 'Rights and Remedies in Implementation of EU Policies by Multi-Jurisdictional Networks' (2014) 20 *European Public Law* 147, 152.

international protection in one country or to be transferred in another based on the rules on the allocation for the responsible Member State for the examination of an application, or the chances of their visa, residence permit or travel authorization application to be accepted, or on their entry on the EU/Schengen territory, or even their implication in a criminal investigation. Nonetheless, the question of whether the legal instruments governing the large-scale IT systems as multi-jurisdictional information networks ensure effective judicial remedies has rarely been addressed. As regards ETIAS and VIS, which entrench algorithmic profiling, the next chapter deals precisely with this matter. For this chapter, emphasis will rather be placed on the operational SIS and Eurodac, where certain safe conclusions can be drawn regarding the limits of judicial protection based on their operation in practice.

The very nature of IT systems display interstate technology-based trust, whereby Member State authorities collect, store and exchange various personal data, the administrative authorities presume that at the time when a record/file/alert was inserted the personal data were lawfully collected, that the rights of third-country nationals are safeguarded, and overall that the entry of the personal data is accurate, of high quality, up-to-date and compliant with the rights to dignity, respect for private life and personal data protection. However, experience demonstrates that disputing the reliability of the underlying data in the IT systems when these have been recorded and entered by an authority in another Member State is not straightforward. In the case of Eurodac, the trust in national administrations seems to be shared by national courts too, whose hands are tied due to the limits in assuming jurisdiction and reviewing the alleged unlawfulness of administrative acts, such as the insertion of a Eurodac record in the system by non-national authorities. Indeed, national courts are in principle competent to review only the acts emanating from the authorities falling within their jurisdiction.[93] As a result, national courts may have no other option but to show trust in the administrative practices of other Member States and instead impose limits in the practices of their own administrations. The gap in judicial protection for applicants for international protection is evident, as research has unveiled only one case at the national level where a national court directly reviewed the irregular registration in Eurodac and thus annulled the transfer decision. In particular, in 2016 a Dublin transfer on the basis of a Eurodac match was disputed before the Administrative Tribunal of Nantes. The case involved a Cameroonian who, after having been subject to an expulsion order from Spain for having entered irregularly, applied for international protection in

[93] Mariolina Eliantonio, 'Information Exchange in European Administrative Law – A Threat to Effective Judicial Protection' (2016) 23 *Maastricht Journal of European and Comparative Law* 531, 536–537.

France.[94] The prefecture of Vendée ordered the transfer of the applicant to Spain, which had accepted the 'take back' request, in accordance with the Dublin III Regulation.[95] The Tribunal found that the prefecture had justified the transfer decision based on the applicant's fingerprints being recorded in Eurodac, which established that he had previously filed an application for asylum in Spain. However, other documents in the file, including an interview carried out by the Spanish authorities, showed that he had in fact been apprehended for an irregular border crossing and had not filed an asylum claim in Spain. Therefore, the transfer decision was based on erroneous information and was thus quashed, also because the applicant's personal circumstances were not examined. The wrongful categorization of the applicant's situation as an asylum applicant, instead of an irregular entrant, had significant implications on the Dublin transfer as, pursuant to the then Dublin rules, the responsibility for examining the application for international protection ceases 12 months after the date on which the irregular border crossing took place.[96] In this case, the French court did not hesitate to expressly review the lawfulness of the Eurodac registration of the applicant by the Spanish authorities as an asylum seeker where he was, in fact, an irregular migrant. As the French authorities based their administrative decision to transfer on the mistaken categorization of the applicant by the Spanish authorities, the decision was ultimately challenged and annulled. By reviewing the Eurodac entry, the French court was able to quash the transfer decision.

Other cases demonstrate tension between trust in modern technologies and administrative procedures, such as the registration of fingerprints in Eurodac or the insertion of a SIS alert, which take place in other Member States, which may not be infallible, and the need to safeguard the fundamental rights of asylum seekers, particularly their right to an effective remedy. The French case is an exceptional example of a national court directly reviewing the legality of the Spanish administrative act of inserting the record in Eurodac. In other cases, though, the courts are silent about the reviewability of the foreign acts and provided guidance to the administrative authorities on how

---

[94] Tribunal Administratif de Nantes, Jugement du 18 février 2016, No. 1600829, https://www.asylumlawdatabase.eu/sites/default/files/aldfiles/TA%20Nantes%20-%2018022016%20-%20defaut%20examen%20%28Dublin%20Espagne%29%20-%20copie%202_0.pdf, accessed 12 October 2024.

[95] Regulation (EU) No 604/2013 of the European Parliament and of the Council of 26 June 2013 establishing the criteria and mechanisms for determining the Member State responsible for examining an application for international protection lodged in one of the Member States by a third-country national or a stateless person (recast) [2013] OJ L 180/1.

[96] Ibid art 13(1).

to treat Eurodac matches and circumscribed the degree of technology-based interstate trust by noting the need for further evidence to corroborate a match and requiring the delivery of prompt administration.[97]

These findings in connection with Eurodac are also confirmed in the case of SIS. Brouwer,[98] Tidghi[99] and Eliantonio[100] have highlighted the limited reviewability of information provision measures in the framework of SIS. Article 54 of the SIS Regulation for border checks and Article 68 of the SIS Regulation regarding police and judicial cooperation in criminal matters provide for remedies before any competent authority, including a court, under the law of any Member State to access, rectify, erase, obtain information or obtain compensation in connection with an alert relating to them. However, this avenue 'does not cover the actual placing of the alert in the system and the threat assessment made in it'.[101] Thus, if a SIS alert is issued and a final measure is taken based on that alert, such as expulsion, it is not possible for the individual to challenge the alert directly before the national court that has jurisdiction on the executing authority, as the alert will probably be considered not to be reviewable because of its preparatory nature.[102] Consequently, alleged unlawfulness of a SIS alert resulting in the annulment of the national decision of refusal of entry or stay on national territory has been scarcely reviewed, with the decision in *Forabosco* by the French Court of State being pivotal in this context.[103] In that case, the French Conseil d' Etat quashed decisions denying Ms Forabosco a visa due to her being listed in SIS by the German authorities on the sole basis that her application for asylum in Germany had been rejected. The Conseil d' Etat held that this fact was not a reason for refusal of entry under the predecessor of the current SIS rules, Article 96 of the Convention Implementing the Schengen Agreement.

Overall, there is no legal certainty that national courts will directly review possible irregularities of records in EU IT systems. The gap in

[97] ECLI:NL:RVS:2016:2441, Raad van State, 201604335/1/V3, https://www.raadvanstate.nl/@105053/201604335-1-v3/, accessed 12 October 2024; see ECLI:NL:RVS:2014:3127, Raad van State, 201304293/1/V4, https://uitspraken.rechtspraak.nl/inziendocument?id=ECLI:NL:RVS:2014:3127, accessed 12 October 2024. For an analysis see Niovi Vavoula, 'Information Sharing in the Dublin System: Remedies for Asylum Seekers Between Gaps in Judicial Protection and Interstate Trust' (2021) 22(3) *German Law Journal* 391.

[98] Brouwer (n 1).

[99] Morgane Tidghi, *Networks of Information in the European Union: Multi-Level Administrative Cooperation in Composite Decision-Making Procedures* (PhD Thesis, University of Luxembourg 2013) 124.

[100] Eliantonio (n 93) 541–542.

[101] Ibid.

[102] Ibid.

[103] CE 9 June 1999, M. et Mme. Forabosco, no. 190384.

judicial protection remains, with the only available remedy being to seek compensation for damages caused as a result of an unlawful processing operation or any act incompatible with the underlying rules of the IT systems. As Hofmann and Todghi have noted, this mechanism is also problematic as it does not indicate the substantive and procedural conditions applicable to these liability claims, and there is no mechanism to ensure that the Member State required to pay compensation will in fact do so.[104]

The entrenchment of the interoperability components adds significant layers of complexity for individuals who are left to navigate a labyrinthine landscape marked by considerable legal uncertainty, both as regards identifying instances of processing of their personal data and in terms of authorities being provided with an effective remedy against interoperable administration.[105] It is entirely unclear whether and how individuals could foresee how their personal data are processed, by which interoperability components, and pinpoint at exactly what level of administration mistakes are made in order to seek judicial protection. The quest of maximizing the operational value of the personal data stored in the underlying systems comes at the expense of the rule of law, with the structure and operation of the systems profoundly changing, and the interpretation of legal principles, such as purpose limitation, being altered.[106] These challenges are bound to further exacerbate as interoperability will no longer be centred on large-scale IT systems to encompass decentralized avenues of information exchange in the law enforcement context.

6 Conclusion

This chapter aimed to provide a concise analysis of fundamental rule of law challenges posed by the establishment, operation and reconfiguration of large-scale IT systems for third-country nationals, which are bound to become interconnected in various ways and with other decentralized information exchange systems in the field of migration and security. The analysis has demonstrated the increased complexity in the legal framework stemming and exacerbated by various factors; firstly, by the default technical nature of the IT systems, which has been severely boosted by interoperability. This technical understanding shifts the focus from the legal implications of the systems particularly in terms of the protection of fundamental rights, which extend beyond privacy and data protection, and underlines the technical efficiency at the expense of the rule of law. The management of

[104] Hofmann and Tidghi (n 92) 159.

[105] EDPS, Opinion 4/2018, paras 23–24.

[106] Ibid para 25.

the IT systems by a technical agency, with poor legal expertise and data protection – let alone fundamental rights – culture is testament to this approach. Interoperability has further led to de-politicizing and de-legalizing the IT systems through technical components and jargon that is confusing and does not allow clear understanding of the emerging landscape of IT systems. Even the extent to which the interoperability components entail the creation of new databases has not been clarified in law. The dominance of the technical over the legal has been further exacerbated by the emergence of increasing, sometimes secret, non-legislative instruments, which make the legal framework of all IT systems impossible to grasp even by expert readership, let alone by the public, including the third-country nationals subject to the underlying rules, as well as non-governmental organizations and legal practitioners who wish to assist them. The secrecy and opacity surrounding the operation of IT systems is a significant rule of law gap, which will only increase with the further expansion of interoperability. Whereas navigating the legal framework is a laborious task, it is clear that law enforcement access to the large-scale IT systems, particularly after the changes brought by the Interoperability Regulations and the integration of non-migration related decentralized systems, creates confusion as to the true nature of the databases, which not only assimilate different groups of third-country nationals for the sake of streamlining the legislation, but also blur the boundaries between different policy fields in the EU Area of Freedom, Security and Justice (AFSJ). Finally, the chapter has captured the difficulties for individuals who wish to contest unlawful records in the IT systems to seek judicial protection essentially reviewing the legality of a foreign administrative measure due to the traditional limits of horizontal separation of jurisdictions. Only a handful of cases exist whereby national courts have directly reviewed a foreign administrative measure, such as the registration of an alert, which points to the direction that digitalization through the creation of IT systems creates an additional layer of denying individuals access to justice.

9

From Digitalization to Algorithmization in European Border Management: Automation, Artificial Intelligence and the Rule of Law

1 Introduction

Chapters 7 and 8 focused on the rule of law challenges stemming from the proliferation of digital technologies developed in the context of European border management. However, in recent years, border management at European level – both European Union (EU) and individual European countries – is marked by the proliferation of tools of automation, and increasingly of autonomy, with various layers of sophistication and complexity as a means of making sense of and exploiting the full potential of the large quantities of personal and non-personal data collected and stored.[1]

An ally in these efforts has been the exponential increase in computing power leading to the emergence of novel techniques, particularly artificial intelligence (AI). The latter could be described as a set of (computing) techniques and approaches aimed at developing machines that can approximate (or even surpass) some aspect(s) of human cognition, such as algorithms to enable automated image, speech or pattern recognition, to

[1] The boundaries between the two terms are not always neatly distinguishable and a system may incorporate both automated and 'autonomous' components. Automation means that the respective system applies pre-determined rules to fulfil a single, specified purpose. By contrast, advanced artificial intelligence (AI) systems are programmed to mimic human intelligence. To achieve this goal, AI systems process vast amounts of data from which they learn using sophisticated algorithms. Hence, they constantly adapt their inner workings to produce the desired outputs.

produce classifications, predictions, recommendations or decisions with the aim of supporting or replacing human tasks. In the AI Act, AI is broadly defined as a machine-based system that is designed to operate with varying levels of autonomy and that may exhibit adaptiveness after deployment, and that, for explicit or implicit objectives, infers, from the input it receives, how to generate outputs such as predictions, content, recommendations or decisions that can influence physical or virtual environments.[2]

In the field of immigration control, broadly including immigration, asylum and border control, AI has the potential to revolutionize the way states manage mobility, decision-making and foreign community integration.[3] AI promises modernized identity checks and border controls, as well as expedited and more efficient decision-making in relation to applications for visas, residence permits or asylum applications.[4] It can also be used for more efficient refugee resettlement in the country to increase their integration prospects, or for various types of risk assessments with the aim of evaluating whether irregular migrants or asylum seekers should be placed in administrative detention.[5] This may be achieved through various AI-based systems: tools that verify the authenticity of documents provided by applicants; emotion or speech recognition tools to test the veracity of applicants' claims regarding their country of origin or their background stories; data-driven algorithms to optimize matching between refugees' personal characteristics and resettlement sites and opportunities; or via algorithms that perform risk assessments based on the information provided or requested by the foreigners concerned. AI tools may also be used for more evidence-based policy making through the prediction and prevention of influxes of refugees and migrants

---

[2] Regulation (EU) 2024/1689 of the European Parliament and of the Council of 13 June 2024 laying down harmonised rules on artificial intelligence and amending Regulations (EC) No 300/2008, (EU) No 167/2013, (EU) No 168/2013, (EU) 2018/858, (EU) 2018/1139 and (EU) 2019/2144 and Directives 2014/90/EU, (EU) 2016/797 and (EU) 2020/1828 (Artificial Intelligence Act) [2024] OJ L2024/1689 (AI Act), art 3(1). For a commentary, see Tervel Bobev, 'Defining AI in the AI Act: Pin the Tail on the System' (*CiTiP*, 2 April 2024), https://www.law.kuleuven.be/citip/blog/defining-ai-in-the-ai-act-pin-the-tail-on-the-system/, accessed 12 October 2024.

[3] Petra Molnar, 'Technology on the Margins: AI and Global Migration Management from a Human Rights Perspective' (2019) 8(2) *Cambridge International Law Journal* 305.

[4] Niovi Vavoula, 'Artificial Intelligence (AI) at EU Borders: From Automated Processing to Algorithmic Profiling and Facial Recognition in the Era of Techno-Solutionism' (2021) 31(4) *European Journal of Migration and Law* 457; Ludivine Stewart, 'Fair and Efficient Asylum Procedures and Artificial Intelligence: Quo Vadis Due Process?' (2024) 55 *Computer Law & Security Review*.

[5] Meltem Ineli-Ciger, 'Resettlement by Algorithm: Can Artificial Intelligence Uphold Human Rights?' (2024) 55 *Computer Law & Security Review*.

based on predictive analytics;[6] or for enhanced situational awareness around the borders by analysing surveillance footage collected by various sensors deployed at states' frontiers and transforming it into actionable information and alerts for border and coast guard authorities.

The move towards more sophisticated tools of automation and autonomy should be viewed from a 'techno-solutionist' perspective, where technology is deemed as neutral and as a panacea for the lack of human capacity in processing the large amounts of data generated by other technological advents, coupled with increased human mobility – with Europe having become a 'global migration magnet',[7] requiring swift decision-making and, importantly, increased efforts to sort out, filter and sift the *bona fide* travellers, migrants or refugees from the *mala fide* ones. In this respect, AI has been deemed as a means of leveraging the wealth of information and providing additional insights and new potential to the data, beyond their original purposes to inform future policy making.

Whereas research in this area has been on the rise with legal scholars increasingly looking into these developments emphasizing the risks for the principle of non-discrimination,[8] the rule of law challenges are under-researched.[9] As highlighted by Burgess, the rule of law has traditionally constrained the arbitrary exercise of power, however it has only ever been deployed to set limits to human decision-making. This raises concerns as to whether and how the rule of law can and should apply to non-human decision-making.[10] In this research, he places the concept of explainability at the heart of a modern approach to the rule of law due to inherent opacity

[6] Ana Beduschi, 'International Migration Management in the Age of Artificial Intelligence' (2021) 9(3) *Migration Studies* 576.

[7] Mathias Czaika and Hein De Haas, 'The Globalization of Migration: Has the World Become More Migratory?' (2014) 48 *International Migration Review* 283, 314.

[8] For example, see Charly Derave, Nathan Genicot, and Nina Hetmanska, 'The Risks of Trustworthy Artificial Intelligence: The Case of the European Travel Information and Authorisation System' (2022) 13(3) *European Journal of Risk Regulation* 408; Timo Zandstra and Evelien Brouwer, 'Fundamental Rights at the Digital Border: ETIAS, the Right to Data Protection, and the CJEU's PNR Judgment' (*Verfassungsblog*, 24 June 2022), https://verfassungsblog.de/digital-border/, accessed 12 October 2024.

[9] See Amanda Musco-Eklund, 'Rule of Law Challenges of "Algorithmic Discretion" & Automation in EU Border Control – A Case Study of ETIAS Through the Lens of Legality' (2023) 25 *European Journal of Migration and Law* 249; 'Limits to Discretion and Automated Risk Assessments in EU Border Control: Recognising the Political in the Technical' (2024) 30 *European Law Journal* 103. Also see Alexandra Karaiskou and Niovi Vavoula, 'AI Risk Assessments in EU Large-Scale IT Systems for Third-country Nationals and Access to Remedies: A Bumpy Road Ahead' in *Data Protection, Privacy and Artificial Intelligence: To Govern or to be Governed, that is the Question* (forthcoming).

[10] Yavar Bathase, 'The Artificial Intelligence Black Box and the Failure of Intent and Causation' (2018) 31(2) *Harvard Journal of Law and Technology*.

of AI – the so-called black box effect. Indeed, such tools are designed on the basis of the end users' instructions to the developers, but how the tool is programmed to do this is opaque, non-transparent and frequently guarded as commercial property.[11] This chapter aims to contribute to these emerging debates[12] by providing an anthology of rule of law challenges stemming from the progressive shift towards AI-fication of European borders. As with the previous chapter, the research does not aspire to an exhaustive analysis, but rather provides concrete cases of rule of law challenges. It focuses on issues relating to the principle of legality, understood as encompassing foreseeability and clarity of the law, legal certainty, the prohibition of arbitrariness of the executive powers and the existence of effective judicial protection through access to judicial remedies.[13] To draw more precise conclusions about the rule of law deficit, the research focuses on both national and EU-level developments.

Against this backdrop, the chapter is structured as follows: the next section provides a concise synopsis of the experimentation of European states with algorithms and AI to inform the subsequent analysis. Then, the analysis focuses on algorithm-powered risk assessments for visa applications (so-called triaging), using as an example the deployment of such tools by the Netherlands and the UK. Section 3 looks into the forthcoming deployment of algorithms in EU migration, asylum and border management with the aim to provide a bird's eye view into how large-scale IT systems will rely on algorithms by focusing on algorithmic risk assessment in the context of the European Travel Information and Authorisation System (ETIAS) and the Visa Information System (VIS), discussed in the previous chapter, the possibility of deploying facial recognition technology, and the elusive role of interoperability in the shift towards algorithmization and AI.

2 The manifold experimentation with algorithms in European states: terminological ambiguities and lack of foreseeability

To illustrate the magnitude of experiments in European states with tools of automation and AI, this section provides a concise overview of the different

[11] Saurabh Bagchi, 'What is a Black Box? A Computer Scientist Explains what it Means when the Inner Workings of AIs are Hidden' (*The Conversation*, 22 May 2023), https://theconversation.com/what-is-a-black-box-a-computer-scientist-explains-what-it-means-when-the-inner-workings-of-ais-are-hidden-203888, accessed 25 September 2025.

[12] Ronan Kennedy, 'The Rule of Law and Algorithmic Governance' in Woodrow Barfield (ed), *The Cambridge Handbook of the Law of Algorithms* (Cambridge University Press 2020).

[13] Case C-156/21 *Hungary v European Parliament and Council of the European Union* (16 February 2022) EI:C:2022:97, para 232.

tools piloted, tested and deployed followed by an in-depth examination of algorithmic risk assessments of visa applicants in two European countries, the Netherlands and the UK.

2.1 A bird's eye view into national initiatives at the borders

Since the past decade, a highly technologized model of migration management, encompassing migration, asylum and border management, is already a reality in various countries – primarily of the Global North.[14] For example, in Canada, the use of algorithmic decision-making in immigration and refugee status determination has been promoted since 2014,[15] whereas at the US–Mexico border, the assessment as to whether an irregular migrant must be placed in pre-deportation detention is determined on the basis of an algorithm.[16] At European level, various European countries have relied on their own means to develop and test new tools, with new technologies deployed to control mobility both before their arrival to Europe and at the borders. Certain EU Member States have invested in tools providing predictions to assist in human decision-making or to influence policy making or approximating other administrative tasks preparatory to human decision-making. Emphasis has been placed on various forecasting tools predicting future immigration and displacement towards Europe (Germany,[17] Sweden[18] and Denmark).[19] In 2023, it was found that the Dutch authorities implement an algorithm to assess short-stay (Schengen) visa applications, which was criticized as discriminatory as it labelled all young men from Suriname for intensive assessment.[20] In

---

[14] For an overview, Derya Ozkul, 'Automating Immigration and Asylum: Mapping the Landscape of New Technologies in Europe' (Working Paper AFAR, January 2022).

[15] Petra Molnár and Lex Gill, 'Bots at the Gate: A Human Rights Analysis of Automated Decision Making in Canada's Immigration and Refugee System' (University of Toronto and the Citizen Lab-Munk School of Global Affairs and Public Policy, 2018) 14–15.

[16] Robert Koulish, 'Immigration Detention in the Risk Classification Assessment Era' (2017) 16 *Connecticut Public Interest Law Journal* 3.

[17] The PREVIEW project monitors ongoing conflicts, and its long-term aim is to develop a forecasting tool for future events. See Commission, 'Feasibility Study on a Forecasting and Early Warning Tool for Migration based on Artificial Intelligence Technology' (November 2020) 36.

[18] The PREDICT project used supervised machine learning techniques to predict migration flows to Sweden, the processing times of different types of cases (such as asylum, residency permit, work permit), and settlement of migrants across Sweden in different months of the year.

[19] Ozkul (n 14).

[20] 'Dutch Foreign Ministry Using Discriminatory Algorithm for Visa Applications' (*NL Times*, 2 May 2023), https://nltimes.nl/2023/05/02/dutch-foreign-ministry-using-dis criminatory-algorithm-visa-applications, accessed 12 October 2024.

Norway[21] and Sweden,[22] tools have been developed to automate the processing of short- and long-term residence and citizenship applications, but in both cases, the systems are less advanced and do not entail machine learning. Another popular AI-based software enables checking whether travellers' or applicants' identities and other supporting documents are genuine and thus detects possible identity fraud. This is the case in the Netherlands,[23] but similar tools are under development in Belgium and France. This does not mean that after arrival, experimentation is less advanced. Additional tools have been developed with name transliteration, that is, converting asylum applicants' names into the Latin alphabet, dialect recognition and mobile phone data analysis, which are gaining momentum.[24]

2.2 The case of triaging visa applications in the Netherlands and the UK

A key issue that has emerged raising significant rule of law challenges stems from the lack of transparency as to the *actual* deployment of AI tools or simpler algorithms, which do not fall within the definition of AI under the AI Act and by the Organisation for Economic Co-operation and Development. This has significant implications in various respects: the applicability of a dedicated legal framework aimed at regulating the use of AI, such as the AI Act; and, second, on ensuring accountability, for example, through proper supervision by national supervisory authorities (data protection or AI-related). The secrecy concerning the precise nature and complexity of the tools used to assist, streamline and standardize human decision-making adds to the inherent opacity of the AI systems, whereby individuals do not know exactly how the AI tool reaches the recommendation and what precise criteria are taken into consideration and how these weigh against each other. Without knowledge as to whether and to what extent those algorithms qualify as AI or not, it becomes impossible for individuals to foresee whether, how and which law applies. This raises significant challenges

---

21 Two robots can register documents, 'filter and mark applications and send out confirmations of legal residence'. See Ozkul (n 14) 22–23.

22 This concerns a rule-based system to verify the age of the applicant or in the case of applications for a work permit, verifying the presence of sponsorship and checking the eligibility of the applicant.

23 This software uses pattern recognition and augmented intelligence and classifies documents according to their risks based on features of the presented document; See Ozkul (n 14) 25.

24 Helene Hohn, 'Digital Identification Systems and the Right to Privacy in the Asylum Context: An Analysis of Implementations in Germany' (Master's Thesis, Leuphana Universität Lüneburg, 2020) 40; Francesca Palmiotto and Derya Ozkul, '"Like Handing My Whole Life Over": The German Federal Administrative Court's Landmark Ruling on Mobile Phone Data Extraction in Asylum Procedures' (*Verfassungsblog*, 28 February 2023), https://verfassungsblog.de/like-handing-my-whole-life-over/, accessed 12 October 2024.

for legal certainty and foreseeability, which are significantly heightened when the tools employed, the rules on how they function and any safeguards regarding the protection of personal data and other human rights are not foreseen in national legislation.

2.2.1 The Dutch 'Informatie Ondersteund Beslissen' algorithm

The case of the Dutch algorithm designed to assess short-stay (Schengen) visa applications is a paradigmatic example of bending the principle of legality and adding to the inherent opacity of algorithm assisted decision-making. The algorithm, referred to internally as Informatie Ondersteund Beslissen, has been deployed by the Dutch Ministry of Foreign Affairs since 2015 as a profiling system designed to calculate the risk score of short-stay (Schengen) visa applicants applying to enter the Netherlands and, consequently, the Schengen area.[25] Its deployment, driven by interests in cutting costs, was completely secretive and unknown to the public and resulted in the profiling of millions of visa applicants using variables like nationality, gender and age.[26] The use of algorithmic profiling for risk prediction is a technique which can be significantly impacted by technological evolution. However, it shifts the assessment focus from someone's individual behaviour to their socio-demographic identity and can result in excluding them from opportunities simply because of who they are and whether their characteristics match the profiles of other individuals who have been deemed in the past as risky, rather than the actual risky behaviour they may display. This probabilistic logic devoid of concrete evidence can result in high false error rates, which may not lead to a ban on the use of profiling, but according to the Court of Justice of the European Union (CJEU) require heightened safeguards.[27] In the Dutch case, applications were categorized as 'low risk', 'moderate risk' and 'high risk' and converted into tracks: fast track, regular track and

---

[25] 'Ethnic Profiling: Whistleblower Reveals Netherlands' Use of Secret and Potentially Illegal Algorithm to Score Visa Applicants' (*Lighthouse Reports*, 23 April 2023), https://www.lighthousereports.com/investigation/ethnic-profiling/, accessed 12 October 2024.

[26] Rijksorganisatie voor Ontwikkeling Digitaliseringe en Innovatie, 'Bias-toetsing "Kort Verblijf Visa" aanvragen' (April 2023), https://racismandtechnology.center/wp-content/uploads/202304-rijks-ict-gilde-bias-toetsing-kort-verblijf-visum-aanvragen.pdf, accessed 12 October 2024; Racism and Criminology Center, 'Dutch Ministry of Foreign Affairs Dislikes the Conclusions of a Solid Report that Marks their Visa Process as Discriminatory so Buys a Shoddy Report Saying the Opposite' (May 2024), https://racismandtechnology.center/2024/05/28/dutch-ministry-of-foreign-affairs-dislikes-the-conclusions-of-a-solid-report-that-marks-their-visa-process-as-discriminatory-so-buys-a-shoddy-report-saying-the-opposite/, accessed 12 October 2024.

[27] Case C-817/19 *Ligue des droits humains ASBL v Conseil des ministers* (21 June 2022) EU:C:2022:491.

intensive track, a method commonly known as 'triaging'. Applicants scored as 'high risk' were automatically moved to an 'intensive track' that can involve extensive investigation and delay. The Data Protection Officer of the Ministry warned of potential ethnic discrimination and advised the Ministry to 'immediately stop profiling visa applicants to distinguish them partly on the basis of nationality and then treating them unequally on the basis of that distinction'.[28] Indeed, research demonstrates that the Dutch algorithm has resulted in family members of Dutch citizens with a migration background being prevented from securing a short-stay visa. Especially applicants from Suriname and Morocco found significant obstacles in obtaining a visa; examples of so-called 'risk profiles' used by the algorithm include Surinamese men aged between 26 and 40 who applied from Paramaribo and unmarried Nepalese men aged around 35–40 who applied for a tourist visa.[29] Officials claim that the risk profiles are also based on data from third parties to see if a group of individuals from the same nationalities attempted to apply for asylum. Overall, statistical data from the Ministry suggest that being flagged as a high risk can carry significant consequences: 33 per cent of applications in the intensive, 'high risk' track were rejected, whereas only 3.5 per cent of applications in the normal, 'low risk' track were rejected. The intensive track also signifies that the examination of the visa application is prolonged for months, thus creating a discouraging, hostile environment of extreme bureaucracy.[30]

The Dutch case illustrates various rule of law challenges; the reference to the vaguer term 'algorithm' blurs the picture as to the use of AI, thus putting into question whether the protective safeguards of the AI Act will apply once the Regulation comes into force. Indeed, all sources consulted on the operation and the discrimination challenges posed by the Dutch tool very carefully make no reference to the term AI. This includes the study commissioned by the Ministry and conducted by auditors who provided an *ex post* rubberstamping of the algorithm, which recommended a continuation of the practice subject to certain recommendations and modifications.[31] The study came after an internal auditor. The commissioned study referred to the algorithm as the BAO Classification Model, an even more technical term, which 'does not utilize a learning algorithm and does not adapt based on historical case outcomes. Instead, it operates within the confines of the

[28] *Lighthouse Reports* (n 25).

[29] Ibid.

[30] Ibid.

[31] SigmaRed, 'Report on Algorithmic Bias Assessment' (7 February 2024), https://racismandtechnology.center/wp-content/uploads/20240227-sigmared-report-algorithmic-bias-visum-aanvragen.pdf, accessed 12 October 2024.

established guidelines'.[32] It was described as a rules-based system, with the rules established under the foreign ministry's guidelines, not learning from past cases as per its design, but rather built on a set of fixed rules and that does not evolve with new data.[33] This finding points to the direction that the Dutch algorithm is not a machine learning tool, whereby the tool is learning from data, and is classified as a 'rules-based' system, whereby the machine merely follows an instruction whereby 'if x then y'. This does not mean that such systems do not fall within the definition of the AI Act, which is broad enough and can encompass rules-based systems, which combine automated inferences based on data training methods. The audit report does not explain in the necessary detail how the algorithm is designed or where the criteria come from; a vague reference to the Ministry's Guidelines is not sufficient to provide foreseeability for individuals. Instead, the study found that there was no disproportionate discrimination based on age, marital status or gender. Notwithstanding the concerns regarding specific nationalities, as mentioned earlier, the study only found that the risk profiles in connection to nationals of Yemen displayed bias due to the rejection rates in respect of their applications. It also revealed a 'notable correlation between BAO Profile and visa application outcomes', in other words, that the visa officers heavily relied on the outcome of the algorithm in their final decision-making on the application. Hiding behind the more ambiguous term 'algorithm' is an interesting practice as it avoids the loaded term of AI, but also allows significant flexibility and discretion on upgrading initially simpler algorithms – for example, those that are rules-based – to more complex machine learning ones. This is a point to which this chapter will return.

Importantly, the secretiveness of the tool is highly questionable; it challenges the principle of legality due to the lack of embedding the tool into legal requirement and frustrates the foreseeability of the applicable law; Schengen visa applications are regulated by the EU Visa Code[34] and – in the form of soft law – the Visa Handbook,[35] all of which create some legal

32 Ibid 13.

33 Ibid.

34 Regulation (EC) No 810/2009 of the European Parliament and of the Council of 13 July 2009 establishing a Community Code on Visas (Visa Code) [2009] OJ L 243/1, as amended by the Regulation 2019/1155 of the European Parliament and of the Council of 20 June 2019; Regulation (EU) 2019/1155 of the European Parliament and of the Council of 20 June 2019 amending Regulation (EC) No 810/2009 establishing a Community Code on Visas (Visa Code) [2019] OJ L 188/25.

35 ANNEX to the Commission Implementing Decision amending Commission Decision C (2010) 1620 as regards the replacement of the Handbook for the processing of visa applications and the modification of issued visas (Visa Code Handbook I) C (2024) 4319 final.

certainty as to the process that is followed, the criteria that are used and the exercise of remedies by the failed visa applicants. The processing of personal data of Schengen visa applicants is regulated by VIS, as discussed in the previous chapter, which at the time when the Dutch Ministry deployed the algorithm had not even conceived the automated processing of visa applications through the use of algorithmic profiling; the revised VIS proposal was only adopted in 2018[36] and Regulation (EU) 2021/1134 – the revised VIS Regulation – was adopted in 2021.[37] Algorithmic profiling has not yet been put in place at EU level, yet at national level, the Dutch have already gone beyond the EU requirements. It is true that the field of migration constitutes a shared competence among the EU and its Member States and, therefore, the Dutch Ministry could have the discretionary power to deploy algorithmic profiling to streamline the processing of visa applications. Yet, the complete opacity at the national level as to how this algorithm operates, exemplified by the lack of documentation – let alone a legal instrument detailing its use, the data used to create the risk profiles, and a clear statement as to whether the tool deployed qualifies as AI or not poses challenges to the rule of law, which prevent individuals from having any indication about how their application has been handled, what criteria are taken into account in examining the application, how these are weighed and what safeguards are in place to prevent violations of fundamental rights, notably discriminatory treatment, of visa applicants. Ultimately, the information that a rejected visa applicant receives is laid down in the Visa Code and does not contain any requirement for referencing the use of algorithmic profiling.[38]

2.2.2 The UK litigation

The case of the UK is very similar to the Dutch one, with one significant difference being the inapplicability of EU law due to non-participation of the UK in the Schengen area. In 2020, two non-governmental

[36] Commission, 'Proposal for a Regulation of the European Parliament and of the Council amending Regulation (EC) No 767/2008, Regulation (EC) No 810/2009, Regulation (EU) 2017/2226, Regulation (EU) 2016/399, Regulation XX/2018 [Interoperability Regulations], and Decision 2004/512/EC and repealing Council Decision 2008/633/JHA' COM (2018) 302 final.

[37] Regulation (EU) 2021/1134 of the European Parliament and of the Council of 7 July 2021 amending Regulations (EC) No 767/2008, (EC) No 810/2009, (EU) 2016/399, (EU) 2017/2226, (EU) 2018/1240, (EU) 2018/1860, (EU) 2018/1861, (EU) 2019/817 and (EU) 2019/1896 of the European Parliament and of the Council and repealing Council Decisions 2004/512/EC and 2008/633/JHA, for the purpose of reforming the Visa Information System [2021] OJ L 248/11 (revised VIS Regulation).

[38] See Section 3.3.

organizations, Foxglove and the Joint Council for the Welfare of Immigrants, challenged the use of a UK Home Office algorithm designed to sift through visa applications as a tool for assisting visa officers working in selected West African states to reach decisions quickly.[39] This is another form of a 'traffic light method',[40] whereby markers such as nationality, country of birth, age, travel history, and so on, were used to assign colour codes, sorting applications into those needing further scrutiny and those eligible for approval by classifying them as red ('high risk'), amber ('medium risk') or green ('low risk').[41] A red etiquette to a visa application would entail heightened suspicion by the visa officer, resulting almost always in an automatic rejection – in a similar fashion as the Netherlands – there was high correlation between the output of the algorithm and the final decision by the visa officer.[42] An application coloured in amber would be further examined and a green one would result in virtually automatic approval. The streaming tool was not explicitly classified as AI, in clear attempts to confuse the public and there was no legislation allowing for individuals to foresee first the existence of the streaming tool and the criteria and safeguards which underpinned its operation. In the litigation, it was alleged that a secret list of nationalities in respect of which any application made by a person from one of those countries were classified as red and thus would result in quasi-automatic refusal. Furthermore, an inevitable feedback loop was in the making: visa decision rates determined the countries on the list of 'suspected nationalities', heightening the likelihood of rejection for applicants from these countries.[43] This approach constitutes a form of digitalized, structured discrimination, possibly on

---

39 The UK legal basis of the challenge was the Equality Act 2010 and the prejudicial consequences of the AI tool's operation.

40 Independent Chief Inspector of Borders and Immigration, 'An Inspection of the Home Office's Network Consolidation Programme and the "Onshoring" of Visa Processing and Decision Making to the UK' (September 2018–August 2019), https://assets.publishing.service.gov.uk/government/uploads/system/uploads/attachment_data/file/863627/ICIBI_An_inspection_of_the_Home_Office_s_Network_Consolidation_Programme.pdf, accessed 12 October 2024.

41 For an analysis, see Catriona Barclay and Elspeth Guild, 'Brexit, Personal Data and Aliens' (2023) 37(3) *Immigration, Asylum and Nationality Law* 271.

42 Ibid.

43 Racism and Technology Center, 'Racist Technology in Action: The UK Home Office's Sorting Algorithm and the Racist Violence of Borders' (2024), https://racismandtechnology.center/2024/04/01/racist-technology-in-action-the-uk-home-offices-sorting-algorithm-and-the-racist-violence-of-borders/, accessed 12 October 2024; Foxglove, 'Home Office Says it Will Abandon Racist Algorithm – After We Sued Them' (4 August 2020), https://www.foxglove.org.uk/2020/08/04/home-office-says-it-will-abandon-its-racist-visa-algorithm-after-we-sued-them/, accessed 12 October 2024.

the grounds of ethnic origin and race.[44] The litigation was a first-class opportunity for the Home Office to disclose the inner workings of the streaming tool, but it instead chose to scrap the tool rather than defend it before the Administrative Court. Home Secretary Priti Patel pledged a full review of the system, including for issues of 'unconscious bias' and discrimination.[45]

The UK case exemplifies a multitude of rule of law challenges; compared to the Dutch case, here the muddy landscape as to the nature of the algorithm remains, given that the Home Office has deliberately sealed the 'black box' retaining the opacity of the algorithms and the subsequent decision-making. The lack of law explicitly foreseeing the use of the streaming tool and providing a basic understanding as to its operation is also astonishing. Overall, the foreseeability for visa applicants as to how their application would be handled, effectively allowing them to understand the inner workings of the algorithm was impaired. Ultimately, seeking judicial protection in case of suspected discriminatory treatment – arguably the 'suspect nationalities' list approach showcases a complete disregard for the principle of non-discrimination in the design and operation of the system – was made impossible.

3 The shift towards algorithmization and AI at EU level: the case of interoperable large-scale IT systems

The six interoperable large-scale IT systems, examined in Chapter 8, also merit further analysis from the perspective of deploying AI systems. The rule of law challenges here emerge already from the lack of any reference to the term 'artificial intelligence' in the legal instruments governing the databases, including non-legislative delegated and implementing acts, which provide for a series of technical specifications. No legal instrument governing the IT systems or interoperability and no implementing or delegated act mention the term 'AI'. This is notwithstanding the fact that Article 111 of the AI Act states that 'AI systems which are components of the large-scale IT systems ... that have been placed on the market or put into service before 2 August 2027 shall be brought into compliance with this Regulation by 31 December 2030'. The legal instruments governing the databases and their interoperability are listed therein. This delay in bringing the large-scale IT systems within the scope of the AI Act, coupled with Article 83 of the Commission Proposal for an AI Act which *ab initio* excluded them from the scope, points to the direction that the IT systems will rely on AI

[44] Ibid.

[45] Ibid.

tools.[46] But where exactly? And how will it work? The lack of reference to AI creates significant foreseeability concerns, as individuals cannot be certain as to whether, where and to what extent the IT systems and the interoperability components will operate based on AI or not. Thus, at EU level, the problem does not lie in the existence of law, but rather its quality, hindering foreseeability, as to the deployment – current or future – of AI. Other rule of law challenges involve the lack of applicability of the AI Act for a period of some years, as well as the significant discretionary power provided to Frontex and European Union Agency for the Operational Management of Large-Scale IT Systems in the Area of Freedom, Security and Justice (eu-LISA), as well as the significant obstacles for individuals to seek judicial remedies *ex post* in a meaningful manner.

3.1 Automated processing of applications for Schengen visas and travel authorizations and the central role of the CRRS

A synopsis of the basic functions of ETIAS and VIS was provided in Chapter 8.[47] Suffices here to mention that Regulations 2018/1240 on ETIAS[48] and 2021/1134 on the revised VIS[49] foresee the automated processing of applicants for travel authorizations (for visa-free nationals) and Schengen visas (not long stay-visas or residence permits) as a pre-empting control mechanism enabling extraterritorial border control.

In particular, the ETIAS Regulation requires visa-free travellers to apply online for travel authorization prior to travelling to the Schengen area and disclosing a series of personal data including biographical data, travel arrangements, home and email address, phone number, level of education and current occupation.[50] Based on this information, the data provided will be subject to automated checks against:

- the other IT systems, Europol data and the Interpol databases, Stolen and Lost Travel Document database and the Interpol Documents Associated

[46] Commission, 'Proposal for a Regulation of the European Parliament and of the Council laying down Harmonised Rules on Artificial Intelligence (artificial intelligence act) and amending certain union legislative acts' COM(2021) 206 final (AI Act proposal).

[47] See Chapter 8, Section 2.2.

[48] Regulation (EU) 2018/1240 of the European Parliament and of the Council of 12 September 2018 establishing a European Travel Information and Authorisation System (ETIAS) and amending Regulations (EU) No 1077/2011, (EU) No 515/2014, (EU) 2016/399, (EU) 2016/1624 and (EU) 2017/2226 [2018] OJ L 236/1 (ETIAS Regulation).

[49] Revised VIS Regulation (n 37).

[50] ETIAS Regulation, art 17.

with Notices databases – this cross-checking will be facilitated by one of the interoperability components – the European Search Portal;[51]
- screening rules, enabling profiling on the basis of risk indicators;[52] and
- a dedicated watchlist of persons suspected of terrorist or serious crime.[53]

Whereas automated processing of ETIAS applications against databases and the watchlist will assist in identifying known individuals, the screening rules, which will be developed by the ETIAS Central Unit, established in Frontex,[54] aim to identify persons who are unknown to the competent national authorities. Both functions will rely on different types of algorithm; whereas the first two functions are also algorithm-reliant enabling data matching, it is the third type of automated processing that is of concern here, as it relies on a considerably higher level of automation, involving *data mining*.[55] Flagging an applicant as potentially risky will take place not because of any specific actions they have engaged in, but because they display particular category traits.[56] The screening rules are to be created as follows: by means of a delegated act, the Commission must define the risks related to security, 'illegal immigration' and high epidemic risk, on the basis of various statistical data, including data provided by the IT systems themselves.[57] This should result in a set of characteristics of specific groups of travellers associated with these risks.[58] The Commission must then specify the risks by means of an implementing act on which the specific risks indicators shall be based.[59] In the case of ETIAS, the independent variables used as risk indicators are demographic and socio-economic

[51] In addition to Article 20 of the ETIAS Regulation, see Regulation (EU) 2021/1152 of the European Parliament and of the Council of 7 July 2021 amending Regulations (EC) No 767/2008, (EU) 2017/2226, (EU) 2018/1240, (EU) 2018/1860, (EU) 2018/1861 and (EU) 2019/817 as regards the establishment of the conditions for accessing other EU information systems for the purposes of the European Travel Information and Authorisation System [2021] OJ L 249/15.

[52] ETIAS Regulation, arts 20(5) and 33.

[53] Ibid art 34.

[54] Ibid art 7.

[55] Karaiskou and Vavoula (n 9).

[56] Susie Alegre, Julien Jeandesboz and Niovi Vavoula, 'European Travel Information and Authorisation System (ETIAS): Border Management, Fundamental Rights and Data Protection' (Study for the European Parliament, 2017) 23–26.

[57] ETIAS Regulation, art 33(2). See Commission Delegated Decision of 23 November 2021 on Further Defining Security, Illegal Immigration or High Epidemic Risks, C (2021) 4981 final.

[58] ETIAS Regulation, art 33(3)–(4).

[59] Commission Implementing Decision of 23 November 2021 on Specifying Risks Related to Security, Illegal Immigration or High Epidemic Risk as Defined in Regulation (EU) 2018/1240 of the European Parliament and of the Council, C (2021) 4980.

characteristics of visa-exempt travellers (namely, age, sex, nationality, country and city of residence, educational level and occupation group) associated with security, irregular immigration and high epidemic risks.[60] After determining the risk profiles based on statistical data from ETIAS itself and the Entry/Exit System (EES), including information on overstayers or refusals of entry or refusals of travel authorizations and information provided by Member States.[61]

If automated processing reveals a hit, Articles 21 and 22 of the ETIAS Regulation provide that the ETIAS Central Unit shall be consulted to verify the hit. If the hit is verified then the application will be processed manually (human in the loop) by the responsible ETIAS National Unit.[62] Otherwise, if no hit is reported, the travel authorization will be automatically granted.[63] Ultimately, automated processing will allow reallocating screening resources to 'risky' individuals prior to their departure, while facilitating travel for low-risk profiles.[64]

In the case of VIS, the revised VIS Regulation foresees largely similar rules on algorithmic profiling, with some differences. For example, even if automated processing does not reveal any hits with other information systems or databases or algorithms (which in the case of VIS are called specific risk indicators and not screening rules), the visa application will be processed manually at national level and there is no automated positive decision-making.[65] Furthermore, the risk indicators differ in that: (1) education level is not included therein (because education level is not requested in a visa application); and (2) additional travel-related data are also included, namely the Member State of destination, the Member State of first entry, and the purpose of travel.[66] These additional risk indicators can be used to infer risk rules about suspicious travel patterns.

The reference to the vague term 'algorithm' is noteworthy: another example of efforts to avoid the loaded term of 'AI' or leaving this issue open for introducing AI in the future. Even the term algorithm has been contested; Frontex has insisted that it would actually be more appropriate to refer to filtering queries than algorithms, and that no sophisticated analysis methods or any form of AI is involved in the risk assessment.[67] As Zandstra

---

[60] ETIAS Regulation, art 33(4).

[61] Ibid art 33(3).

[62] Ibid arts 25–32.

[63] Ibid art 21.

[64] Matthias Leese, 'The New Profiling: Algorithms, Black Boxes, and the Failure of Anti-discriminatory Safeguards in the European Union' (2014) 45(5) *Security Dialogue* 494.

[65] Revised VIS Regulation, art 9j.

[66] Ibid art 9j (4).

[67] Derave et al (n 8).

and Brouwer have stressed, this approach is at odds with the very wording of the legal instruments and exemplifies the politics around the use of AI in this field, aimed at blurring the landscape and ultimately obstructing scrutiny.[68]

The potential of using AI in the implementation of the ETIAS screening rules and the VIS specific risk indicators may be found in the Central Repository for Reporting and Statistics (CRRS),[69] aimed to 'provide cross-system statistical data and analytical reporting for policy, operational and data quality purposes'.[70] A (non-publicly available) report by eu-LISA states that CRRS that will collect and store (among others) statistical data from VIS, EES and ETIAS of overstayers and information regarding refusals of entry of third-country nationals can use AI tools to enhance the identification of risks for specific groups of travellers by identifying patterns or a set of common characteristics from the analysis of historical data in the CRRS related to security, irregular migration and high epidemic risks.[71] Furthermore, in the Report of the Future Group on Travel Intelligence and Border Management by Europol and Frontex,[72] it is stated that in cooperation with eu-LISA and other partner agencies, the joint analysis capability could leverage the full potential of CRRS as a data source for analytical purposes and develop appropriate analytical tools for risk assessment with the support of AI. The possibility that CRRS could use AI tools to assist in the design of risk profiles for ETIAS and VIS demonstrates the true potential of the interoperability components, which is not exhausted in aggregating data from the underlying systems, as mentioned in the previous chapter, but entails putting them into novel uses beyond the contours of their operation.

Apart from the nature of the algorithm, its actual design and content of the specific risk indicators are not foreseeable. They are not written in law, which only contains the categories of data that will be used for their creation and therefore individuals could only have a very vague idea of how the profiling takes place. The lack of clarity and foreseeability as to the nature, design and content of the risk assessment of travellers through the algorithm

[68] Zandstra and Brouwer (n 8).

[69] Alexandra Karaiskou, *Immigration and Algorithmic Discrimination in Europe* (PhD Thesis, European University Institute).

[70] Interoperability Regulations, art 39(1).

[71] eu-LISA, 'AI in CSSR in the Context of ETIAS and the Revised VIS Final Report' (2022), https://www.eulisa.europa.eu/Publications/Information%20Material/eu-LISA%20-%20Year%20In%20Review%202022.pdf, accessed 12 October 2024.

[72] Europol and Frontex, 'Future Group on Travel Intelligence and Border Management – Final Report' (2021) 65, https://www.europol.europa.eu/cms/sites/default/files/documents/1127634-_public_version_of_1031161.pdf, accessed 12 October 2024.

resonates with what Hildebrandt has referred to as 'code-driven' and 'data-driven' law, which is in contrast to written legal norms.[73]

The use of AI in CRRS for the determination and verification of the risk profiles raises additional questions regarding the application of the AI Act. Arguably, CRRS constitutes a high-risk AI system, which is subject to specific safeguards on risk management,[74] human oversight,[75] pre-market conformity assessments[76] and post-market monitoring.[77] Furthermore, both providers and deployers also need to register specific information of the high-risk AI systems in an EU database managed by the Commission in collaboration with the Member State concerned.[78] However, high-risk AI systems in the area of migration, asylum and border control management will be registered in a non-public database only accessible to the Commission and competent national authorities.[79] Furthermore, certain important pieces of information, such as the training data used or a summary of the fundamental rights impact assessment, do not need to be entered at all.[80] From a rule of law perspective, this is a particularly important exception because it may perpetuate the lack of transparency and lack of foreseeability regarding the use of AI in ETIAS and VIS. As a result, we may never have full information regarding the application of AI in CRRS.

3.2 Significant discretionary power to Frontex and eu-LISA

A key requirement of the principle of legality is putting sufficient limits on the discretionary powers of public authorities.[81] Whereas the Commission will specify the risks, it is for Frontex to establish the specific risk indicators. For example, a screening rule could capture all males from New Zealand between the ages of 18 and 30 occupied in agriculture, which means that all ETIAS applicants falling within this risk profile could be flagged as potential threats whose application merits manual examination by the responsible ETIAS National Unit. As argued by Musco-Eklund,[82] both ETIAS and

73 Mireille Hildebrand, 'The Adaptive Nature of Text Driven Law' (2021) 1(1) *Computational and Text-driven Law*.

74 AI Act, art 9.

75 Ibid art 14.

76 Ibid art 17.

77 Ibid art 72.

78 Ibid art 49 in conjunction with art 72.

79 Ibid art 49(4).

80 Ibid in conjunction with Annex VIII.

81 Musco-Eklund (n 9) 255.

82 Ibid.

VIS Regulation allows significant discretion to the agency as they merely require that the specific risk indicators are:

- based on the Commission's risk specification;
- consist of a combination of certain data categories; and
- are targeted, proportionate and non-discriminatory.[83]

These requirements do not say anything as to 'how personal traits and data will be weighed against each other in the risk assessment'.[84] A great degree of discretion is also enjoyed by eu-LISA, which, as explained in Chapter 8, is the technical developer and manager of ETIAS and VIS and is developing the software enabling the profiling.[85] The only limitation on the developer is that the algorithm shall enable profiling by comparing risk indicators with data in the application file, without further specifying the actual design.[86] The fact that private companies hired by eu-LISA are involved in the development of the algorithm raises additional questions of foreseeability for the individuals.

3.3 Elusive judicial protection against discriminatory decision-making

The case of automated risk assessments, potentially relying on AI, poses significant challenges to individuals' rights, particularly non-discrimination. As highlighted elsewhere, specific groups of travellers are likely to be disadvantaged compared to others based on protected characteristics (namely age, sex, nationality, or social origin and combinations thereof) resulting in indirect discrimination and a presumption of 'guilt', even if they have done nothing wrong. Considering that immigration decision-making is already intertwined with ethnic and social stereotypes, profiling may further reify them in a vicious circle of self-fulfilling prophecies, resulting in serious discrimination concerns.[87] Furthermore, the principle of individualized assessment of applications and the duty to give reasons, an essential requirement of good administration as a general principle of EU law, enshrined in Article 41(2c) of the EU Charter, may be compromised to

[83] ETIAS Regulation, art 33(4)–(5) and revised VIS Regulation, art 9j(4).

[84] Musco-Eklund (n 9) 259.

[85] ETIAS Regulation, arts 6(1), 73(3) and 74(1); Revised VIS Regulation, art 26.

[86] Musco-Eklund (n 9) 260.

[87] For an analysis see Niovi Vavoula, 'Tr-AI-nsforming Migration, Asylum and Border Management in the EU: The Roles of the AI Act, Interoperable Large-scale IT Systems and EU Migration Agencies' (Computer Law & Security Review, forthcoming; Niovi Vavoula, 'Algorithmic Profiling and Ineffective Remedies: The Cases of ETIAS and VIS' (2023) 3 *ASYL* 13; Karaiskou and Vavoula (n 9).

the extent that adverse decisions are adopted primarily on the basis of such profiles.[88] Moreover, even if the facts of each case are taken into consideration during the manual assessment, the automated 'hits' produced by ETIAS or the revised VIS are likely to impair independent human evaluation.[89]

The aforementioned considerations suggest that the ability of individuals to seek effective judicial remedies, as enshrined in Article 47 of the EU Charter, is important for safeguarding the rule of law. In *R.N.N.S and K.A*, concerning the rejection of two visa applications on the ground of risk to public policy, internal security or public health, the CJEU held that summary justifications based on predetermined lists of grounds did not meet this threshold of specificity, as the statement of reasons must indicate not only the applicable ground, but also the essence of the reasons of the refusal.[90] Furthermore, in *Ligue des droits humains* on the algorithmic risk assessment of air passengers' Passenger Name Record data, the CJEU stressed Member States must ensure that the affected person can understand how those criteria and those programmes work, without necessarily disclosing to him/her what these are during the administrative procedure, so that he/she can 'decide with full knowledge of the relevant facts whether or not to exercise his or her right to … judicial redress'.[91] The competent national court and the person concerned, unless in case of threats to state security, must have the opportunity to examine all the grounds and evidence on the basis of which the decision was taken.[92]

Regrettably these standards do not exist in either the ETIAS Regulation or the revised VIS Regulation.

Article 38 of the ETIAS Regulation requires individuals to be informed about the grounds for refusal, and Article 37 states that the predetermined grounds for refusal include, among others, those both clear and specific, such as the existence of a Schengen Information System (SIS) alert, and less clear grounds such as that the applicant poses a security, irregular immigration or high epidemic risk. The applicant will receive a standardized form for

88 Karaiskou and Vavoula (n 9); see also Case C-255/90, *Jean-Louis Burban v European Parliament* (31 March 1992) ECR I-2253; Case T-167/94, *Detlef Nölle v Council of the European Union and Commission of European Communities* (18 September 1995) ECR II-2589; Case T-231/97, *New Europe Consulting and Michael P. Brown v Commission of the European Communities* (9 July 1999) ECR II-2403.

89 Saar Alon-Barkat and Madalina Busuioc, 'Human-AI Interactions in Public Sector Decision-Making: "Automation Bias" and "Selective Adherence" to Algorithmic Advice' (2023) 33(1) *Journal of Public Administration Research and Theory* 153.

90 Joined cases C-225/19 and C-226/19, *R.N.N.S. and K.A. v Minister van Buitenlandse Zaken* (24 November 2020) EU:C:2020:951.

91 Case C-817/19 *Ligue des droits humains ASBL v Conseil des ministers* (21 June 2022) EU:C:2022:491, para 210.

92 Ibid para 211.

the refusal of the travel authorization which replicates the grounds under Article 37.[93] However, it is unclear what information a rejected ETIAS applicant will receive through the standardized form when they will be 'captured' by the screening rules, even though the standardized form *requires* the ETIAS National Unit to fill in a free-text box stating the relevant facts and additional reasoning underlying the decision.[94] There is potential offered in the handbook foreseen in Article 93 of the ETIAS Regulation, aimed at providing any concrete guidelines on the implementation of ETIAS and which could address such concerns to control.[95] In the case of VIS, things are even more complicated as the examination of a Schengen visa application takes place in accordance with the Visa Code. However, a potential rejection of a Schengen visa application based on the use of algorithms has not been accompanied by any changes in the information provided to rejected applicants. Annex VI of the Visa Code includes the standard form for refusal of visa applications, but it has not been adapted to the introduction of algorithmic profiling through VIS.

3.4 Facial images: the hidden shift towards facial recognition

Aside from the term 'algorithm', which blurs the landscape as to the deployment of AI in the case of algorithmic profiling, the legal framework of large-scale IT systems is equally confusing as to the use of AI in the processing of biometric data, namely fingerprints (or broadly dactyloscopic data) and facial images. With the exception of ETIAS, IT systems will process different types of biometric data, with emphasis on verification (one-to-one recognition) and identification (one-to-many recognition) initially through fingerprints and more recently facial images. In particular, fingerprint identification already takes places in Eurodac, VIS and SIS to verify the identity or identify third-country nationals at the borders or on national territory.[96] There is also desire to make the most of facial images, through the deployment of facial recognition technology (FRT), which is more invasive as it happens at a distance, without contact, with people in motion, without their awareness or consent. Indeed, all EU large-scale systems, except ETIAS, will process facial images.

Regulation 2017/2226 on EES foresees two types of biometric identifiers – four fingerprints and a facial image – and has provided for the use of facial

[93] Commission Implementing Decision (EU) 2022/102 of 25 January 2022 laying down forms for refusal, annulment or revocation of a travel authorisation [2022] OJ L 17/59.

[94] Karaiskou and Vavoula (n 9).

[95] ETIAS Regulation, art 93.

[96] Vavoula (n 4).

recognition technology for verification purposes at the border and on national territory.[97] EES will rely on machine learning techniques for biometric matching. Facial images may also be used in combination with fingerprints to identify individuals and border authorities or immigration authorities shall have access to search with the fingerprint data or the fingerprint data combined with the facial image, for the sole purpose of identifying any third-country national who may have been registered previously in EES under a different identity or who does not fulfil or no longer fulfils the conditions for entry to, or for stay on, the territory of the Member States.[98]

In addition, Regulation (EU) 2024/1358 on the revised Eurodac foresees the recording of facial images in addition to fingerprints in respect of individuals falling within the personal scope of the database (applicants for international protection, refugees, irregular migrants, beneficiaries of temporary protection, individuals rescued following a search and rescue operation, and individuals who have been admitted in according with EU or national resettlement schemes). Both fingerprints and facial images will be used for comparison to maximize high degree of accuracy in identifying individuals,[99] but it is possible to record facial images only due to bad quality or unavailability of fingerprints.[100]

Furthermore, Articles 22–23 of the Regulation (EU) 2018/1861 concerning the SIS regulate the processing of photographs, facial images and dactyloscopic data that fulfil minimum data quality standards and technical specifications and must be processed following a data quality check.[101] Facial images will not only be used to confirm the identity of a person, but also 'as soon as it becomes technically possible, and while ensuring a high degree

[97] Regulation (EU) 2017/2226 of the European Parliament and of the Council of 30 November 2017 establishing an Entry/Exit System (EES) to register entry and exit data and refusal of entry data of third-country nationals crossing the external borders of the Member States and determining the conditions for access to the EES for law enforcement purposes, and amending the Convention implementing the Schengen Agreement and Regulations (EC) No 767/2008 and (EU) No 1077/2011 [2017] OJ L 327, art 23(2).

[98] EES Regulation, art 26. Also, according to Articles 24 and 25, facial images may be used as search keys to conduct searches in EES for the purposes of examining a visa application or having access to facilitation programmes.

[99] Ibid art 27.

[100] Ibid art 28. In that case a verification by a trained expert is necessary. See Article 38.

[101] Regulation (EU) 2018/1861 of the European Parliament and of the Council of 28 November 2018 on the establishment, operation and use of the Schengen Information System (SIS) in the field of border checks, and amending the Convention implementing the Schengen Agreement, and amending and repealing Regulation (EC) No 1987/2006 [2018] OJ L 312/14 (SIS Regulation for border checks). The Commission will adopt those standards and specifications. Ibid art 32(4). Also see Regulation 2018/1860, art 4.

of reliability of identification' facial images may be used to identify a person in the context of regular border-crossing points.[102]

Similarly, with respect to the European Criminal Record Information System for Third-country Nationals (ECRIS-TCN), which will also be used for border management purposes, Article 6 of the ECRIS-TCN Regulation foresees that in the first stage, facial images may be used only to confirm the identity of a third-country national who has been identified as a result of an alphanumeric search or a search using fingerprint data.[103] In the second stage and following a Commission delegated act, facial images will be used for the purpose of identifying third-country nationals in order to determine the Member States holding information on previous convictions concerning such persons.

Finally, in the revised VIS Regulation, the collection of live facial images is foreseen during the application process to enable biometric matching using facial recognition technology.[104] Furthermore, in rules mirroring the EES Regulation, facial images will be used to verify the identity of a visa holder at the borders or to identify them in combination with their fingerprints.[105] However, it is explicitly stated that facial images shall not be the only search criterion.[106]

Notwithstanding the rather elaborate provisions, the legal instruments make *no single reference* to the FRT, leaving the reader to guess about the tools deployed. It has been through the reports of eu-LISA that the use of FRT is confirmed, the legal instruments do not provide any clear information to the average public. The legal landscape becomes even more convoluted with the adoption of the Interoperability Regulations, which foresee the creation of a shared Biometric Matching Service (sBMS), which will store biometric templates of all the biometric data stored in the underlying IT systems.[107] It is expected that sBMS will play a pivotal role in deploying FRT in border crossing using the biometric data stored in the IT systems, but this does not flow from the legal framework, either the legislation or the delegated acts. This shocking finding confirms the analysis of the previous chapter on how interoperability creates an ecosystem of extreme

102 Ibid art 33(4).

103 Regulation (EU) 2019/816 of the European Parliament and of the Council of 17 April 2019 establishing a centralised system for the identification of Member States holding conviction information on third-country nationals and stateless persons (ECRIS-TCN) to supplement the European Criminal Records Information System and amending Regulation (EU) 2018/1726 [2019] OJ L 135/1.

104 2021 VIS Regulation, art 22a(1)(j).

105 Ibid art 18.

106 Ibid art 20.

107 Interoperability Regulations, arts 12–16.

opacity and lack of transparency to promote data maximization. It is rather confirmed by eu-LISA itself.[108] In the case of EES, eu-LISA further states that the system will rely on machine learning techniques for biometric matching.[109] In the case of SIS, the processing of facial images will take place by 'plugging CCTV cameras into an AI-enabled, EU-wide police database so that wanted or suspected individuals can be tracked down via their faces or vehicle number plates'.[110]

The lack of foreseeability does not concern only the type of technologies used for the performance of certain tasks, but also the uses of this technology. As mentioned earlier, in principle, biometric data will be used for biometric recognition, including verification and identification.[111] However, in the case of SIS, things are far more complex. As mentioned earlier, biometric recognition will take place first to confirm the identify of a person and 'as soon as it becomes technically possible, and while ensuring a high degree of reliability of identification' facial images may be used to identify a person in the context of regular border crossing points.[112] Before the implementation of this functionality, the Commission shall present a report on the availability, readiness and reliability of the required technology. The Parliament shall be consulted on the report. In delegated acts, the Commission will also determine 'other circumstances in which photographs and facial images may be used to identify persons'.[113] The wording of these provisions is vague, particularly the last part which leaves the door open to the Commission to enable live facial recognition technology at the borders without the knowledge of the persons affected. The Parliament's limited role in ensuring democratic scrutiny is problematic, even more so since the introduction of facial images – and generally the adoption of the revised SIS framework – was not accompanied by an impact assessment evaluating the necessity and proportionality of this new functionality. The impetus towards the

---

[108] eu-LISA, Schengen Conference Session 8: AI but also Interoperable and Automated and Conclusion of the Conference – Intervention by Luca Tagliaretti, Deputy Executive Director of eu-LISA, https://www.youtube.com/watch?v=Kab2ZRy4B4s, accessed 12 October 2024.

[109] eu-LISA, 'Artificial Intelligence in the Operational Management of Large-scale IT Systems' (July 2020), https://op.europa.eu/en/publication-detail/-/publication/6173f7a8-d78a-11ea-adf7-01aa75ed71a1, accessed 12 October 2024.

[110] EuroMed Rights, 'Europe's Techno Borders' (July 2023), https://euromedrights.org/wp-content/uploads/2023/07/EuroMed-Rights_Statewatch_Europe-techno-borders_EN-1.pdf, accessed 12 October 2024.

[111] Biometric identification is considered as a high-risk AI system, but biometric verification is classified as of limited risk.

[112] SIS Regulation for border checks, art 33(4).

[113] Ibid.

incorporation of facial images in SIS is high. The Joint Research Centre of the Commission conducted a study in this respect noting that 30 per cent of alerts in SIS contain facial images already (out of the 965,000 alerts on persons stored in SIS)[114] and concluding that facial recognition technology could be integrated in SIS, listing 19 recommendations for the rollout of the technology, including different measures to ensure the highest possible quality of the stored data.[115]

3.5 The Multiple Identity Detector: an artificial intelligence-powered interoperability component?

Another example of how interoperability conceals the potential recourse to AI systems concerns the operation of the Multiple Identity Detector (MID), the basic modalities of which were analysed in Chapter 8.[116] The operation of MID involving the cross-checking of personal data against all records and the automated creation of links among datasets and the fingerprint matching in national Automated Fingerprint Identification Systems may also entail the use of AI. First, according to Article 27(2) of the Interoperability Regulations, where a record contains biometric data, the detection will be performed through sBMS. Thus, FRT will be used for comparing the biometric templates created from new data to the templates already stored to determine whether data of the same person are already stored in the Common Identity Repository or SIS. Second, with regard to alphanumeric data, searches in the European Search Portal will take place using different combinations of certain biographical data or travel document data.[117] In that regard, according to Recital 41 of the Interoperability Regulations, small transliteration or spelling mistakes will be detected in a manner to avoid creating any unjustified inconvenience for the person in question. Indeed, Delegated Regulation (EU) 2023/333 stresses the need to ensure that the number of cases in which yellow links are generated by MID and therefore require manual verification are limited.[118] To that end, the Delegated Regulation provides an exhaustive list of rules for when identity data shall be considered as similar. These

[114] eu-LISA, 'SIS II – 2020 statistics' (March 2021).

[115] Joint Research Centre of the European Commission, 'Study on Face Identification Technology for its Implementation in the Schengen Information System' (2019) 9.

[116] Chapter 8, Section 2.4.

[117] Interoperability Regulations, art 27(3)–(4).

[118] Commission Delegated Regulation (EU) 2023/333 of 11 July 2022 supplementing Regulation (EU) 2019/817 of the European Parliament and of the Council as regards determining cases where identity data are considered as same or similar for the purpose of the multiple identity detection [2023] OJ L 47/17.

rules concern, for example, known transliteration of names, inversions of name and surname, cases of the order of letters being inversed, or where a difference is found due to the use of hyphens, inversion of date and month when these match.[119] The rules must be applied by eu-LISA, assisted and advised by the Interoperability Advisory Group, 'by means of an algorithm in consultation with the Commission, assisted and advised by the Interoperability Subgroup of the Expert Group on Information Systems for Borders and Security'.[120] eu-LISA shall monitor the impact of the application of the algorithm and report, on a regular basis, to the Expert Group. Where necessary, to limit the number of cases in which yellow links generated by the MID would need to be turned into white links by the responsible authorities, the Commission, assisted and advised by the Expert Group, shall request eu-LISA to adjust the algorithm by prioritizing the yellow links created between identity data that are considered more similar.

The Delegated Decision uses the term 'algorithm' without specifying whether it falls under the definition of AI. But research shows that this could well be AI,[121] specifically AI for text comparison and detection of similarities and differences. Furthermore, it is not clear whether it should be considered as a migration or a law enforcement tool. MID is a paradigmatic example of how cramming divergent objectives within the function of large-scale IT systems challenges the rule of law and can lead to downgrading or removing legal safeguards. MID is by default designed as a hybrid tool aimed not only at flagging cases of potential identity fraud, but a tool that assists in identification of third-country nationals. Whereas the latter points to the direction that MID will function as an administrative tool, the detection of identity fraud relates to law enforcement with significant criminal law consequences. This hybrid nature of MID creates challenges as to the exact articles of the AI Act that apply. In particular, MID could be deemed as a risk assessment tool to determine whether a third-country national poses a risk of irregular migration or security either within the migration-related provisions of the AI Act, namely Annex III.7(b). This category relates to profiling, whereby here the profiling performed by MID involves an analysis of aspects concerning that natural person's reliability or behaviour in accordance with Article 3(4) of the General Data Protection Regulation and Article 3(4) of the Law Enforcement Directive. Equally, MID could

[119] Ibid.

[120] Ibid.

[121] Francesca Tassinari, *The External Reach of the Interoperability of Large-Scale IT Systems in the AFSJ* (PhD Thesis, University of Granada, 2022) 429.

be classified under the law enforcement related provisions of the AI Act, thus applying Article 5(1)(d). The latter foresees as high-risk AI systems used to assess or predict the risk of a natural person committing a criminal offence, based solely on profiling or on assessing their personality traits and characteristics. Furthermore, MID is a tool designed for 'the purpose of detecting, recognising or identifying natural persons' under Annex III.7.(d), as it will enable the correct identification of *bona fide* persons. The categorization has significant implications: Article 6(3) of the AI Act allows for declassifying a high-risk AI system under certain requirements, with the exception of AI systems performing profiling. In the case of MID, if it is classified as a profiling tool then it cannot be declassified, whereas if considered as an identification tool such decategorization can take place. The decategorization will signify that the increased safeguards of high-risk AI systems will not apply to MID.

Overall, there are two inter-related rule of law challenges posed by the design of MID. On the one hand, the inherent opacity of the inner workings of MID generates lack of foreseeability as to the nature of MID, which challenges the legality principle; the omission of the legislation is coupled with deliberate lack of specificity through the use of a vague term in the delegated act. On the other hand, the hybrid nature of MID creates significant legal of uncertainty as to first whether the AI Act applies in the first place and, if so, which provisions (and corresponding safeguards) apply in particular.

3.6 The curious case of Article 111 of the AI Act

Another facet of the AI Act that merits further examination is its Article 111. The latter prescribes that AI systems which are components of the large-scale IT systems shall be brought into compliance with this Regulation by 31 December 2030.[122] The requirements of the AI Act must be taken into account in the evaluation of each large-scale IT system and where those legal acts are replaced or amended.[123] This is the amended version as Article 83(1) of the AI Act excluded the systems from the scope of the AI Act 'unless the replacement or amendment of those legal acts leads to a significant change in the design or intended purpose of the AI system or AI systems concerned'. However, its requirements shall be taken into account, *where applicable*, in the evaluation of each database.[124]

122 AI Act, art 111(1).

123 Ibid.

124 For an analysis on the challenges of this provision, see Vavoula (n 4).

Reading between the lines, both the Commission proposal and the finalized Regulation foresee a temporary exclusion of the IT systems from the scope of the AI Act. However, the proposal did not meet the requirements of legal certainty because the temporariness of the exclusion could not be determined; it was unclear as to when the legal instruments regulating the operation of the IT systems would be replaced or amended. It is true that the 2020 Commission report on opportunities and challenges for the use of AI in border control, migration and security provides some indications about the future direction of IT systems; additional algorithms could be used in order to further assist human decision-making, whereby the flagged applications will be further classified depending on the degree of risk, a process called triaging.[125] However, it is also clear that the main preoccupation has been on putting in place the refurbishment of the operational databases and the setting up of the new databases, as well as the establishment of interoperability, which has already faced delays and is scheduled for full operationalization in 2027. The oxymoron is that one of the arguments presented referred to the exclusion as a means of ensuring legal certainty.[126] Most likely, the need for the exclusion stemmed from the fact that the legal instruments of the IT systems were adopted between 2017 and 2021 and therefore the preparations were already underway, and this could lead to significant delays. Besides, various legal instruments were adopted without a Fundamental Rights Impact Assessment, which is foreseen in Article 27 of the AI Act and therefore application of the AI Act could arguably require revisiting the legislative process altogether.

Article 111 of the AI Act, adopted at the behest of the European Parliament,[127] provides more clarity as to the deadline of this exclusion, with the end of 2030 being the deadline within which the systems need to be brought in compliance with its requirements. This approach is helpful because the application of the AI Act was not dependent upon any further revisions to the legal instruments of the large-scale IT systems or interoperability. Yet, this does not mean that this provision does not present significant rule of law challenges. A divide between AI systems operational at the national level created an unjustified divide between AI systems deployed at the national level and those deployed at EU level which remains unexplained. Furthermore, the operationalization of the revamped IT system

[125] European Commission, 'Opportunities and Challenges for the Use of Artificial Intelligence in Border Control, Migration and Security' (May 2020).

[126] See n 110.

[127] Parliament, 'Artificial Intelligence Act Amendments adopted by the European Parliament on 14 June 2023 on the proposal for a regulation of the European Parliament and of the Council on laying down harmonised rules on artificial intelligence (Artificial Intelligence Act) and amending certain Union legislative acts (COM (2021) 0206 – C9-0146/2021 – 2021/0106(COD))' P9_TA (2023)0236 (14 June 2023).

architecture will take place gradually; EES is scheduled to start its operations in a phased manner,[128] ETIAS in late-2026 and the full implementation of interoperability is, as mentioned earlier, expected by 2027. With the majority of the AI Act rules applying from 2 August 2026, there is an expected three- to four-year gap in the application of the AI Act.

Article 111 has two main consequences; first, it deprives affected individuals from the complementary remedial system offered by the AI Act. In particular, Article 85 of the AI Act states that without prejudice to other extrajudicial and judicial remedies, individuals having grounds to consider that there has been an infringement of the AI Act may submit complaints to the relevant market surveillance authority, which will ensure that products in the market conform with the AI Act. This means that individuals will have to rely on remedies offered by data protection and administrative law, which, as highlighted by this chapter, may not be sufficient.

The delay in applying the AI Act in the context of interoperable IT systems is highly problematic for an additional reason: CRRS is likely to use AI tools in the compilation of tailor-made, cross-system statistical data and analytical reporting for policy, operational and data quality purposes. Statistical data are anonymized data that will be drawn from the individual systems and stored in the CRRS pursuant to Article 39 of the Interoperability Regulations. Because they are anonymized, they do not qualify as personal data and therefore are not subject to EU data protection law, including the rules on supervision by national supervisory authorities and the European Data Protection Supervisor (EDPS). Halting the application of the AI Act signifies that the supervision of AI tools at the national level, as envisaged in the AI Act aimed at ensuring accountability, is also delayed. The result will be that CRRS will not be subject to any supervision, either from the perspective of EU data protection law or from the AI Act until 2030. This accountability gap is particularly significant; it means that for a number of years, the operation of this interoperability component will essentially become a black site. From 2030 onwards, the supervision of AI systems will include the systems as well and will probably encounter additional difficulties through *ex post* conduct audits on the CRRS.

4 Conclusion

This chapter aimed to highlight how algorithms and AI are bound to transform not only the management of migration, asylum and border controls, but

128 Rebecca Ann Hughes, 'Is the Entry/Exit Scheme Delayed Again? What Travellers Need to Know about New EU Border Checks' (*Euronews*, 20 September 2024), https://www.euronews.com/travel/2024/09/20/from-november-some-travellers-will-face-new-eu-border-controls-as-entryexit-scheme-launche, accessed 12 October 2024.

importantly these developments multiply the rule of law challenges raised by 'traditional' digitalization tools. The chapter looked at both national and EU initiatives, all of which demonstrate (at least for now) impenetrable secrecy and opacity into the precise nature of the algorithms employed and the extent to which they qualify as AI, within their meaning under the AI Act. This secrecy is argued to be a deliberate policy choice to create confusion through terminological ambiguities and potentially downgrade the importance of the shift towards algorithmization, hinder democratic scrutiny, avoid legal obligations and ultimately shrink the protection offered to the individuals affected. The case of the UK Home Office, which withdrew the visa triaging system rather than providing further information in the litigation, is telling of this opacity, which significantly hinders any foreseeability of how decision-making is taking place. At the EU level, the tactic has been the preference towards the more neutral term algorithm to shift the attention or leave flexibility for the future deployment of AI. This chapter aims to demonstrate the true, hidden potential of interoperability, a debate which did not feature *at all* in the negotiations towards the adoption of the Interoperability Regulations. Such a blunt disregard for the rule of law via concealing that interoperability components are *prerequisites* or *motors* for the deployment of AI is particularly significant, orchestrated also via the temporary exclusion of interoperable IT systems from the scope of the AI Act (even though there are already various shortcuts taken, for example, the lack of impact assessments). The chapter also demonstrated the significant obstacles that different groups of third-country nationals face in obtaining meaningful information regarding the decision-making process behind their travel authorization or visa application and therefore seeking judicial protection will be particularly obstructed; after all, if individuals do not know what went wrong with their application, how can they challenge it? Ultimately, this chapter serves to reinforce the arguments made in Chapters 7 and 8 about the emergence of 'rule of technology', rather than a rule of law approach, whereby technical feasibility dictates the legal and policy developments in an opaque manner, which creates the illusion of consistency and administrative efficiency, where it actually erodes the rule of law and leaves third-country nationals at its margins.

Conclusion: Restoring the Rule of Law on the Border

The analysis contained in this book demonstrates a paradox in the evolution of contemporary border control. On the one hand, border controls have been constantly proliferating, with states' focus on preventing migrants from reaching their territory leading to multiple borders: in the territory of third countries, on the high seas, at the external border, in the territory of the state of destination or transit, and in the digital sphere. On the other hand, this proliferation of borders has been accompanied not by more, but by less law: a key focus of states has been the negation of the application of law, and the negation of the rule of law, to migrants in this process. It is true that digitalization in itself constitutes a means through which individuals become visible and accounted for; the processing of their personal data within databases and Eurosur is a way in which their journey towards or presence in Europe cannot be denied. However, the analysis demonstrates that bringing individuals within the sphere of European Union (EU) (migration) law does not signify the application of the rule of law through opaque and highly technical rules with significant loopholes that can hardly be contested. Besides, human rights and refugee law standards applicable in countries of destination are either wholly inapplicable or partially applicable to migrants, with systems designed to minimize the legal responsibility and accountability of states in the operation of border control: leading thus to lawless borders.

The analysis aims to contribute towards redressing this rule of law deficit in contemporary immigration control and towards bringing migrants firmly within a rule of law framework in terms of the full application of constitutional and human rights norms in border control. To do so, our thinking must engage both with addressing the current rule of law deficit in terms of lawlessness – in terms of the negation of law – and with ensuring meaningful legal responsibility as well as political and judicial accountability of states and the EU in cases of violations of constitutional law, fundamental rights and international law in border control.

In terms of addressing lawlessness, our analysis has demonstrated the urgency of ensuring the full application of key protective instruments such as the EU Charter of Fundamental Rights and the European Convention on Human Rights (ECHR) in the operation of border control. The analysis has demonstrated the conscious efforts by states, and by Frontex, to generate 'legal black holes' negating their legal responsibility for border control operations, which may have profoundly negative consequences for the fundamental rights of migrants, including their access to asylum. In revisiting this rule of law deficit, it is essential to adopt a meaningful concept of jurisdiction under the ECHR, which will ensure its application on the basis of the impact that border control, including extraterritorial and externalized border control, has on the individual. An impact-focused conception of jurisdiction would assert the applicability of the law in cases where states – or the EU – attempt to evade their responsibility through omission (for example, failure to search and rescue at sea) or through support action in third countries which does not constitute directly coercive border control (such as training, the provision of financial support or surveillance intelligence) and render the ECHR applicable when these actions have the effect of violating international law. In this context, a holistic approach to state obligations under international law is advocated, including international refugee law, international human rights law and international law of the sea (including search and rescue at sea), with the positive obligations they entail. In terms of EU law, the implementation of the Pact for Migration and Asylum must be fully compliant with international obligations and with EU constitutional law, including the right to asylum and its underpinning requirement of access to asylum.

In terms of ensuring responsibility and accountability for human rights violations in border control, greater use of criminal law is hereby advocated. Criminal law will be used here not to target irregular migrants,[1] but rather to prosecute state authorities and EU officials for human rights violations in border control. The EU has competence under Article 83(2) of the Treaty on the Functioning of the European Union (TFEU) to adopt legislation criminalizing the failure to comply with international law of the sea, and in particular with search and rescue obligations.[2] There exists a legal basis under Article 83(2) TFEU in order to achieve the effective implementation of EU transport policy, inspired by the use by the CJEU of a transport policy framework to counter state arbitrariness in targeting non-governmental organizations who conduct search and rescue at sea in

[1] On this trend, see Valsamis Mitsilegas, *The Criminalisation of Migration in Europe* (Springer 2015).

[2] Elspeth Guild and Valsamis Mitsilegas, 'The Duty of the EU to Criminalise Failure to Rescue at Sea' (*EU Migration and Asylum Law Blog*, 23 December 2022), https://eumigrationlawblog.eu/the-legal-duty-of-the-eu-to-criminalise-failure-to-rescue-at-sea/, accessed 12 October 2024.

the *Sea-Watch* case.[3] This approach has been debated by Di Martino, who has argued that Article 83(2) TFEU could be used to adopt legislation for the effective implementation of immigration, and not transport policy. Di Martino further argues in favour of the use of Article 83(1) TFEU, under the heading of corruption, for the EU to adopt criminal law for abuse of power in border control. Di Martino's contribution is important in that it focuses on the criminal liability of EU public officials.[4] The proposal would extend criminalization also to public officials of Member States, and Article 83(2) TFEU would provide an appropriate legal basis for this objective. In addition to a transport framing, indeed we could consider an emphasis on the effective implementation not of immigration, but specifically of EU asylum law, which requires at its core effective access to asylum.

As regards the practices of EU external border controls, it is critical that the EU acknowledge and address the legal deficit regarding what law its border agency, Frontex, is applying. National border agencies are required to apply their national law on border crossing, but each Member State has different laws and rules, consistent with its exercise of a state sovereignty claim to control those borders. While the EU has a Borders Code which sets out the conditions for the crossing of the EU's external borders by persons (which, as a regulation, must be applied by the Member States) its border agency is not obliged to ensure the correct application of this regulation. Indeed the regulation which constitutes the legal foundation of Frontex makes scant reference to the Code as if the legal conditions for crossing EU external borders and the agency charged with policing these crossings are unrelated. This means that on the one hand the legal framework of EU external border crossing provides for an individual decision on each attempt by a person to cross an external border where in the event of refusal there is a duty to provide a written notice of refusal and information on entitlements to appeal. This framework excludes from its scope anyone who seeks international protection whose claim must be assessed in accordance with the Common European Asylum System. On the other hand, the Frontex regulation does not oblige the agency to ensure that the Code rules are respected. Instead there is an ambiguous concept of shared responsibility at the heart of the regulation which creates a zone of effective non-law where both national border police and Frontex seem to be able to avoid responsibility for harm which results from their coordinated efforts to prevent some people seeking to cross borders from doing so.

---

3 Joined Cases C-14/21 and C-15/21 *Sea-Watch eV v Ministero delle Infrastrutture e dei Trasporti and Others* [2022] EU:C:2022:604.

4 Alberto di Martino, 'Does the European Union's Rule of Law Require the Criminalisation of EU Public Officials? A First Appraisal' (2024) 30(1–2) *European Law Journal* 181.

As for the digitalization and algorithmization of border controls, our analysis has demonstrated that the more widespread is the application of a 'techno-solutionist' mentality, whereby the reliance on highly sophisticated technological means is based on the perception of technology as neutral and as a panacea for resolving pathogenic administrative procedures, the deeper the rule of law challenges. A 'rule of technology' approach results in highly complex, opaque legal instruments, leading to significant lack of clarity as to the impact on third-country nationals and manifold fundamental rights challenges that extend beyond the rights to respect for private life and the protection of personal data to cover the rights of the child, the right to human dignity and right to effective remedies.

Whereas it may not be feasible to halt recourse to digital technologies and particularly the use of AI, there exist various mechanisms that could enable bringing the different faces of digitalization within the rule of law. Firstly, full transparency is needed in the legal instruments regulating the use of digital technologies, including the disclosure of the precise nature of the tools used in Eurosur and the disclosure of the nature of algorithms in large-scale IT systems and interoperability. This necessitates legislative intervention to clarify opaque parts of the legal instruments or insertion of additional provisions, where necessary. Secondly, it is imperative that trust in digital technologies and human agents verifying their results is overturned and that the recording of personal data by one Member State is not treated as by default lawful, allowing national courts to review the lawfulness and legality of records inserted by authorities (or EU agencies) operating in other Member States. Thirdly, the supervision and overall oversight of Eurosur and large-scale IT systems must become an ongoing process, on the ground, following the pathways of personal data by national data protection authorities and the European Data Protection Supervisor.[5] The role of the Schengen Evaluation and Monitoring Mechanism, which is designed to ensure that the Schengen area functions well and whether the participating states implement correctly the Schengen *acquis*, cannot be underestimated as well.[6] Regrettably, Eurodac and the European Criminal Record Information System for Third-country Nationals are not part of that *acquis*, however, as both of them are part of the interoperability ecosystem and are accessed at the external borders they are indirectly part of border management and thus could be scrutinized in terms of rule of law deficits. As digitalization

[5] Niovi Vavoula, 'Algorithmic Accountability through the "Human over the Loop" in Interoperable and AI-reliant Large-scale IT Systems' (2025) *European Papers*.

[6] Council Regulation (EU) 2022/922 of 9 June 2022 on the establishment and operation of an evaluation and monitoring mechanism to verify the application of the Schengen acquis, and repealing Regulation (EU) No 1053/2013 [2022] OJ L 160/1.

and algorithmization pose challenges beyond data protection-related ones, it may be useful to consider supervision as a more holistic exercise which encompasses more broadly all fundamental rights and the rule of law, thus the involvement of other national oversight mechanisms such as the National Committees for Human Rights, could be an option. Finally, considering the huge investments in funding these systems, other agencies, such as the European Anti-fraud Office, could be mobilized to scrutinize the rule of law challenges of Eurosur and IT systems, in a manner similar to their work as regards Frontex's complicity in fundamental rights violations.

The EU external border remains a space under construction filled with various state, EU and private sector entrepreneurs but lacking a coherent and human rights consistent legal framework. This lack of a coherent legal structure with the individual at the centre results in a startling lack of legal remedies for those harmed by national and EU practices in external border control. The harm is both highly visible in the form of shipwrecks and loss of life at sea with all parties claiming that they had a lack of sufficient knowledge to perform their search and rescue duties (notwithstanding the capacities of Eurosur) and almost completely invisible in algorithms making 'recommendations' for refusing individuals access to the EU with no legally accessible grounds which can be the subject of an appeal. It is time for the EU to take up the challenge of human rights compliance in border control and to put in place an effective legal framework bringing an end to this lawless regime.

Index

References to footnotes show both the page number and the note number (231n3)

A

A.A. and Others v North Macedonia 23
'abusive' asylum seekers 38
accelerated border procedures 38, 41, 42, 46
administrative law 63–65, 217
Adriana 96, 107, 122
Advanced Passenger Information data 184
Aegean 84–86
AI (artificial intelligence) 172, 190–218, 222
AI Act 191, 195, 197, 198, 201, 202, 215–217
aircraft identification numbers 155, 156
Al Chodor 52
Albania 32–35
algorithmic profiling 185, 196–199, 200
algorithmization 190–218, 222
Amnesty International 121
Apatzidou, V. 38
Appulonappa case 61–62
Area of Freedom, Security and Justice (AFSJ) 92, 189
Article 1 ECHR 14, 18
Article 2 ECHR 19, 33
Article 2(2) Protocol 4 33
Article 3 ECHR 13, 14, 33
Article 4 Protocol No 4 13, 14, 21, 23, 33
Article 5 ECHR 33
Article 6 of Directive 2013/32 25
Article 13 ECHR 33
Article 16 of the International Law Commission's Articles on State Responsibility 20
Article 17 of the International Law Commission 20
Article 18 of the Charter 24
Article 19 of Charter 24
A.S. and others v. Italy and Malta 17n31
Asylum Procedures Regulation 39, 41–42, 46
asylum/asylum applications
  derogations 49
  Frontex 85
  instrumentalization of migration 46
  jurisdiction 14
  'non-entry' fiction 37–43
  outsourcing refugee status determination 25–32
  pre-entry phase of asylum applications 38
  pushbacks at the border 22
  rejection of asylum applications 38, 42
  right to asylum 20, 21
  Treaty on the Functioning of the European Union (TFEU) 24
autonomous concepts 51, 53
Aviat, M. 151, 152

B

B.A. v Cyprus 54n125
Baltic states 4n7
Bathase, Y. 192
Belarus 4n7, 44, 131, 132
Bellingcat 90–91, 125
Bigo, D. 178, 184
biometric data 39, 143, 162, 164, 166–168, 180, 183, 209–213
'border abroad' 11
border guards 80, 81, 83, 106, 128, 130, 132, 149
border violence 4–5, 4n7, 20–21, 108, 111–133
Brexit 35, 78
Brouwer, E. 187, 205
Bulgaria 78

C

Canadian Supreme Court 61–62
Canary Islands 4n7
capacity building 20
Cassarino, J.-P. 40, 53n122
Central Repository for Reporting and Statistics (CRRS) 168, 172, 202, 205–206, 217
Charter of Fundamental Rights
  algorithmic profiling 207–208

criminalization of legal advice 67
evolution of extraterritorial immigration control 19
extraterritorial immigration control 24
Frontex 81, 98, 99, 114, 127, 129, 130
full application of 219–220
instrumentalization of migration 50
interoperable large-scale IT systems 184
chilling effects 59, 66, 67, 91
civil society
Frontex 94, 98, 107, 112
hostile environment 56, 57, 62, 65
coast guards 17–19, 76, 90, 107, 119, 124–125
coercive powers
detention 51–52
extraterritorial immigration control 16, 17, 18, 19
Frontex 73, 74
rise of 2
collective expulsion of migrants 14–15, 21, 23, 24, 87
Commission v Council (31 March 1971) 34n127
Commission v Hungary [2020] 51, 130
Commission v Hungary [2022] 67n62
Common European Asylum System (CEAS) 33–34, 35, 130, 131, 163–164, 221
Common Identity Repository (CIR) 168, 172, 183, 213
Common Security and Defence Policy 150
competences 2
see also shared competence
complaints mechanisms 81, 105, 108–109
Consultative Forum (Frontex) 81, 94, 103–104, 105, 112, 120, 130
contactless control 20
Convention Implementing the Schengen Agreement 187
Convention on the Law of the Sea 64
cooperation mechanisms 19, 144
Corte di Cassazione 62–63
Council of Europe 6n14
Council of Europe Commission for Human Rights 34, 59, 94
Council Regulation (EC) No 2007/2004 138, 139, 154
Court of Appeal 30
Court of Auditors 95, 119, 126
Court of Justice of the European Union (CJEU)
AI (artificial intelligence) 196
algorithmic profiling 208
criminalization of facilitation of unauthorized entry 61
detention 50, 51–52, 53
facilitation of unauthorized entry 59
Frontex 73–77, 84, 89, 97, 112, 130–132, 133
hostile environment 64, 67
IT systems 181
pushbacks at the border 24
Sea-Watch 63–64
transport policy 220–221
crimes against humanity 97
'crimes of disobedience' 62
criminal law
blurred with immigration law 179–180
Eurosur 158
Frontex scrutiny 112, 126–127, 129, 132
hostile environment 57–63
human rights violations 220–221
IT systems 162, 166
Multiple Identity Detector (MID) 214–215
criminalization of provision of legal advice 67
crisis and force majeure 48, 49
cross-border crime 75, 101, 131, 141, 144, 148, 152n90, 158
cybercrime 101
Cyprus 78

D

data mining 203
data protection rules 144, 145, 154, 171, 181, 183, 217, 222
deaths on migration routes 4n6, 18, 19, 94, 107, 121, 122, 223
dehumanization 48
delegated and implementing acts 174–177, 211
den Heijer, M. 15
denial of the rule of law 20–21
Denmark 78, 194
deprivation of liberty 50
derogations 46, 49
detention
Common European Asylum System (CEAS) 131
detention centres 32, 33
Hungary 130
normalization of 50–54
not considered 'entry' 40
Pact on Migration and Asylum 42, 46, 47, 55
refugees 26
safeguards 52
of ships 65
deterritorialization 40
DG HOME 80, 128, 129
Di Martino, A, 221
digitalization 160–189, 219, 222
Dijstelbloem, H. 149
discrimination 80
Divisional Court 30
drones 141, 153, 156

Dublin transfers 185–186
duty to rescue 33, 62–63

E

Eliantonio, M. 187
emergency, states of 45–47, 50, 52, 131
Entry/ Exit System (EES) 160, 164–165, 179, 204, 205, 210, 212, 217
equality 80
ERTA doctrine 34
EU aid 75
EU Border Assistance Mission Moldova and Ukraine (EUBAM) 74–75
EU Borders Code 79, 221
EU Charter of Fundamental Rights
  algorithmic profiling 207–208
  criminalization of legal advice 67
  evolution of extraterritorial immigration control 19
  extraterritorial immigration control 24
  Frontex 81, 98, 99, 114, 127, 129, 130
  full application of 219–220
  instrumentalization of migration 50
  interoperable large-scale IT systems 184
EU cooperation mechanisms 19
EU Data Protection Regulation (EUDPR) 145, 154–155
EU destabilization agendas 44, 45, 48
EU Fundamental Rights Agency (FRA) 94, 96–97, 119, 171
EU law
  autonomous concepts 51
  criminalization of facilitation of unauthorized entry 57–63
  detention 53
  Frontex 118, 124, 131
  instrumentalization of migration 46, 48, 49
  Italy-Albania 33–34
  personal data processing 154–155
  right to asylum 220
  Schengen Borders Code 79, 221
  search and rescue 220
  secondary EU law 50–51, 64
  transport law 63–64, 220
EU Observer 125
EU Satellite Centre 152
EU Visa Code 198
EUAA 171
EU–Albania Stabilisation and Association Agreement 34
eu-LISA (European Union Agency for the Operational Management of Large-Scale IT Systems in the Area of Freedom, Security and Justice) 169–170, 172–173, 205, 206–207, 211–212, 214
Eurodac 160, 163–164, 170, 173–174, 179, 181, 185, 210, 222
Eurojust 142, 143, 144
European Anti-fraud Office (OLAF) 77, 81, 82, 83, 90, 93, 95–96, 97, 99, 105–106, 109, 111–112, 118n41, 119, 121, 123–129, 132, 223
European Arrest Warrant 182
European Center for Constitutional and Human Rights 98
European Commission
  AI (artificial intelligence) 206, 216
  border surveillance 139
  facial recognition technology 212
  Frontex oversight 93, 98–99, 101, 115–118, 122, 123, 126, 129
  instrumentalization of migration 44
  integrated border management 74
  Italy-Albania 34
  'non-entry' fiction 38
European Convention on Human Rights (ECHR)
  evolution of extraterritorial immigration control 11, 13–15, 219–220
  Illegal Migration Act 2023 26
  Italy-Albania 33, 35
  non-refoulement 27
European Council 44, 80, 95, 100, 171
European Council on Refugees and Exiles (ECRE) 47n78
European Court of Human Rights (ECtHR)
  cross-border crime 158
  detention 54
  and EU law 24
  evolution of extraterritorial immigration control 12–13, 16, 17, 20, 22
  Frontex 86
  instrumentalization of migration 46–47
  Italy-Albania 33
  N.D. and N.T. v Spain 21, 23, 24, 36, 40, 47
  pushbacks at the border 21
  'serious crime' 158, 182
  and state sovereignty 36
  UK-Rwanda model 31, 35
  UNHCR evidence 30
European Criminal Record Information System for Third-country Nationals (ECRIS-TCN) 160, 165–166, 179–180, 211, 222
European Data Protection Supervisor (EDPS) 96, 97, 140, 156, 183, 217, 222
European Economic Community Treaty 73
European External Action Service (EEAS) 143
European Integrated Border Management (EIBM) 100
European Maritime Safety Agency 152
European Ombudsman 96, 107, 109, 119, 122, 126, 133
European Parliament
  AI Act 216

facial recognition technology 212
Frontex oversight 80, 92, 94–95, 97, 100, 111, 113–123, 125–126, 132, 133
technological reform 173
European Parliament's Committee on Civil Liberties, Justice and Home Affairs (LIBE Committee) 111, 118–123, 125, 128, 133
European Public Prosecutor's Office (EPPO) 95–96, 126–127, 129, 132
European Search Portal 167, 203
European situational picture (ESPs) 149, 150–151, 157
European Surveillance Room 108
European Travel Information and Authorisation System (ETIAS) 1, 145, 160, 165, 169–170, 173–176, 179, 185, 202–208, 217
European Union Agency for Asylum (EUAA) 4n7, 142, 160
European Union Agency for the Operational Management of Large-Scale IT Systems in the Area of Freedom, Security and Justice (eu-LISA) 169–170, 171, 172–173, 205, 206–207, 211–212, 214
Europol
Eurodac 164
interoperable large-scale IT systems 171, 202
personal data processing 178
Report of the Future Group on Travel Intelligence and Border Management 205
Schengen Information System (SIS) 180
technology-led border surveillance 139, 140, 142, 143, 144, 146, 150
visa policies 163
Eurosur 7, 20, 106, 122, 127, 137–159, 219, 222, 223
Eurosur Regulation 147–148, 154, 157, 158
EU-Turkey Deal 98
evidence-based policy making 191–192
Expert Group on Information Systems for Borders and Security 214
expulsion of aliens 14, 32, 88, 89
extension of time restrictions 49
extraterritorial immigration control 11–36

F

facial recognition technology (FRT) 156, 162, 209–213
facilitation of unauthorized entry 57–63
'facilitators' package' 57, 59
False and Authentic Documents Online (FADO) system 143, 144
feasibility studies 146, 147, 170
fingerprints 163, 186, 209–213
Finland 50n95
flag states 64
FMS v Orszagos Idegenrendezeti Főigazgatosag Del-alfoldi Regionalis Igazgatosag (n 102) 52n104
Forabosco 187
Foxglove 200
France 4n7, 186, 187, 195
free movement 73, 78, 101, 161, 179
Frontex
accountability 152–153
AI (artificial intelligence) 206–207
Consultative Forum (Frontex) 81, 94, 103–104, 105, 112, 120, 130
Eurosur 7, 146–147
external oversight 111–133
internal oversight 93–110
interoperable large-scale IT systems 171, 203, 204
migration information hub 139–146
power and accountability 71–92
Report of the Future Group on Travel Intelligence and Border Management 205
research role of Frontex 100, 102, 116, 153
rule of law deficit 221
small boats 1
Frontex Data Protection Officer (DPO) 140, 146
Frontex Fundamental Rights Officer (FRO) 77, 81–85, 94, 100, 104–109, 112, 120–121, 126–128, 131, 132
Frontex Regulation 2007 140
Frontex Regulation 2016 154
Frontex Regulation 2019
Article 46 130–132
breaches of 128
cooperation duties 144
delayed implementation of 126
European Anti-fraud Office (OLAF) 147
Eurosur 137
external oversight 111, 113
fundamental rights 122
informational tasks 142–146
Interinstitutional Agreement 123
internal oversight 96–97, 99, 100, 101, 103, 104, 107, 108
personal data processing 145–146, 154–155, 156–157
power and accountability 72, 73, 74, 76–77, 79, 80, 83
scrutiny powers 115, 118
SSP (specific situational picture) 150–151
transparency 120
Frontex Scrutiny Working Group (FSWG) 97, 109, 118–123, 126, 131, 132
Frontex Situation Centre 147
fundamental rights abuse allegations
Frontex external oversight 112, 114, 117–118, 119–129, 130–132

Frontex internal oversight 96, 97, 99, 102–103, 105–106
Frontex's power 77, 80, 81–91
personal data processing 155
'techno-solutionism' 222
Fundamental Rights Agency (FRA) 94, 96–97, 119, 171
fundamental rights monitors 104–105, 108, 118, 119–120
Fusion Services 151–152, 154–155, 157

G

General Court 84–86, 87, 89, 90, 97, 133
General Data Protection Regulation–GDPR 154, 157, 181, 214
Geneva Convention 1951 34
Germany 194
ghost landings 89
Giuffré, M. 16, 20
Greece 83, 85, 89, 96, 107, 118, 124–125
Greek–Turkish land border 4n7
Guild, E. 11

H

Hague Programme 170, 178
Hamoudi v Frontex [2022] 89n58, 105–106
Hickman, T. 27
high seas 12–20, 32–35, 58, 121
High-Level Expert Group on Information Systems and Interoperability 171
Hildebrandt, M. 206
Hirsi Jamaa and Others v Italy 12, 13n9, 15–16, 18, 36
Hofmann, H.C.H. 188
hostile environment 56–68
human rights
extraterritorial immigration control 12, 16, 18
hostile environment 56, 59
Illegal Migration Act 2023 26
international human rights bodies 17
Italy-Albania 32–33, 35
lawlessness 36, 220
UK-Rwanda model 30–31
Human Rights Act 27
Human Rights Council 5n9
humanitarian assistance 48–49, 58, 61, 62, 63
see also search and rescue
Hungarian–Serbian border 4n7
Hungary 22, 23, 24, 67, 121, 130
hybrid threats 44, 48, 55

I

I. L. v Politsei-ja Piirivalveamet [2022] 52n112
Iceland 78
Illegal Immigration Bill 66
Illegal Migration Act 2023 25–26
Immigration Acts 27
impact assessments 147, 150, 170, 206, 212, 216
incident reporting 81–82, 120, 122
see also serious incident reports (SIRs)
individualisation of jurisdiction 15–16
'Informatie Ondersteund Beslissen' algorithm 196–199
(in)security continuum 178, 184
instrumentalization of migration 22, 43–50, 52, 55
integrated border management 73–77, 99–101, 115–116
interception at sea 97
Interinstitutional Agreement 123
International Convention for the Safety of Life at Sea (SOLAS Convention) 64
International Criminal Court 97, 98
international human rights bodies 17
international law
definition of Member State borders 2
and the ECHR 220
Illegal Migration Act 2023 26
International Convention for the Safety of Life at Sea (SOLAS Convention) 64
migrant smuggling/ facilitation of unauthorized entry 57, 58, 61
migrants assisting other migrants 59
non-refoulement 27
refugee law 26, 27
state responsibility 20
International Law Commission 20, 121–122
International Organization for Migration (IOM) 4n6, 94
international treaties 13
Interoperability Regulations 167, 170, 172–173, 177–178, 183, 184, 211, 213, 217, 218
interoperable large-scale IT systems 160–189, 201–206, 216, 217, 222
Interpol 202
Ireland 78
IT systems 160–189, 201–206
Italy
Adriana 107
extraterritorial immigration control 12, 17–18, 19
Italy-Albania 32–35
joint operations 151
and Libya 114n14, 118
Rackete case 62–63
Steccato di Cutro shipwreck 121
Tribunale di Bologna 61

J

joint asylum and return procedures 38, 86–87, 120
Joint Council for the Welfare of Immigrants 200

joint operations 130–132, 139, 140, 141, 143, 151
judicial accountability 26, 29–30
judicial remedies 184–188, 207–209
judicial review 31
jurisdiction 14, 15–17, 18–19, 20

K

Kennedy v UK 158, 182
Kinsa (Kinshasa) 61
Krajcíková, K. 154

L

Lampedusa 12
large-scale IT systems 160–189
Latvia 44
law enforcement
  EU Border Assistance Mission Moldova and Ukraine (EUBAM) 75
  Eurodac 164
  information exchange 149
  IT systems 166, 168, 180
  Multiple Identity Detector (MID) 214
  personal data processing 178–179
  technology-led border surveillance 141, 144, 145
  visa data 163
Law Enforcement Directive 214
law of the sea 17, 19
lawful entry procedures 23
lawlessness 36, 219–220
legal black holes 36, 220
legal personality 80
legal profession 65–68
LIBE Committee (European Parliament's Committee on Civil Liberties, Justice and Home Affairs) 111, 118–123, 125, 128, 133
Libya 13, 14, 17–18, 97, 114n14, 118
Liechtenstein 78
Lighthouse Reports 121
Ligue des droits humains ASBL v Conseil des ministers 196n27, 208
Lithuania 44, 131
Luxembourg Court 63

M

M.A. v Valstybės sienos apsaugos tarnyba 25n74, 50n96, 52n109, 131n96
Macedonia 23
Malta 12
Mann, I. 15n21
Marin, L. 40, 53n122, 154
Maritime Rescue Coordination Centre (MRCC) 18
martial law 50, 52, 131
M.B. v The Netherlands 54
Medvedyev v France 12–13
M.H. and Others v Croatia 23n63
migrant smuggling/ facilitation of unauthorized entry 57
migrants assisting other migrants 59, 62
migration databases 39
militarization 22, 44–45
Missing Migrants Project 4n6
Mitsilegas, V. 184
Moldova 74–75
Montenegro 151
Moreno-Lax, V. 16–17, 18, 20
Morocco 4n7
Multiple Identity Detector (MID) 167–168, 171, 172, 213–215
Musco-Eklund, A. 206–207

N

National Committees for Human Rights 223
National Coordination Centres (NCCs) 141, 146, 149, 157
national security 30, 44, 45, 47, 48, 55
national situational picture (NSPs) 149–150, 154, 155, 156
N.D. and N.T. v Spain 21, 23, 24, 36, 40, 47
Netherlands 194, 195, 196–199
New York Protocol 1967 34
'non-entry' fiction 37–43
non-governmental organizations (NGOs)
  evolution of extraterritorial immigration control 16
  Frontex 84, 103, 119, 129, 133
  hostile environment 56, 58, 64
  illegal expulsions 89
  Sea Watch 98
  and the technological ecosystem 174
non-refoulement principle 24, 27–29, 33, 34, 86–87, 152
Norway 78, 195

O

OLAF (European Anti-fraud Office) *see* European Anti-fraud Office (OLAF)
Organisation for Economic Co-operation and Development (OECD) 195
organized crime 57, 58, 60, 62
outsourcing refugee status determination 25–32
'own conduct' 21–22, 23

P

Pact on Migration and Asylum 26, 37–55, 220
Palermo Convention on Transnational Organized Crime 57, 58
Papastavridis, E. 19
Passenger Name Record (PNR) data 182, 184, 208
'path trackers' 163–164

personal data processing 139–146, 153–158, 160–189, 199
physical border controls 20–25
Poland 22, 44, 131
Poland-Belarus border 4n7, 44
policing 77–78, 80, 90, 118n41, 121, 149, 183
  see also Europol
port authorities 64–65
Poseidon operation 89
predictive tools 153, 192, 194
pre-emptive risk assessment 152, 179
pre-entry phase of asylum applications 38–39, 53
preventive paradigm 15, 20, 24, 38–40, 45–46, 54, 58, 152
proportionality 50, 52, 53, 65, 181
Prüm 184
public health 145
pullback practices 16, 20, 35, 155
pushbacks at the border 20–25, 35, 90, 118–121, 124–125, 130–131, 155

Q

Quintel, T. 144

R

R on the application of AAA and Others [2023] 26n81, 28n91
Rackete case 62
Ras Jadir 18
reaction capabilities 150
Reception Conditions Directive 53, 54
refoulement 21, 24, 27–29, 30, 31, 86–87
Refugee Convention 27, 114n14
refugee law 26, 28, 33
Regulation on a return border procedure 42
removal of aliens 38, 40, 43
repatriation, risk of arbitrary 13
Report of the Future Group on Travel Intelligence and Border Management 205
rescue operations 12–13, 17–18, 33, 39, 62–63
  see also search and rescue
research role of Frontex 100, 102, 116, 153
residence requirements for asylum seekers 41–42
Return Directive 52
returning migrants 38, 88, 142, 144, 162, 164
right to asylum 20, 21, 24, 38, 50, 61, 220
right to remain 42
rights of appeal 32
rights of the child 87
risk assessment 43, 47, 65, 107, 141, 145, 146, 152, 180, 191, 196
risk profiles 168, 197–199, 204, 205
R.N.N.S and K.A 208
Romania 78
Rome Statute 98
Rwanda 25–32, 35

S

S and Marper v UK 181
'safe and legal routes' 26
safeguards 40, 46, 47, 52
Safety of Rwanda (Asylum and Immigration) Act 2024 31
Salzano, L. 95, 121
sanctions 63, 64
Sarantaki, A.-M. 98–99
Schengen *acquis* 78, 222
Schengen area
  ETIAS (European Travel Information and Authorisation System) 145
  free movement 161
  Frontex 101, 102
  secondary movement 101
  territorial nature of 2
Schengen Borders Code 24, 25, 43, 44, 46, 72, 79
Schengen Evaluation and Monitoring Mechanism 222
Schengen Evaluation Mechanism Regulation 79
Schengen Information System (SIS) 39, 160, 162, 166, 168, 179, 180, 185, 187, 208, 210–213
Schengen Strategy 100
Schengen visas 202, 209
Sciences-Po Paris 97
screening procedures 39, 43, 53, 143, 165, 203, 205
Screening Regulation 43
search and rescue
  criminalization 57, 61
  duty to rescue 33, 62–63
  EU law 220
  evolution of extraterritorial immigration control 16, 17–18
  Frontex 121, 122
  hostile environment 56, 63–64, 223
  information exchange 149
  Pact on Migration and Asylum 39, 41
  situational awareness pictures 154
Sea-Watch 18, 63, 98, 221
Sea-Watch 3 62–63
secondary movement 101
securitization 22, 44–45, 178
security risks 39, 41, 45, 145, 164
selective suspension of the law 38
serious incident reports (SIRs) 81–82, 83, 103, 105, 120, 124–125, 126, 127, 129
Shachar, A. 54
Shahzad v Hungary 23n62

shared Biometric Matching Service (sBMS) 167–168, 172, 211
shared competence 76–77, 80, 199
shared responsibility 73–77
ship identification numbers 154, 155, 156
short-stay visas 1n2, 162, 197
Single European Act 78
SIRENE 162
situational awareness pictures 141, 147–148, 149–153, 154, 155, 192
small boats 1, 17–18, 32, 90, 105, 118, 121, 156
smuggling 57, 61, 62, 144
SOLAS Convention (International Convention for the Safety of Life at Sea) 64
Spain 21, 186
specific situational picture (SSP) 149, 150–151
SS & ST v Frontex [2022] 84n47
S.S. and Others v Italy 17–18, 19
standing corps 72, 83, 115n26, 142–143
state sovereignty 2, 14, 36, 56
stateless persons 42, 49, 67
states of emergency 45–47, 50, 52, 131
Steccato di Cutro shipwreck 121
substantive asylum interviews 41
Supreme Court 26–31
surveillance
  AI (artificial intelligence) 192
  diversion of 127
  Eurosur 146–158
  external oversight of Frontex 118n41, 121, 122, 124
  extraterritorial immigration control 20
  Frontex 90–91, 96, 101, 106
  instrumentalization of migration 46n73
  IT systems as complex ecosystem 169
  'non-entry' fiction 39
  SSP (specific situational picture) 151
  technology-led 137–159
Sweden 194, 195
Switzerland 78
Syria Justice and Accountability Centre 97–98
Syrian refugees 86–88, 89

T

'take back' requests 186
'techno-solutionism' 164, 173, 192, 222
terrorism 144, 164, 166, 181–182, 203
thermal cameras 153, 156
third countries
  Eurosur 152
  extraterritorial immigration control 12–20
  Frontex 116, 124, 142, 152–153
  integrated border management 74
  large-scale IT systems for third-country nationals 160–189
  outsourcing refugee status determination 25–32
  personal data processing 139, 155, 156
  safe 13
  and Schengen 79
threat, third-country nationals as 41, 43, 44, 47, 55
Tidghi, M. 187, 188
trafficking 34, 66, 144
transfers of migrants 185–186
transit zones 22, 24, 41, 43, 46, 47, 51, 130
transport policy 220–221
Treaty on the Functioning of the European Union (TFEU) 24, 78, 84, 85, 98, 220, 221
Tribunale di Bologna 61
Turkey 86, 89, 90, 105, 127
Turkish-Greek sea border 89

U

UK v Council 181n79
UK visa applications 195, 199–201, 218
Ukraine 2, 74–75
UK-Rwanda model 25–32, 35, 66
UN Special Rapporteur on the Human Rights of Migrants 16n26, 114, 148
United Nations Convention against Torture and Other Cruel, Inhuman or Degrading Treatment or Punishment 27
United Nations General Assembly (UNGA) 6n12, 6n13, 17n31
United Nations High Commissioner for Refugees' (UNHCR) 28, 30
United Nations International Covenant on Civil and Political Rights 27
unwanted third-country nationals 38, 41–43
'unworthiness' of migrants 38
US Extraordinary Rendition Program 33

V

Vested-Hansen, J. 40
violence 45, 111–113, 129
Visa Code 79, 209
Visa Handbook 198–199
Visa Information System (VIS) 146, 160, 162–163, 170, 174, 176–177, 179, 185, 199, 202, 204, 205, 207, 211
visa policies 79, 162–163, 195–196, 198–199, 200
vulnerability assessments 115

W

watchlists 145, 165, 169, 203
WhatsApp 106, 112, 132
Working Group on Fundamental Rights and Legal Operational Aspects of Operations (WG FRaLO) 102–103, 125
WS v European Coast Guard Agency 86n50, 88n54, 109

Z

Zandstra, T. 204

Printed and bound by CPI Group (UK) Ltd, Croydon, CR0 4YY

15/09/2026

14962385-0008